Lecture Notes in Computer Science   6708

Commenced Publication in 1973
Founding and Former Series Editors:
Gerhard Goos, Juris Hartmanis, and Jan van Leeuwen

Editorial Board

Sven Apel
Ethan Jackson (Eds.)

Software
Composition

10th International Conference, SC 2011
Zurich, Switzerland, June 30 - July 1, 2011
Proceedings

 Springer

Volume Editors

Sven Apel
University of Passau
94032 Passau, Germany
E-mail: apel@uni-passau.de

Ethan Jackson
Microsoft Research
Redmond, WA 98052-6399, USA
E-mail: ejackson@microsoft.com

ISSN 0302-9743   e-ISSN 1611-3349
ISBN 978-3-642-22044-9   e-ISBN 978-3-642-22045-6
DOI 10.1007/978-3-642-22045-6
Springer Heidelberg Dordrecht London New York

Library of Congress Control Number: 2011929855

CR Subject Classification (1998): D.2, F.3, C.2, D.3, D.1, H.3

LNCS Sublibrary: SL 2 – Programming and Software Engineering

Typesetting: Camera-ready by author, data conversion by Scientific Publishing Services, Chennai, India

Printed on acid-free paper

Springer is part of Springer Science+Business Media (www.springer.com)

Preface

SC 2011 was the tenth occurrence of the International Conference on Software Composition. Since its inception SC has been a conference for investigating software composition from many perspectives. This year we continued this tradition with a diverse Program Committee and a broad spectrum of publications. Topics such as functional programming, aspect-oriented programming, interfaces, components, and robotics can be found in this year's proceedings. We accepted ten full papers and two short papers with an overall acceptance rate of 37%. Each paper went through a rigorous review process, with between three to four reviews per paper.

This edition of SC was collocated with the 49th International Conference on Objects, Components, Models, and Patterns (TOOLS Europe). It included a joint session with TOOLS to help facilitate interaction between theoreticians, practitioners, and tool builders. The event was held at ETH in Zürich, Switzerland, and provided an excellent venue for collaborative thought and idea exchange. In addition to TOOLS Europe, SC was also collocated with the 5th International Conference on Tests and Proofs (TAP) and the 4th International Conference on the Theory and Practice of Model Transformations (ICMT). This LNCS volume contains the proceedings of SC 2011, which was held from June 30 to July 1, 2011 at ETH in Zürich, Switzerland.

First, we would like thank the authors for their hard work and cutting-edge contributions. Their work is crucial to maintain SC's role as a vibrant venue to discuss software composition. We would also like to thank the Program Committee and their secondary reviewers for their thorough reviews and detailed feedback. Their expert opinions allow SC to host ideas from many different viewpoints while maintaining a high standard. We express our tremendous thanks to Bertrand Meyer and his team for organizing the venue at ETH. We express the same thanks to Judith Bishop and Antonio Vallecillo for their assistance in coordinating with TOOLS Europe.

July 2011

Sven Apel
Ethan Jackson

Organization

Program Chairs

Sven Apel   University of Passau, Germany
Ethan Jackson   Microsoft Research, USA

Program Committee

Don Batory   The University of Texas at Austin, USA
Benoit Baudry   INRIA Rennes, France
Nikolaj Bjørner   Microsoft Research, USA
Eric Bodden   Technische Universität Darmstadt, Germany
Jan Bosch   Intuit, USA
Manfred Broy   Technische Universität Munich, Germany
Pascal Costanza   Vrije Universiteit Brussels, Belgium
Kathi Fisler   Worcester Polytechnic Institute, USA
Jeff Gray   University of Alabama, USA
Volker Gruhn   University of Leipzig, Germany
Robert Hirschfeld   HPI, Germany
Wouter Joosen   Katholieke Universiteit Leuven, Belgium
Christian Kästner   Philipps University of Marburg, Germany
David H. Lorenz   Open University of Israel, Israel
Welf Löwe   Växjö University, Sweden
Ina Schaefer   Chalmers University of Technology, Sweden
Joseph Sifakis   Verimag, France
Yannis Smaragdakis   University of Massachusetts at Amherst, USA
Stefan Sobernig   Wirtschaftsuniversität Wien, Austria
Janos Sztipanovits   Vanderbilt University, USA
Clemens Szyperski   Microsoft, USA
Stavros Tripakis   The University of California at Berkeley, USA
Salvador Trujillo   IKERLAN, Spain
Eric Wohlstadter   University of British Columbia, Canada

Steering Committee

Uwe Aßmann   Dresden University of Technology, Germany
Judith Bishop   Microsoft Research, USA
Thomas Gschwind   IBM Zürich Research Lab, Switzerland
Oscar Nierstrasz   University of Berne, Switzerland
Mario Südholt   INRIA – École des Mines de Nantes, France

Table of Contents

Composition and Interfaces

Deriving Functional Interface Specifications for Composite
Components.. 1
   Perla Velasco Elizondo and Mbe Koua Christophe Ndjatchi

Comparing Machine Learning Approaches for Context-Aware
Composition 18
   Antonina Danylenko, Christoph Kessler, and Welf Löwe

An Implementation of Composable Memory Transactions in Haskell 34
   André Rauber Du Bois

Synthesizing Glue Operators from Glue Constraints for the
Construction of Component-Based Systems 51
   Simon Bliudze and Joseph Sifakis

Aspects and Features

A Sequence of Patterns for Reusable Aspect Libraries with Easy
Configuration 68
   Maarten Bynens, Eddy Truyen, and Wouter Joosen

Pluggable Aspect Instantiation Models 84
   David H. Lorenz and Victor Trakhtenberg

Composing Event-B Specifications - Case-Study Experience 100
   Ali Gondal, Michael Poppleton, and Michael Butler

Applications I

A Formal Approach for Incremental Construction with an Application
to Autonomous Robotic Systems.................................... 116
   Saddek Bensalem, Lavindra de Silva, Andreas Griesmayer,
   Felix Ingrand, Axel Legay, and Rongjie Yan

Towards Incremental Cycle Analysis in ESMoL Distributed Control
System Models 133
   Joseph Porter, Daniel Balasubramanian, Graham Hemingway, and
   János Sztipanovits

Assuring Architectural Properties during Compositional Architecture
Design... 141
   Constanze Deiters and Andreas Rausch

Applications II

Coherence and Performance for Interactive Scientific Visualization
Applications.. 149
    Sébastien Limet, Sophie Robert, and Ahmed Turki

Toward Validated Composition in Component-Based Adaptive
Middleware 165
    Annie Ressouche, Jean-Yves Tigli, and Oscar Carrillo

Author Index... 181

Deriving Functional Interface Specifications for Composite Components

Perla Velasco Elizondo[1] and Mbe Koua Christophe Ndjatchi[2]

[1] Centre for Mathematical Research (CIMAT), Zacatecas, Zac., 98060, Mexico
[2] Polytechnic University of Zacatecas (UPZ), Fresnillo, Zac., 99059, Mexico

Abstract. An interface specification serves as the sole medium for component understanding and use. Current practice of deriving these specifications for composite components does not give much weight to doing it systematically and unambiguously. This paper presents our progress on developing an approach to tackle this issue. We focus on deriving functional interface specifications for composite components, constructed via composition operators. In our approach, the composites' interfaces are not generated in an *ad hoc* manner via delegation mechanisms, but are derived systematically, consistently and largely automatically via a set of functions on the functional interfaces of the composed components. Via an example, we illustrate the aforementioned benefits as well as the fact that our approach provides a new view into the space of interface generation.

1   Introduction

A *component's interface specification*, or a component specification for short, defines the component and serves as the sole medium for its understanding and use by answering questions such as: What services are provided and required by the component?, How can these services be used?, What quality characteristics do the offered services fulfill? And so on. There is a common agreement about the information elements that a component specification should include [5,1]: (i) the *instantiation* mechanisms, (ii) the *functional* properties, i.e. the component's provided and required services, (iii) the *non-functional* properties, i.e. the component's quality attributes and (iv) the *context dependencies*, i.e. the information about the component's deployment environment. Independently from their form, all these elements are crucial for setting up and validating a component composition.

The idea of constructing *composite components* is recognised as a good practice in component-based development (CBD) because it is a means to maximise reuse [6]. By composite components we mean *reusable general-purpose* components made up of an assembly of two or more atomic components.[1] The issue of being a composite should be transparent for a user, as the composite should be utilised in the same manner as an atomic one. Thus, the availability of the specification of a composite component is crucial to allow its reuse, as it is the ability to consistently derive it to scale the development techniques of any CBD approach.

Ideally, the information of a composite's specification should be derived from the specifications of its constituents and the semantics of their composition [11,6]. Unfortunately, current practice of deriving specifications for composite components does not

---

[1] We consider an atomic component the most basic kind of component in a component model.

S. Apel and E. Jackson (Eds.): SC 2011, LNCS 6708, pp. 1–17, 2011.
© Springer-Verlag Berlin Heidelberg 2011

give much weight to doing so in a more systematic and unambiguous manner. This paper, besides extending our previous work, presents our progress on developing an approach to tackle this issue.

We have introduced an approach to CBD and demonstrated the construction of composite components in practice, e.g. [13]. In this approach composites are constructed via *composition operators*. Previously, the process of composites' interface generation was vaguely outlined, required a lot of human intervention and resulted in interfaces with only one service, which is not natural for the users of the composites. Thus, in this paper we present an approach where the composites' interfaces are derived considering both, the functional specifications of their constituents and the semantics of the operators utilised in their composition. The main contribution in this piece of work is a set of *operator-specific functions* to support an approach for consistently deriving functional interface specifications instead of generating them in an *ad hoc* manner via delegation mechanisms. Via an example we will show that our approach (i) provides a *new view* into the space of interface generation, which increases the number of services offered by a composite, (ii) has simple but formal *algebraic basis*, which makes interface derivation more precise, consistent and systematic and (iii) can be *largely automated*, which mitigates derivation effort.

This paper is organised as follows. In Section 2, we discuss composite components in current CBD approaches. In Section 3, we review the foundations of this work. Next, we present some of the defined functions to generate the functional specification of composite components. In Section 5, we demonstrate the use of these functions via an example. In Section 6, we discuss the benefits of our approach and briefly survey relevant related work. Finally, in Section 7, we state the conclusions and future work.

2   Composite Components in CBD Approaches

The idea of constructing reusable composite components has been recognised as a good practice in CBD. However, it is not a trivial task. We believe that a fundamental issue to enable their generation is the availability of an *algebraic approach to composition*. That is, an approach that when putting components together in some way, results in a new component that preserves some of the properties of its constituents. The lack of such an approach might be the reason why, although component composition is supported, only in some CBD methods it enables the construction of reusable composites [8].

To clarify the former, consider composition in JavaBeans [2,8]. In JavaBeans *beans* (i.e. atomic components) are Java classes which adhere to design and syntactic conventions. These conventions make their storage, retrieval and visual composition possible. When components are composed, the resulting "composition" takes the form of an *adaptor class*.[2] However, this class does not preserve the properties of a bean class; it does not correspond to an entity that can be specified in terms of its properties, its events and its methods as it can be done for its constituent beans. As a corollary, the adaptor class cannot be stored, retrieved and (re)used as a bean class can.

There are CBD approaches that are closer to our notion of composite components. However, there are still some issues that make it difficult to formalise a method to consistently specify them. For example the Koala component model [2,8], which is used

---

[2] In JavaBeans, an adaptor class is a wrapper class utilised to wire the composed components.

in the consumer electronics domain, supports the construction of composites from pre-existing specifications. Specifications are written in some sort of definition language and can be stored in and retrieved from a repository to be reused for composite component definition. Koala supports the specification of various elements relevant to a component. In the example depicted in Fig. 1 we focus on the provided and required services (i.e. the functional properties), as they are the target of the work presented in this paper. Fig. 1 shows (a) the ITuner interface specification, (b) the CTunerDriver component specification –in terms of a set of pre-existing interface specifications (e.g. ITuner), (c) the CTVPlatform composite component specification –in terms of a set of pre-existing component specifications (e.g. CTunerDriver) and (d) the CTVPlatform composite's graphical representation in Koala notation.

```
(a) interface ITuner{
        void SetFrequency(int f);
        int GetFrequency(void);
    }

(b) component CTunerDriver{
        provides ITuner ptun;
                 IInit pini;
        requires II2c ri2c;
    }
```

```
(c) component CTVPlatform{
        provides IProgram pini;
        provides IMem pos;
        requires II2c fast;
        contains
            component CFrontEnd cfre;
            component CTunerDriver ctun;
            component CMemDriver cmem;
        connects
            pini = cfre.pini;
            pos = cmem.pos;
            cfre.rtun = ctun.ptun;
            cmem.rif = ctun.pini;
            ctun.ri2c = fast;
    }
```

Fig. 1. (a) An interface, (b) an atomic and (c) a composite component specifications and (d) a composite component's graphical representation in Koala

We already mentioned the idea of consistently generating composites' functional specifications from the information in the functional specifications of their constituent components as well as the semantics of their composition. We consider that this is not achieved in Koala at all. The CTVPlatform composite is specified in the same manner in which its constituents are (i.e. it defines its functionality in terms of a set of pre-existing interfaces). However, the exposed interfaces IProgram, IMem and II2c result from manually forwarding them, via *delegation mechanisms*, from the inner components to the enclosing one according to the developer's needs.[3] This is in contrast to doing so based on the semantics of the components and their composition.

We also observe that, because of the manner in which they are generated, the possibility of reusing these composites in a different development is limited. An alternative to generate a highly-reusable composite is that of providing a mean to invoke a number of valid sequences of services offered by its constituents [6]. By adopting a composition approach as the one depicted in Fig. 1, not all the constituents' services are available to invoke in the resulting composite if the constituents' interfaces have not been forwarded, e.g. the ptun interface. Although it is useful for the construction of certain types of composites, this *ad hoc* manner of hiding and exposing the constituents' interfaces could represent a shortcoming for maximising reuse. Note, however, that by

---

[3] This method follows the semantics of delegation operators in UML 2.0.

forwarding all the constituents' interfaces, which can be a remedy to fix the aforementioned situation, one could violate the composition semantics as it could lead to allow invoking invalid sequences of services.

3   The Foundations of This Work

The composites for which our approach is meant to work are constructed according to the semantics of a new component model [7]. In this model *components* are passive and general-purpose. They have an *interface specification* and an *implementation*. The interface describes the component's *provided services* (i.e. the functional properties) in terms of a *name*, the types of *input parameters* and the types of *output parameters*. Additionally, this interface describes the *non-functional* properties and the *deployment context dependencies* related to these services. The implementation corresponds to the services of the component coded in a programming language. We distinguish between atomic and composite components. The latter are constructed from atomic (or even composite) components via *composition operators*. These operators encapsulate *control-* and *data-flow* schemes; many of them analogous to well-known *patterns*, e.g. [10,4]. The operators are *first-class units*, at both design and implementation time, that admit some sort of parametrisation to indicate the components they compose and the services that must be executed in the composed components.

Fig. 2 shows a system's structure in this component model. In this hierarchical structure, composites can be seen as atomic components and can in turn be a subject of further composition by using another operator (see the inner dotted boxes). As in Koala, the composite's interface elements (e.g. their provided services) are recreated from a lower level to an upper level. However, it is done via a *composition algebra* rather than via traditional delegation mechanisms.

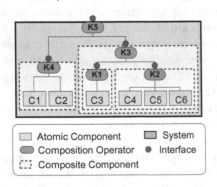

Fig. 2. A system's structure in the new component model

A catalogue of operators to allow component composition within this context has been presented [14]. The table on the left-hand side of Fig. 3 lists the operators in the catalogue. They are organised in (i) *adaptation*, (ii) *basic* and (iii) *composite operators*. Adaptation operators are *unary* operators which adapt the component in the sense that before any computation takes place inside the component, the execution of the control-flow scheme encapsulated by the operator is executed first. Basic composition operators are n-*ary* operators used to support component composition. While basic operators provide only one type of control- and data-flow scheme, composite operators combine many types. These operators have already been implemented and their usefulness demonstrated by constructing a variety of prototype systems, e.g. [13].

Due to lack of space, we do not explain all the operators in the catalogue. However, for clarification purposes, we describe the operators that we will use in the example in Section 5. The descriptions are in terms of the notation on the right-hand side of Fig. 3. The dotted boxes represent the resulting assemblies. The computation boxes represent the computation in the composed/adapted component. Arrows represent the control-flow. Data required in the assembly to perform the corresponding computation is denoted as the *input* label, while the assembly computation result is denoted as the *output* label.

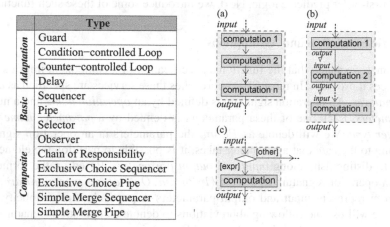

Fig. 3. The catalogue of operators and the behaviour of the assemblies resulting from the (a) *Sequencer*,(b) *Pipe* and (c) *Guard* operators

Both the *Sequencer* and *Pipe* composition operators can be used to compose two or more components, so that the execution of a service in each one of them is carried out in a *sequential* order, see Fig. 3 (a) and (b). The *Pipe* operator also models internal data communication among the composed units, so that the *output* generated by the execution of a component's service is the *input* to the next one in the chain. Fig. 3 (c) depicts the case of the *Guard* adaptation operator. Any computation in the adapted component is conditional upon the value of a Boolean expression (expr) being *true*.

Now that we have defined the generalities of our previous work, let us focus on our approach to derive functional interface specifications.

4   The Proposed Approach

We have outlined a new view of composition where operators are utilised to compose software components. In general, if a set of atomic components are composed by using our approach, then the user of the resulting composite should be able to execute a number of service sequences in terms of the services offered by the composed components. The nature and number of all possible sequences (i.e. the composite's services) should be determined from both the functional specifications of the atomic components and the semantics of the operator utilised in their composition.

The resulting composite should provide a functional specification informing about these service sequences. Ideally, the composite's functional specification should be offered in the same form as that of an atomic component. That is, as a set of provided services. Although in this case, these services should be abstractions denoting valid service sequences to invoke within the composite's constituents and their corresponding requirements and outcomes (i.e. their input and output parameters).

The composition algebra in our composition approach makes it easier to develop a set of operator-specific functions to specify how to generate the composites' functional specifications as outlined above. The semantics of these functions is based on algebra of sets and first-order predicate logic. Next, we introduce some of these such functions.[4]

4.1 Basic Formalism and Assumptions

In Section 1 we stated that the functional specification of a component informs about the services it provides. In most CBD approaches these services are specified as *operation signatures*. An operation signature is defined by an *operation name* and a number of *parameters*. Each one of these parameters is defined by a *parameter name* and a *parameter type*. We will denote as *Param* the parameters in an operation signature. According to the *role* that a parameter takes, it is possible to partition the elements in *Param* to distinguish among *input* and *output parameters*. Based on the former, we define an operation signature as a tuple $\langle InParam, OutParam \rangle$ where $InParam$ and $OutParam$ represent input and output parameters respectively. For simplicity, from now on we will use the following abbreviations to denote an operation signature (Sig) and a component's functional specification ($FSpec$), i.e. a set of operation signatures: $Sig == \langle InParam, OutParam \rangle$ and $FSpec == \mathbb{P}\, Sig$.

Note that in these definitions we do not make the operation name of the signature explicit. However, we assume that each operation signature in a $FSpec$ is associated to an operation name which works as an identifier for it. Thus, a functional specification $FSpec$ could contain identical tuples $\langle InParam, OutParam \rangle$ as long as these tuples are associated to different operation names.

In this basic formalism we will treat $Param$ and its partitions as *bags* instead of sets to allow for duplication of parameters. A composite component could be generated from a set of instances of the same component type. For example, consider the case of composing three instances of a Dispenser Component (e.g. one for water, one for milk and one for coffee) into a Coffee Dispenser composite component. This results in a composition scenario involving a number of functional specifications $FSpec$ with the same operation signatures. When composing these specifications via certain type of operators, it could be required to have multiple occurrences of the same parameter. Note, however, that we assume that operation signatures are well formed meaning: $Sig == \langle InParam, OutParam \rangle$ such that $InParam \cap OutParam = \emptyset$. We also assume that parameters with the same name and type are semantically equivalent.

Considering the former, we have defined a set of helper and operator-specific functions to derive the functional specifications of composite components. Helper functions perform part of the computation in operator-specific ones. In this paper we only present the functions utilised in the example in Section 5. However, detailed descriptions of all the defined functions can be found in [15].

---

[4] We assume basic knowledge of set theory, first-order predicate logic and the Z language syntax.

4.2 The Helper Functions

The function parameter complement (*param_comp*) maps a group of parameters to their complementary *role*, i.e. either input or output. On the other hand, the functions signature input parameter and signature output parameter (*sig_in* and *sig_out* respectively) get the input and output parameters of an operation signature respectively.

$$param\_comp : Param \rightarrow Param$$

$$param\_comp = p_1, p_2, \ldots, p_n \in Param \bullet \bigcup_{i=1}^{n} \sim p_i$$

$$sig\_in, sig\_out : Sig \rightarrow Param$$

$$s : Sig \bullet sig\_in(s) = InParam \wedge sig\_out(s) = OutParam$$

The function signature concatenation (*sig_concat*) works on a set of operation signatures to generate one whose input and output parameters result from the concatenation of the input and output parameters on the participating ones. To specify the issue of having duplicated elements in *InParam* and *OutParam*, we use the $\uplus$ operator.

$$sig\_concat : Sig \times \ldots \times Sig \rightarrow Sig$$

$$sig\_concat = s_1, s_2, \ldots, s_n : Sig \bullet \langle \biguplus_{i=1}^{n} sig\_in(s_i), \biguplus_{i=1}^{n} sig\_out(s_i) \rangle$$

The functions add input parameter and add output parameter (*add_in* and *add_out* respectively) add input and output parameters to an operation signature respectively. The function signature (*sig_match*) verifies whether there are common elements among the output parameters of one operation signature and the input parameters of another. Finally, the function signature bound (*sig_bound*) works on a set of operation signatures and results in one consisting of the union of the given signatures, but with the parameters in the participating signatures that are complementary removed.

$$add\_in, add\_out : Param \times Sig \rightarrow Sig$$

$$p : Param; \ s : Sig \bullet$$
$$add\_in(p, s) = \langle \{p \cup sig\_in(s)\}, sig\_out(s) \rangle \wedge$$
$$add\_out(p, s) = \langle sig\_in(s), \{p \cup sig\_out(s)\} \rangle$$

$$sig\_match : Sig \times Sig \rightarrow Boolean$$

$$sig\_match = s_1, s_2 : Sig \bullet sig\_out(s_1) \cap sig\_in(s_2) \neq \varnothing$$

$$sig\_bound : Sig \times \ldots \times Sig \rightarrow Sig$$

$$sig\_bound = s_1, s_2, \ldots, s_n : Sig \bullet$$
$$\langle \{sig\_in(s_1) \uplus$$
$$(sig\_in(s_2) \setminus param\_comp(sig\_out(s_1))) \uplus$$
$$(sig\_in(s_3) \setminus param\_comp(sig\_out(s_2))) \uplus$$
$$\ldots \uplus$$
$$(sig\_in(s_n) \setminus param\_comp(sig\_out(s_{n-1})))\}, sig\_out(s_n) \rangle$$

Now that we have presented the helper functions, next we present the operator-specific ones.

4.3 The Operator-Specific Functions

The *guard_composite_fspec* function generates the functional specification of an assembly created via a *Guard* operator. Besides the functional specification of the adapted component, this function also takes one input parameter, which represents the value to be evaluated by the *Guard*'s Boolean expression. This parameter is added to the input parameters of each one of the operation signatures of the adapted component via the *add_in* helper function.

$$guard\_composite\_fspec : InParam \times FSpec \rightarrow FSpec$$

$$
\begin{aligned}
&guard\_composite\_fspec = \\
&\quad s_1, s_2, \ldots, s_n : Sig; \\
&\quad f : FSpec; \\
&\quad p : InParam \mid \#p = 1; \\
&\quad (s_1, s_2, \ldots, s_n) \in f \bullet \bigcup_{i=1}^{n} add\_in(p, s_i)
\end{aligned}
$$

The *seq_composite_fspec* function generates the functional specification of a composite component created via the *Sequencer* operator. The helper function *sig_concat*, makes each operation signature contain the input and output parameters of the participating signatures. Finally, the *pipe_composite_fspec* function generates the functional specification of a composite component created via the *Pipe* operator. The helper functions *sig_match* and *sig_bound* verify that the signatures in the participating specifications meet the requirements for internal data communication and remove the occurrences of the complementary parameters in the resulting signatures respectively.

$$seq\_composite\_fspec : FSpec \times \ldots \times FSpec \rightarrow FSpec$$

$$
\begin{aligned}
&seq\_composite\_fspec = \\
&\quad s_1, s_2, \ldots, s_n : Sig; \\
&\quad f_1, f_2, \ldots, f_n : FSpec; \\
&\quad (s_1, s_2, \ldots, s_n) \in f_1 \times f_2 \times \ldots \times f_n \bullet \\
&\qquad \bigcup_{(s_1,\ldots,s_n) \in \prod_{i=1}^{n} f_i} sig\_concat(s_1, s_2, \ldots, s_n)
\end{aligned}
$$

$$pipe\_composite\_fspec : FSpec \times \ldots \times FSpec \rightarrow FSpec$$

$$
\begin{aligned}
&pipe\_composite\_fspec = \\
&\quad 1 \leq i < j \leq n; \\
&\quad s_1, s_2, \ldots, s_n : Sig; \\
&\quad f_1, f_2, \ldots, f_n : FSpec; \\
&\quad \forall s_i, s_j \in (s_1, s_2, \ldots, s_n) \in f_1 \times f_2 \times \ldots \times f_n \mid sig\_match(s_i, s_j) \bullet \\
&\qquad \bigcup_{(s_1,\ldots,s_n) \in \prod_{i=1}^{n} f_i} sig\_bound(s_1, s_2, \ldots, s_n)
\end{aligned}
$$

Next we present the design of some composite components by using these functions.

5 Example

We will define some composites meant to be used to construct different versions of a Drink Vending Machine system (DVM). We chose this simple and small size example as it is enough to illustrate the use of our functions.[5] The DVM is limited to two general actions: (1) *to sell a drink* and (2) *to maintain the dispensers*. (1) involves receiving the customer request and payment as well as delivering the drink. (2) involves filling and emptying the dispensers of the drinks' ingredients.

Fig. 4 shows the proposed composites to use in the DVM as well as their behaviours. Fig. 4 (a) shows a **Coffee Card Cashier** composite, which is made of the Card Reader (CR) and Billing Component (BC). CR is responsible for getting coffee cards' identifiers and BC for debiting the cards. By composing these components with a *Pipe* P and a *Guard* G operators we can generate a composite that, once a coffee card has been inserted in the coffee machine's slot and the amount to debit to it has been specified (e.g. *amt*), it retrieves the card's identifier by executing a service in CR (e.g. getCardId). The obtained result can be passed up via P to G to check its value. If it has a valid value (e.g. *if cardId ! = null*), then the card can be debited by executing a service in BC (e.g. debit) and the result can be returned (e.g. *errorCode*).

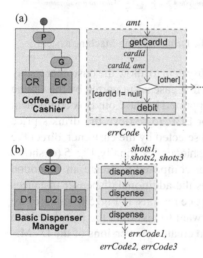

The **Basic Dispenser** composite, shown in Fig. 4 (b), is made up of three instances of the dispenser component and one *Sequencer* operator SQ. A Water (D1), a Coffee (D2) and a Milk Dispenser (D3) have been considered. The composite allows the sequential execution of one service in each one of these components, e.g. the dispense service. *Shots1-shots3* denote the number of shots to be dispensed by each dispenser, while *error-Code1-errorCode3* denote the resulting values of each one of these executions.

Now we describe how we use these composites in the DVM system. We have organised the DVM design into three subsystems: a *Cashier*, a *Drink Maker* and a *Maintenance*. The first two will deal with the function (1) and the last one will support the function (2). Fig. 5 (a) shows a version of the VDM in terms of the three subsystems. The *Cashier Subsystem* comprises the **Coffee Card Cashier** composite and the Payment Manager Component (PMgr) –which manages the drinks menu. The *Drink Maker Subsystem* comprises the **Basic Dispenser** composite and the Recipe Manager Component (RMgr) –which manages the drinks recipes. The *Maintenance Subsystem* comprises the **Basic Dispenser** composite only. If the function (1) is required, then the *Selector* SL will call the *Pipe* P3 and it in turn will call the *Cashier Subsystem* to deal with the drink payment. In this subsystem, the *Pipe* P1 will first retrieve the drink's price by executing a service in PMgr. Then, it will pass up the price when calling the required service in

Fig. 4. Useful composites for the Drink Vending Machine systems and their behaviour

---

[5] Composites providing more sophisticated services can be seen in [13,15].

the Coffee Card Cashier composite. Next, the *Pipe* P3 will pass up the result to the *Drink Maker Subsystem*. In this subsystem, the *Guard* G1 will allow any computation down on the hierarchy only if the drink payment has been processed. In such a case, this operator will call the *Pipe* P2. P2 will first retrieve the drink's recipe by executing a service in RMgr and then call the Basic Dispenser composite to perform the dispense of ingredients accordingly. On the other hand if the function (2) is required, then the *Selector* SL will call the corresponding Basic Dispenser's service.

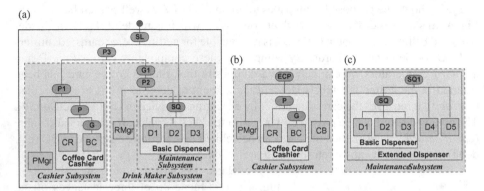

Fig. 5. The outlines of three alternative designs of the Drink Vending Machine system

Fig. 5 (b) shows a new version of the *Cashier Subsystem* to allow the customer to pay for drinks by using either coffee cards or cash. The first case is supported by the Coffee Card Cashier composite, while the second one is supported by the Coin Box component (CB). We use an *Exclusive Choice Pipe*[6] operator ECP to retrieve the drink's price from PMgr and then, based on the payment method selected by the customer, direct the execution of the charge to either the Coffee Card Cashier or CB. Finally, Fig. 5 (c) shows how the Basic Dispenser composite can be further composed to create an Extended Dispenser composite. This new composite includes the additional dispenser instances D3 and D4 for dealing with more ingredients. For space reasons, in Fig. 5 (b) and (c) we did not depict the complete DVM designs, but we want to highlight the fact that these new subsystems can replace the ones in Fig. 5 (a) to create new versions of the DVM.

5.1 Composite Component Generation

For clarity purposes, in Fig. 6 we describe the functional specifications of atomic components in some sort of IDL[7] syntax. The keywords in and out denote the *role* of a parameter in the operation. Next, we describe these specifications using the formalism described in Section 4.1.

Functional Specification of the Coffee Card Cashier Composite. Attending the bottom-up nature of our composition approach, we will start with the assembly involving the *Guard* operator (G) and the Billing Component (BC). Let $p = \{cardId\}$ be

---

[6] The Exclusive Choice Pipe is a composite composition operator that allows executing a computation in a predecessor component and then, the generated output is passed up as input data for the computation of only one component in a set of successor components.

[7] Interface Definition Language.

```
interface Dispenser{                          interface CardReader{
  emptyDispenser ();                            getCardId(out int cardId);
  setTemperature (in int temp, out errCode);  }
  add (in int shots, out int errCode);
  dispense (in int shots, out int errCode);
}

interface BillingComponent{
  credit(in int cardId, in int amt, out errCode);
  debit(in int cardId, in int amt, out errCode);
  getBalance(in int cardId, out int amt);
}
```

Fig. 6. Functional specifications of atomic components

```
(a)                                          (b)
interface BasicDispenser{                    interface CoffeeCardCashier{
  op1();                                       op1(in int amt, out errCode);
  op2(in int temp, out errCode);              op2(in int amt, out errCode);
  op3(in int shots, out int errCode);         op3(out int amt);
  op4(in int shots, out int errCode);        }
  ...
  op63(in int shots, in int shots, in int temp,
       out int errCode, out int errCode, out int errCode);
  op64(in int shots, in int shots, in int temp,
       out int errCode, out int errCode, out int errCode);
  op62(in int shots, in int shots, in int temp,
       out int errCode, out int errCode, out int errCode);
}
```

Fig. 7. The interface specifications of (a) the Basic Dispenser and (b) the Coffee Card Cashier

the input parameter to be evaluated by G's Boolean expression, i.e. "*in int cardId*". Let
$f_1 = \{\langle\{cardId, amt\}, \{errCode\}\rangle, \langle\{cardId, amt\}, \{errCode\}\rangle, \langle\{cardId\}, \{amt\}\rangle\}$
be the functional specification of BC. By using the *guard_composite_fspec* function we
can derive the functional specification
$f_2 = \{\langle\{cardId, amt\}, \{errCode\}\rangle, \langle\{cardId, amt\}, \{errCode\}\rangle, \langle\{cardId\}, \{amt\}\rangle\}$
The f_2's tuples denote the signatures of the "guarded" versions of the *debit, credit* and
getBalance operations in the BC composite. As p's and f_1's *cardId* are semantically
equivalent, the *Guard*'s *add_in* helper function kept it in only one occurrence. However,
within the assembly the parameter is utilised as the variable to be evaluated in G's
Boolean expression (e.g. *if cardId ! = null*) and as the input parameter of the operation
signatures.

Once f_2 has been obtained, it can be used together with the functional specification of
the Card Reader component (CR) to generate the functional specification of the Coffee
Card Cashier composite via the *pipe_composite_fspec* function. Thus, let [8]
$f_1 = \{\langle\varnothing, \{cardId\}\rangle\}$
and f_2 be the CR and the guarded BC specifications respectively, we can derive
$f_3 = \{\langle\{amt\}, \{errCode\}\rangle, \langle\{amt\}, \{errCode\}\rangle, \langle\varnothing, \{amt\}\rangle\}$
which represents the Coffee Card Cashier's functional specification. Using the IDL syn-
tax introduced before, this functional specification can be rewritten as shown in Fig. 7
(b). In here, *op1-op3* are signatures abstracting the three valid sequences of operations
to invoke within the composite's constituents, i.e. *getCardId-credit, getCardId-debit*

---

[8] We use the $\varnothing$ symbol to denote both no input parameters and no output parameters.

and *getCardId-getBalance*. Note that, both the input and the output parameters of these operation sequences are entirely derived from the semantics of the *Pipe* operator. The helper function *sig_bound* is utilised to remove the input parameter *cardId* in the resulting signatures, as it is produced internally within the composite, see Fig. 4 (a).

Functional Specification of the Basic Dispenser Composite. Let f_i, i=1,2,3, be the functional specifications of the three Dispenser's instances:

$$f_i = \{\langle \varnothing, \varnothing \rangle, \langle \{temp\}, \{errCode\} \rangle, \langle \{shots\}, \{errCode\} \rangle, \langle \{shots\}, \{errCode\} \rangle\}$$

Applying the *seq_composite_fspec* function, we can derive the one of the **Basic Dispenser** composite component:

$$f_4 = \{\langle \varnothing, \varnothing \rangle,$$
$$\langle \{temp\}, \{errCode\} \rangle,$$
$$\langle \{shots\}, \{errCode\} \rangle,$$
$$\langle \{shots\}, \{errCode\} \rangle,$$
$$\dots,$$
$$\langle \{shots, shots, temp\}, \{errCode, errCode, errCode\} \rangle,$$
$$\langle \{shots, shots, shots\}, \{errCode, errCode, errCode\} \rangle,$$
$$\langle \{shots, shots, shots\}, \{errCode, errCode, errCode\} \rangle\}$$

The f_4's signatures abstract the valid sequences of operation executions within the composite's constituents. The IDL version of f_4 is shown in Fig. 7 (a). The *op*1 and *op*64 abstract the execution sequences *emptyDispenser-emptyDispenser-emptyDispenser* and *dispense-dispense-dispense* respectively. The input and output parameters of these signatures are entirely derived from the semantics of the *Sequencer* operator. Each one of the signatures in the resulting specification is made of a concatenation of the parameters of the composed components' signatures via the *sig_concat* helper function. The duplicated elements in the resulting *InParam* and *OutParam* sets are because of composing several instances of the same component types. This allows, for example, invoking the sequence *dispense-dispense-dispense* with a different number of shots in each one of the dispensers, see Fig. 4 (b).

5.2   Automation and Tool Support

We have generated a new version of our existing composition tool[9] that includes a set of algorithms that implement the defined functions. The tool operates on atomic components that are offered as *binary* files. The binaries correspond to a Java implementation and relate to a functional interface specification written as Java annotations. During component composition, the annotations (together with other component classes' metadata) are read via *reflection techniques*, to determine the content of components' functional specifications and derive the ones for the composites. Composites' specifications are attached to their implementations as Java annotations.

Fig. 8 shows a screenshot of the tool during the generation of the **Basic Dispenser** composite (described in Section 5.1). As can be seen, the names of the resulting signa-

---

[9] The tool enables component composition by dragging, dropping and composing pre-existing components and pre-existing operators into a visual assembler. The generation of Java code for the defined assemblies is also supported, see [13].

tures are generated by concatenating the names of the composed ones, e.g. *dispensedis-pensedispense*. For naming the input and output parameters, the tool uses the ones in the participating signatures. Although having duplicated elements in either the *InParam* or the *OutParam* sets is semantically valid in our approach, it is syntactically invalid at implementation-time, i.e. method signatures in Java cannot have duplicated parameter names. Thus, when this happens a suffix to the original ones is added to differentiate them, e.g. *shots1*, *shots2* and *shots3*.

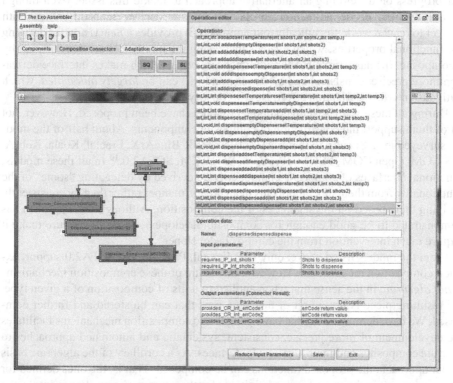

Fig. 8. A visual tool to support the generation of composite components.

Our tool largely automates the functional interface derivation. However, in some cases composite developer intervention could be needed to refine the content and syntax of the resulting specifications. For example, to eliminate signatures representing execution sequences that are invalid or undesirable, the composite developer has to provide the filtering criteria. Taking into consideration the domain context for which the Basic Dispenser composite is built, only 4 out of the 64 operations make sense. These operations are the ones abstracting the sequential execution of the same operation in each one of the dispenser components, e.g. *dispense-dispense-dispense*. Similarly, to allow a better understanding to composite users, the composite developer might want to rename the resulting operations or parameters. The tool provides the means to allow this and some other refinements, e.g. see the lower part of Fig. 8 which allows the composite developer to rename operations and parameters.

6   Discussion and Related Work

Management of both functional and non-functional properties is one of the main challenges in CBD community. Despite the former, the starting point in their management, that is their specification, is not addressed completely in most CBD approaches [11]. With few exceptions, current practice in CBD focuses on components and leaves their interactions specified as lines representing method calls. As illustrated in Section 2, such lines are not enough for defining a method for systematically, consistently and automatically deriving the specifications of component assemblies. We have presented our progress on developing an alternative approach to tackle this issue. Even though we only focus on deriving functional properties, our approach presents differences with respect to related work. Specifically, our approach (i) provides a *new vision* for deriving the functional properties, which enables increasing the number of services offered by a composite, (ii) has simple but formal *algebraic basis*, which makes interface derivation more precise, consistent and systematic and (iii) can be *largely automated*, which mitigates interface derivation effort. Next we justify these claims.

During all these years several component models have been proposed. However, not all of them support the construction of composite components. About half of the models surveyed in [2,8] support them: AUTOSAR, BIP, BlueArX, Fractal, Koala, KobrA, MS COM, Open COM, PECOS, ProCom, SaveCCM, SOFA2.0.[10] In all these models, functional interfaces of composite components are derived by delegating "some" of the functionality from their subcomponents in an *ad hoc* manner rather than by consistently deriving them based on the semantics of the composition. Although this approach has demonstrated to be good enough for composite developers, its *ad hoc* nature make it require much intervention from the composite developer.

From the models listed above, only BIP, Fractal, ProCom and SOFA2.0 support explicit composition mechanisms. However, the nature of these composition mechanisms *is not algebraic* in the sense that when applied to units of composition of a given type, the resulting piece is not a unit of the same type that can be stored and further composed. We have demonstrated that having algebraic composition mechanisms facilitates the development of more precise, consistent, systematic and automated approaches to derivate composites and their functional interfaces. As a corollary of the algebraic basis of our approach, the proposed functions can be composed. That is, the ones defined for basic operators can be reused in the definitions for the composite ones. For example, the *Observer* is a composite composition operator made up of one *Pipe* and one *Sequencer* operators. As can be seen, its corresponding function

$$obs\_composite\_fspec : FSpec \times \ldots \times FSpec \to FSpec$$

$$obs\_composite\_fspec = f_1, f_2, \ldots, f_n : FSpec \bullet$$
$$pipe\_composite\_fspec(f_1, seq\_composite\_fspec(f_2, \ldots, f_n))$$

uses both the $pipe\_composite\_fspec$ and the $seq\_composite\_fspec$ functions accordingly. Thus, we could say that we support some sort of interface composition. This observation leads us to the point of recognising that our work shares some principles and

---

[10] Note that not all the generated composites in these models are meant to be reusable –e.g. in BIP, Fractal and PECOS there is not a notion of repository where the generated composites can be stored to and retrieved from.

goals with algebraic composition mechanisms such as *parameterised modules* (a.k.a. functors) and *traits* [3].

In some functional languages (e.g. ML [12]), a module is characterised by a signature (i.e. an interface specification) and a structure (i.e. an implementation of the signature). A parameterised module denotes a function from structures to structures; that is, it accepts one or more structures of a given signature, and produces a new structure that implements a particular signature. In contrast to our approach, the signature of the new structure is chosen by the programmer in an *ad hoc* manner rather than derived from the parameterised module's arguments. On the other hand, traits are essentially groups of provided and required methods that serve as building blocks for classes by providing first-class representations of the behaviours of a class. Traits can be algebraically composed via the *sum* operator which, generally speaking, has the semantics of some sort of structural union. Thus the number of the behaviours (i.e. methods) in the composite trait is the "sum" of the behaviours in all the composed traits. In our approach, the number of the behaviours is derived differently as each behaviour abstracts a particular form of coordination between the behaviours of multiple components. Thus our approach supports a new notion for deriving the structure and behaviors of a composite.

Our proposal has some drawbacks though. In the example presented in Section 5, we observed that depending on the number of operations provided by the composed components, the application of some functions could explode potentially the number of operations in the resulting interfaces. Although by using our tool a composite developer can filter the number of signatures of the resulting specification by keeping some execution sequences away, it could be desirable to automatically support this filtering by using some sort of behavioural information, e.g. assertions or behaviour protocols.

Additionally, we are dealing with stateless components and we are not considering specifications containing assertions on operations. We are exploring the feasibility of using some formalism in algebraic specification languages to deal with state and assertion composition under the semantics of our composition operators. For example, in the Z specification language [9] schemas specify the state of a module as well as relevant operations on them. Z schemas have a name, a declaration part and a predicate part. The name part gives a name to the aspect of the the module being specified. The declaration part defines a number of variables of certain types. The predicate part defines invariants on these variables. The schema calculus of Z allows extending the schemas and combining them by using logical connectives such as conjunction, disjunction and implication. Conjunction and implication between schemas are defined by combining the declaration parts and taking in conjunction or implication the predicate parts. Schemas can be composed sequentially, which implies that the after-state of the first schema is to be matched with the before-state of the second.

7   Conclusions and Future Work

When the construction of reusable composite components is supported, the ability to derive their interface specifications is crucial to scale the development techniques of any CBD approach. We presented our progress on developing an approach to support this issue. Specifically, we focused on the generation of composites' functional specifications. The composites are constructed via composition operators defined within the context of a new component model. The specification approach is based on a set of operator-specific functions, which allow deriving composites' functional specifications in a systematic, consistent and largely automatic manner. Via an example we have illustrated the aforementioned benefits as well as the fact that our approach provides a new view into the space of interface generation.

In the near future, we plan to extend our approach to deal with more sophisticated behavioural information. Similarly, we have started to work on a similar approach to derive other elements from the composites' interfaces, i.e. the non-functional properties and the information about the deployment environment. So far it seems feasible to derive directly composable non-functional properties as described in [2].

By doing this research we hope to gain more understanding on software composition and its automation, which is the ultimate goal not only for CBD, but also for some other component-based development paradigms such as service composition and software product lines.

References

1. Broy, M., Deimel, A., Henn, J., Koskimies, K., Plasil, F., Pomberger, G., Pree, W., Stal, M., Szyperski, C.: What characterizes a (software) component? Software - Concepts and Tools 19(1), 49–56 (1998)
2. Crnković, I., Sentilles, S., Vulgarakis, A., Chaudron, M.R.V.: A classification framework for software component models. IEEE Trans. on Software Engineering (2010) (pre-Prints)
3. Ducasse, S., Nierstrasz, O., Schärli, N., Wuyts, R., Black, A.P.: Traits: A mechanism for fine-grained reuse. ACM Trans. on Prog. Languages and Systems 28, 331–388 (2006)
4. Gamma, E., Helm, R., Johnson, R., Vlissides, J.: Design Patterns: Elements of Reusable Object-Oriented Software. Addison-Wesley Professional Computing Series. Addison-Wesley, Reading (1995)
5. Geisterfer, C.J.M., Ghosh, S.: Software component specification: A study in perspective of component selection and reuse. In: Proc. of the 5th Int. Conf. on Commercial-off-the-Shelf (COTS)-Based Software Systems. IEEE Computer Society, Los Alamitos (2006)
6. Lau, K.-K., Ling, L., Velasco Elizondo, P.: Towards composing software components in both design and deployment phases. In: Schmidt, H.W., Crnković, I., Heineman, G.T., Stafford, J.A. (eds.) CBSE 2007. LNCS, vol. 4608, pp. 274–282. Springer, Heidelberg (2007)
7. Lau, K.-K., Ornaghi, M., Wang, Z.: A software component model and its preliminary formalisation. In: de Boer, F.S., Bonsangue, M.M., Graf, S., de Roever, W.-P. (eds.) FMCO 2005. LNCS, vol. 4111, pp. 1–21. Springer, Heidelberg (2006)
8. Lau, K.-K., Wang, Z.: A survey of software component models. Preprint CSPP-38, School of Computer Science, The University of Manchester (May 2006)
9. Potter, B., Till, D., Sinclair, J.: An Introduction to Formal Specification and Z, 2nd edn. Prentice Hall PTR, Upper Saddle River (1996)
10. Russell, N., ter Hofstede, A.H.M., van der Aalst, W.M.P., Mulyar, N.: Workflow control-flow patterns: A revised view. Technical Report BPM-06-22, BPM Center (2006)
11. Sentilles, S., Štěpán, P., Carlson, J., Crnković, I.: Integration of extra-functional properties in component models. In: Lewis, G.A., Poernomo, I., Hofmeister, C. (eds.) CBSE 2009. LNCS, vol. 5582, pp. 173–190. Springer, Heidelberg (2009)

12. Ullman, J.D.: Elements of ML programming. Prentice-Hall, Inc., Upper Saddle River (1998)
13. Velasco Elizondo, P.: Systematic and automated development with reuse (2009),
    http://www.cimat.mx/~pvelasco/exo/exotool_en.html
14. Velasco Elizondo, P., Lau, K.-K.: A catalogue of component connectors to support development with reuse. Journal of Systems and Software 83(7), 1165–1178 (2010)
15. Velasco Elizondo, P., Ndjatchi, M.K.C.: Functional Specification of Composite Components. Technical Report I-10-05/24-06-2010(CC/CIMAT), Centre for Mathematical Research (June 2010), http://www.cimat.mx/reportes/enlinea/I-10-05.pdf

Comparing Machine Learning Approaches for Context-Aware Composition

Antonina Danylenko[1], Christoph Kessler[2], and Welf Löwe[1]

[1] Linnaeus University, Software Technology Group,
351 95 Växjö, Sweden
{antonina.danylenko,welf.lowe}@lnu.se
[2] Linköping University, Department for Computer and Information Science,
581 83 Linköping, Sweden
{christoph.kessler}@liu.se

Abstract. Context-Aware Composition allows to automatically select optimal variants of algorithms, data-structures, and schedules at runtime using generalized dynamic Dispatch Tables. These tables grow exponentially with the number of significant context attributes. To make Context-Aware Composition scale, we suggest four alternative implementations to Dispatch Tables, all well-known in the field of machine learning: Decision Trees, Decision Diagrams, Naive Bayes and Support Vector Machines classifiers. We assess their decision overhead and memory consumption theoretically and practically in a number of experiments on different hardware platforms. Decision Diagrams turn out to be more compact compared to Dispatch Tables, almost as accurate, and faster in decision making. Using Decision Diagrams in Context-Aware Composition leads to a better scalability, i.e., Context-Aware Composition can be applied at more program points and regard more context attributes than before.

Keywords: Context-Aware Composition, Autotuning, Machine Learning.

1 Introduction

Context-dependent computation is an essential part of a wide range of application domains, where an application should behave according to the conditions arising during the execution. A technique that enables this type of computation is called Context-Oriented Programming—a programming approach that treats context explicitly and makes it accessible and manipulatable by software [1,2]. In order to get the desirable behavior of the application, a specific composition, called *Context-Aware Composition*, has to be made regarding the current context of the execution. Context-aware composition separates the concerns of defining component variants and the decision in favor of any of these variants in a composition context. The former is done by component designers who develop variants that might be advantageous in certain composition contexts possibly supported by variant generators, generating for instance different schedules. The latter is fully automated. In a learning phase, variants are tested in different contexts, and the champion variant of each context is captured in a generalized Dispatch Table that is later used to compose with this variant in the actual composition context.

S. Apel and E. Jackson (Eds.): SC 2011, LNCS 6708, pp. 18–33, 2011.

The learning and composition phases can be separated (offline learning) or interleaved (online learning) leading to self-adaptive systems.

Context-aware composition can improve performance of software systems considerably as it dynamically composes with the prospected best variant of alternative algorithms, data structures, etc. Composition context can range from domain-specific to technology-dependent attributes, and even include properties that may be based on hardware or software (e.g. number of available processors, problem size, etc.). Hence the number of attributes in Dispatch Table can be very large. Scalability of context-aware composition generally depends on scalability of variants-modeling technique that, in turn, depends on the actual number of contexts. However, Dispatch Tables are not very scalable. Capturing the learned knowledge in Dispatch Tables mapping context attributes to variants can be memory consumptive: the tables grow exponentially with the number of context attributes. Hence, capturing these tables for every composition point, i.e., all calls to a function f of a component with several implementation variants, might lead to problems with the overhead in memory consumption, implying that the amount of required memory for execution of a certain application might be dramatically increased.

To remedy this problem, we enhance the scalability of the variants-modeling technique by introducing technology from machine learning. In fact, we learn decision functions $d_f : X_1, ..., X_n \rightarrow Y$, with X_i a table dimension (i.e., a context attribute) and Y the table entry (i.e., the presumably best algorithm variant of f). The actual composition (dynamic dispatch) then evaluates the function d_f for the actual context attributes and invokes the best variant. Therefore, as always in machine learning, we need to bias:

- Accuracy of the decision: does d_f always decide for the optimal variant, and what is the impact of suboptimal decisions on the overall performance,
- Decision time and its impact on the overall performance,
- Memory size for capturing d_f.

For this work, we assume an offline learning and hence ignore the learning time.

The remainder of this paper is structured as follows: Section 2 introduces the different technologies for learning decision functions and theoretically assesses their memory consumption and decision time. Section 3 assesses their memory consumption and decision overhead practically in a number of experiments, compares their accuracy with Dispatch Tables as the baseline, and shows the speedups of context-aware composition using different decision function implementations. We base our experiments on a sorting problem. Sorting is an extreme problem for context-aware composition in the sense that the ratio of dynamic decisions and payload operations is rather high. However, the insight on this extreme case can deliver a guidance for other cases, since it presents a general overview and interpretation of each learning technology. Section 4 discusses related work, and Section 5 concludes the paper and points out directions of future work.

2   Assessment of Learning Strategies

Learning is the process of constructing, from training data, a fast and/or compact surrogate function that heuristically solves a decision, prediction or classification problem for which only expensive or no algorithmic solutions are known. It automatically abstracts from sample data to a total decision function.

Different learning strategies might be employed; depending on the strategy and the problem to solve, resulting classifiers differ in speed of learning and deciding, their memory consumption, and their decision accuracy. Machine learning strategies are usually chosen based on the problem domain, sometimes even on the sample data [3]. However, bounds on memory and decision overheads can be theoretically estimated for every learning strategy regardless of the specific problem domain. In this section, we present such bounds and compare memory consumption and decision overhead for four classifiers representing three most common used generalization models [4]: Naive Bayes Classifier representing the Probability model; Decision Trees and Decision Diagrams representing the Tree-based model; Support Vector Machines representing the Maximum Margin model. Additionally, we take Dispatch Tables as our baseline decision function implementation.

Dispatch Tables are implemented as n-dimensional arrays, n the number of context attributes. Each dimension i contains entries corresponding to the sample values of the context attribute X_i. Thus, the memory consumption M of the Dispatch Table can be approximated from below by

$$M = size \times m^n$$

where $size$ bytes are necessary to encode all variants in Y, and m is the minimum number of samples of any of the context attributes.

Before making a decision, the closest sample point for each actual context attribute value needs to be computed. Assume we sample discrete attributes completely and continuous attributes with a logarithmic distance. Then we find the index corresponding to a discrete attribute value by a mapping table lookup, and the index of a continuous attribute value by computing the logarithm of the actual attribute value. Additionally, each access to an n-dimension array is basically an access to a 1-dimensional array requiring some offset calculations:

$$offset = base\_address + (((d_1 \times |X_1| + d_2) \times \ldots |X_{n-1}| + d_{n-1}) \times |X_n| + d_n) \times size,$$

where d_i is the index and $|X_i|$ the sample size of the context attribute X_i. Therefore, a decision time for an n-dimensional Dispatch Table can be estimated as

$$T(n) = (log \times k + n) \times T_{flop} + (n - k + 1) \times T_{aa} + c,$$

where k is the number of continuous attributes, log is the number of floating point operations for calculating the logarithm[1], T_{flop} is the time for a flop, T_{aa} is the array access time, and c is a constant time used for small operations. Dispatch Tables capture variants at sample points of continuous attributes. Finding the sample point closest to an actual context attribute value must be done prior to each table lookup. In contrast, classification models learned by different learning strategies can decide on continuous attributes directly as discussed below.

---

[1] Many processors provide the integer $log2$ in a single instruction in hardware; in our Java implementation we need 21 flops.

Decision Trees are trees encoding context attributes in the inner nodes. Each outgoing edge of such a node corresponds to a value (or value range) of the context attribute. Each path from the root node to a leaf in the Decision Tree represents actual context values leading to a classification result. Using a Decision Tree as a dispatch repository for a given context $(X_1, \ldots, X_n)$ is straight forward: in each inner node corresponding to attribute X_i, starting at the root, we use the attribute value x_i^j to decide which child to visit next. Decision Trees could capture Dispatch Tables without any loss of accuracy. However, learning algorithms compute approximations in order to avoid Decision Trees to over-fit the sample data. Most of these algorithms employ a recursive top-down approach that changes the order of the attributes for each path in order to select the most relevant attributes first and possibly ignore the less relevant attributes [5]. Assume an initial data set R of tuples $(x_1, \ldots, x_n) \rightarrow y$ and root node r:

- *Base Case:* If all instances in R belong to the same class label y, then r is a leaf with label y.
- *Recursive:* Otherwise, select one attribute X_i and create a child node $node^j$ for each possible attribute value x_i^j. Partition R into smaller subsets R^j based on their particular value for the attribute X_i. Apply the algorithm recursively on each child node $node^j$ using data sets R^j.

The number of tests necessary to reach a leaf is equal to the *depth* of the Decision Tree. This *depth* varies around the number n of context attributes: for *discrete* context attributes it is at most n; *continuous* attributes can even occur several times on the path due to data partitioning [6]. So, generally, the prediction time is $depth \times T_{aa}$ and we approximate

$$T(n) \approx n \times T_{aa} + c.$$

In the worst case, the memory required for capturing the Decision Tree is even larger than for the corresponding table: k leaves if the table has k entries, and (almost) k inner nodes. This size reduces when the learning strategy approximates the decisions. It can also be reduced if all paths from an inner node lead to the same decision (making this whole subtree redundant). Hence, the memory consumption is

$$M = size \times edges,$$

where *edges* is number of edges in the tree (assuming that *size* bytes are even sufficient to encode all different nodes).

Decision Diagrams represent Decision Trees in a compact way by eliminating redundant subtrees. In particular, diagrams are a generalization of Ordered Binary Decision Diagrams (OBDDs) [7,8], known as a compact representation of Boolean functions. In practice, they reduce the exponential memory consumption of table representations of these functions to acceptable sizes.

We do not have binary but general decisions, since a context attribute could have any domain, and the function (variant) values are not binary either, since there are, in general, more than two variants to choose from. These more general Decision Diagrams are

known as *Multi-Terminal Multi-Valued Decision Diagrams* (MMDDs) [9]. They correspond to rooted directed acyclic graphs with inner nodes representing context attributes
and leaves representing decisions. Generally, decision time and worst case memory
size of diagrams are the same as for Decision Trees. Thus, the worst case memory and
look-up overhead for Decision Trees and Decision Diagrams are equal, but, due to the
elimination of redundancies, the size is expected to be considerably smaller in practice.

A Naive Bayes Classifier is a simple probabilistic classifier based on Bayesian statis-
tics. It naively assumes conditional independence of the context attributes from each
other using a simple classification method which classifies an item by determining a
probability of its belonging to a certain class $y \in Y$ [10,11].

For example, we wish to approximate a target function: $X \rightarrow Y$, or equivalently
$P(Y|X)$. Let us assume that Y is a binary class with values y_1 and y_2 and X is a vector
space of n context attributes. Applying Bayes' rule, $P(Y = y_1|X)$ can be calculated as:

$$P(Y = y_1|X) = \prod_{i=1}^{n} \frac{P(X = x_i|Y = y_1) \times P(Y = y_1)}{P(X = x_i|Y = y_1) \times P(Y = y_1) + P(X = x_i|Y = y_2) \times P(Y = y_2)},$$

where x_i denotes the ith possible vector of X, and the summation in the denominator is
done over all values of class Y.

Naive Bayes classifiers use the sample data and compute all possible probabilities
for each attribute vector x_i over all class values y_k. As a result, a Naive Bayes classifier
is just a set of probabilities that are accessed during classification for computing the
most probable variant. For a discrete attribute X_i, the probability is stored in an array
with $|Y| \times |X_i|$ elements; for a continuous attribute, a *mean* and a *variance* are computed
and stored in two arrays of size $|Y|$. So the memory consumption with k continuous
attributes is

$$M = |Y| \times size \times (2k + 1 + (n - k) \sum_{i=1}^{(n-k)} |X_i|).$$

A decision using a Naive Bayes classifier takes quite some time: it requires 4 flops for
each discrete attribute and 88 flops for each continuous attribute (including
mathematical operations computing Gaussian) for each possible class. Thus, the decision time is estimated as

$$T(n) = (4n + 84k) \times T_{flops} + (2n + k) \times T_{aa} + c.$$

Support Vector Machines (SVM) construct a linear separating hyperplane in the vector space defined by the table dimensions with the maximal margin in a higher dimen-
sional space. If the vectors cannot be separated by planes, artificial dimensions can be
introduced using so-called kernel functions [12].

We refer to LIBSVM [13], a library for Support Vector Machines, as a black box
with a radial basis function for the kernel function and follow the normalization and
parameter finding suggestions detailed in [14].

SVMs can be trained to be very accurate classifiers. However, the training time of
SVMs can be very long, especially on large data sets. Training an SVM requires solving

a constrained quadratic programming (QP) problem which usually takes $O(s^3)$ computations, where s is the number of sample points [15].

More importantly, deciding requires an evaluation of the kernel function that takes for the selected kernel approximately $20 + (n + |Y|)$ flops for each support vector and a number of additional flops for finding the actual variant. The number l of support vectors is usually proportional to s, so we can approximate

$$T(s, n) \approx T(l, n) \approx (20 + n + 2|Y| - 1) \times l \times T_{flops} + l \times (2|Y| - 1) \times T_{aa} + c.$$

The encoded SVM classifier has a quite high memory consumption for capturing the support vectors, approximated with

$$M = 12l + 24|Y| + 4|Y|^2 + 100s$$

double precision values.

Based on these theoretical estimations, we cannot decide which classifier to prefer. It depends on the bias between acceptable decision time and memory overhead, and on the concrete problem, i.e., the number of context attributes, sample points etc. However, once the number of attributes and the sample data points are decided, the above approximations can be used to (pre-)select a preferred classifier. We will discuss this in the next section by instantiating the approximations for a concrete context-aware composition example comparing theoretical assessments with results of practical measurements.

3 Experiments

Algorithm Variants We implemented the well-known sorting algorithms Selection sort, Quicksort, and Merge sort along with two parallel versions of Quicksort and Merge sort, which spawn a new thread for one of the sub-problems in each divide step. We used textbook implementations [16] and did not optimize the variants, especially, we greedily create new threads regardless of the number of cores available. All algorithms are implemented in Java/JDK 1.6.

Platforms All experiments are executed on three different multi-core machines:

M1 a 2 core Dell Latitude PC running Windows XP (2002, SP 3) on an Intel Dual Core T2300 at 1.66GHz and 2GB RAM,
M2 an 8 core IBM Blade Server running Linux (CentOS) on an Intel 8 Core 5450 at 3GHz and 16GB RAM, and
M3 a 2 core MacBook Pro running Mac OS X (10.6.5) on an Intel Core i5 at 2.4 Ghz and 8GB RAM.

All tests are run on the respective native JVMs with setting -Xms128m -Xmx1g.

3.1 Memory Overhead of the Approaches

To compare different classification approaches, we constructed three Dispatch (decision) Tables for our sorting problem for different multi-core machines (M1, M2, M3). The dispatch technique attempts to speed up sorting by selecting the best algorithm

Table 1. Memory overhead of different classification models

	Table	Tree	Diagram	Bayes	SVM
Classifier size in bytes	136	24/40	24/40	80	544

(class) Y for the current context (problem size N, processor availability P), where N is a continuous integer sampled at powers of two between $2^0 \ldots 2^{16}$, P is boolean with 0 and 1 as possible values (encoding whether or not processors are available). Y is a discrete integer in the range $1 \ldots 5$ each representing one of the algorithm variants. The memory needed for storing $2 \times 17 = 34$ entries is rather small, i.e. $M = 4 \times 34 = 136$ bytes, cf. Table 1 for the size of the Dispatch Table and the alternative classifiers constructed as discussed in Section 2. However, for a higher number of context attributes the memory need will grow exponentially.

To encode a Dispatch Table in a Decision Tree or a Decision Graph, we used the FC4.5 learning algorithm, a fast and efficient implementation of the well-known and widely used classification algorithm C4.5 [17]. Decision Trees have a moderate learning effort. The memory compression rate is quite high: $\approx 82\%$ for M1, M2 (6 *edges*, requiring 24 bytes) and $\approx 71\%$ for M3 (10*edges*, 40 bytes).

The Decision Diagram is a redundancy-free encoding of the Decision Trees and, hence, the depth does not change. However, Dispatch Table compression does not improve compared to Decision Trees (the number of edges is the same). In our example, the diagram uses up to 27% fewer nodes than the tree.

The Naive Bayes classifier was the fastest to construct and the encoded Dispatch Tables take only 80 bytes giving a 41% of reduction immediately without any additional optimizations, since the size of the classifier only depends on the context attributes, not their values.

In order to construct an accurate prediction model based on Support Vector Machines, a learning phase requires an optimization of kernel function parameters specific to each problem domain and input sample data. Although done automatically, finding parameters giving an acceptable decision accuracy requires a cross-validation prelearning over the large range of parameter values. In our example, (pre-)learning time was still acceptable in range of a few seconds. The memory required to encode the SVM classifier is 544 bytes (based on the LIBSVM library implementation). This is the highest memory overhead and even 75% larger than Dispatch Table memory consumption.

3.2 Decision Accuracy of the Approaches

In this section, we compare the accuracy of the different decision approaches. As we know the right decision for each actual context (processors available and problem size) only for the sample points measured in the training phase, we can assess accuracy only approximatively: (1) by comparing the decisions of the different approaches at these sample points, and (2) by comparing their decisions with the decisions of the table approach as the baseline. We define a decision error as (1) the ratio of decisions not suggesting the best algorithm variant in the sample points over all decisions, and (2) the ratio of decisions diverging from the suggestion of the decision table over all decisions.

Table 2. Errors of different decision approaches

Platform	Problem	Tree [%]	Diagram [%]	Bayes [%]	SVM [%]
PC 2 cores	Sample points	0	0	15	0
(M1)	10.000	21	21	0	10
	100.000	21	21	4	10
	1.000.000	21	21	100	10
Server 8 cores	Sample points	0	0	9	0
(M2)	10.000	25	25	0	0
	100.000	25	25	1	0
	1.000.000	25	5	100	25
MAC 2 cores	Sample points	0	0	6	0
(M3)	10.000	21	21	0	9
	100.000	21	21	3	9
	1.000.000	21	21	100	9

The Dispatch Table captures the best implementation for the sample points. Hence, its error is 0 in the measure (1). However, we do not know if the Dispatch Table suggests the best variant between sampled problem sizes. Hence, (2) is an accuracy measure relative to the baseline implementation of context-aware composition using Dispatch Tables.

For the different platforms, Table 2 shows the error (1) at the sample points and the error (2) for selected sizes of arrays to sort. All ratios are given in %.

Dispatch Tables (trivially), Decision Trees and Diagrams, and Support Vector Machines (cf. rows "Sample points") are to 100% accurate according to measure (1) and, generally, all decision approaches perform very accurate at the sample points with an error of at most 15%.

The error is somewhat higher for the accuracy measure (2). Independent of the problem size, Decision Trees and Diagrams suggest in 21% to 25% of the cases different algorithm variants than the Dispatch Table (cf. columns "Tree" and "Diagram"). For the Bayesian classifier and the classifier based on Support Vector Machines, the error (2) increases with the problem size. However, it is in most cases smaller than for Decision Trees and Diagrams. Note that the error of 100% for the Bayesian classifier for the very large problems is due to its first (wrong) decision in favor of Selection sort. As Selection sort does not contain any recursive calls, there are no other decision points and this wrong decision is the only one.

As a conclusion, none of the approaches ought to be dropped from further evaluations since their accuracy is comparable with that of Dispatch Tables.

3.3 Decision Overhead of the Approaches

We compare the overhead of the different approaches for decision making first based on our theoretical assumptions and then experimentally.

For the 2-dimensional Dispatch Table based on one continuous and one discrete attribute, the prediction time includes 22 floating point operations and one array access,

Table 3. Decision overhead (# operations) of different classification models

	Table	Tree	Diagram	Bayes	SVM
Flops	22	0	0	46	644
Array access	1	2.5	2.5	5	140

Table 4. Time overhead (in %) of different decision approaches

Platform	Problem size	Quicksort in msec.	Table in %	Tree in %	Diagram in %	Bayes in %	SVM in %
PC 2 cores	10.000	3.62	43	25	22	1161	4099
(M1)	100.000	51.91	28	14	10	816	2871
	1.000.000	998.36	15	8	6	423	1449
Server 8 cores	10.000	1.87	52	34	34	680	1595
(M2)	100.000	22.93	55	29	30	553	1321
	1.000.000	552.51	24	12	12	243	576
MAC 2 cores	10.000	1.99	37	36	33	328	1008
(M3)	100.000	28.08	29	19	18	224	707
	1.000.000	478.55	25	16	15	139	426

that is $T_{flops} \times 22 + T_{aa}$. It is worth mentioning that in our cost model the time for a lookup to any 2-dimension Dispatch Table is constant and does not depend on the number of entries stored, which is a simplification ignoring caching effects. Table 3 shows the floating point operations and the number of array accesses for the classifiers.

The decision time required by Decision Trees and Diagrams depends on the tree's and diagram's depth, respectively. For each of the three Decision Trees (Diagrams) constructed, the decision requires at most three indirect array accesses, since the maximum depth is three for all them (the average depth is 2.5). Thus, the expected overhead can be estimated as $T_{aa} \times 2.5$.

As discussed, a Bayes classifier is quite effective in memory consumption but has quite a high runtime overhead for making decisions. In our setting, it requires 46 floating point operations and 5 array accesses, $T_{flops} \times 46 + T_{aa} \times 5$. This is twice as many flops and five times as many array accesses compared to Dispatch Table, making it a slow classifier for our problem.

Decisions in SVM includes 21 flops that correspond to a kernel function computation calculated for each of the $l = 28$ support vectors and then additional 56 flops for classification. Altogether, the decision phase takes 644 flops and the whole decision time is $T_{flops} \times 644 + T_{aa} \times 140$. This is the highest look-up overhead among all classification models.

Experiments confirm these overhead predictions. In the experiments, we use the fastest homogeneous solution – Quicksort – as the baseline. The third column of Table 4 shows the time for Quicksort for the different platforms and three selected array sizes to sort.

On each recursive invocation of Quicksort (with a certain number of processors still available and a certain sub-problem size), we look up the best algorithm variant in the different decision repositories. However, in order to compare the overhead in a fair way, we always invoke Quicksort even in Context-Aware Composition regardless of the best algorithm variant suggested. Hence, all compared solutions essentially implement Quicksort.

Table 4 shows the execution times of the Context-Aware Composition based on the different decision functions relative to the execution time of Quicksort on the same platform and architecture. For instance, the Dispatch Table (cf. column "Table") introduces an overhead of 43% on the PC with 2 cores and the problem size of 10,000 array elements as it requires $1.43 \times 3.62\text{msec} = 5.18\text{msec}$ of the corresponding Quicksort execution times without table lookup (3.62msec).

There are $O(N)$ expected lookups for problems of size N in Quicksort; the expected work of Quicksort is $O(N \log N)$. The lookup time is $O(1)$; it only depends on the number of algorithm variants, the number of context attributes and the decision repository variant, but it does not grow with the problem size. Hence, for all decision repository variants, the overhead gets smaller with increasing problem size. This is confirmed by the measurements.

The Decision Diagram (column "Diagram") introduces the lowest overhead in almost all cases with the Decision Tree (column "Tree") not far behind. These overheads are between 6% and 36% depending on problem size and platform. The Dispatch Table comes with an overhead between 15% and 55%. Algorithm variant selection using Bayesian classifiers and Support Vector Machines (columns "Bayes" and "SVM", resp.) slows down the execution by factors between 2.4 and almost 42. Quicksort (and other recursive sorting algorithms) are extreme in the sense that ratio between decision points (recursive calls) and workload is rather high. Therefore, we observed a rather high overhead for context-aware composition compared to the homogeneous Quicksort variant. In conclusion, Dispatch Tables, Trees, and Diagrams introduce an overhead that is still acceptable as it can be expected that a clever algorithm variant selection compensates for the overheads. At least for recursive sorting problems, this is not the case for Bayesian classifiers and Support Vector Machines.

As the conclusion, we discard Bayesian classifiers and Support Vector Machines as decision repositories for improving sorting using context-aware composition due to their (too) high decision overhead. As Decision Trees and Diagrams by construction always suggest the same variant and Decision Diagrams are smaller in size and have the slightly smaller overhead, we discard Decision Trees in the final overall assessment.

3.4 Overall Performance

Now we are ready to assess the overall performance of context-aware composition using Decision Diagrams vs. using Dispatch Table. Figure 1 shows the experimental results on the different platforms. As a reference, it also shows how the fastest homogeneous implementation variant (sequential Quicksort) performs on the three platforms.

On the PC with two cores, the optimized version using Decision Diagrams gains a speed-up of 1.47 over sequential Quicksort, on average over all array sizes from $10,000 - 1,000,000$ (step $10,000$) while the optimized version using Dispatch Tables gains a speed-up of 1.46. On the server with 8 cores, the difference between the two implementations is even more pronounced: an average speed-up of 1.92 for the

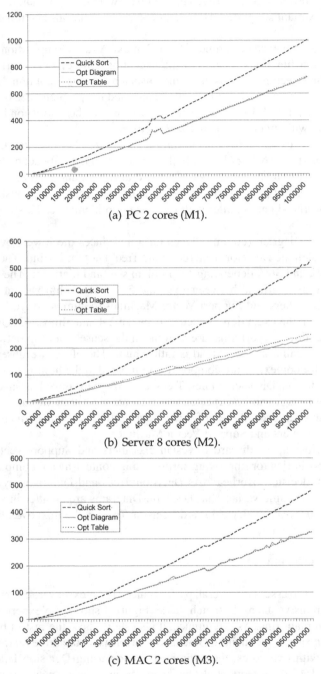

(a) PC 2 cores (M1).

(b) Server 8 cores (M2).

(c) MAC 2 cores (M3).

Fig. 1. Homogeneous Quicksort and Context-Aware Sorting using Decision Diagrams ("Opt Diagram") and Dispatch Tables ("Opt Table"). The x-axis displays the array size, the y-axis the time in *msec*

diagram-based solution vs. 1.79 for the table-based solution. On the MAC with 2 cores, the speed-up results are 1.39 vs. 1.37, again in favor of the diagram-based solution.

Obviously, the decisions of the Dispatch Table are (slightly) more accurate, but this is more than compensated with the lower runtime overhead of the Decision Diagrams. Altogether, the experiments showed that the Decision Diagram is not only smaller by a factor of five than the Dispatch Table, but also (slightly) faster when used as a decision repository in context-aware composition.

4 Related Work

Context-aware composition, i.e., the run-time context dependent binding of a call to a matching callee defined by another component, is gaining importance as a knob for performance optimization, in particular since the stagnation of CPU clock rates puts an urgent need to exploit new sources for performance improvements. Andersson *et al.* compose and optimize special implementations of data structures and algorithms, considering matrix multiplication as a case study [18]. This work may be considered as a generalization of the dispatch mechanism in object-oriented languages, for instance in the sense of Context-Oriented Programming (COP) [19,1,2].

The optimization of libraries for specific functionality such as linear algebra or signal processing is a natural target for optimized composition because the domain and code base is limited and statically known, computations can often be described in a restricted domain-specific language from which variants can be generated and tuned automatically, and because even high off-line tuning times are acceptable due to the high reuse of libraries. Well-known examples include the library generators ATLAS for basic linear algebra computations and FFTW and SPIRAL [20,21] for transforms in signal processing.

More recently, optimized composition has been proposed as an optimization technique also in the more general context of component based systems, where the programmer is responsible for annotating components so that their composition can be optimized for performance. However, only few approaches consider recursive components with *deep composition*, and only few consider the co-optimization of the selection of implementation variants with other variation possibilities, such as the layout and data structure of operands or scheduling.

Li *et al.* [22] implement a library generator for sorting that uses dynamic tuning to adapt the library to the target machine at installation time. They use a number of machine parameters (such as cache size, the size of the input and the distribution of the input) as input to a machine learning algorithm. The machine learning algorithm, a problem-specific combination of two different classifiers, is trained to pick the best algorithm for any considered scenario.

Large-scale distributed memory systems as used in high-performance computing are usually programmed in SPMD (single program, multiple data) style using MPI or partitioned global address space languages to enable tight resource control. Brewer [23] investigated dynamic algorithm selection for such a system for sorting and PDE solving, and also considered limited support for the dynamic selection of array distributions on distributed shared memory systems. The run-time predictor is constructed from measured samples by calibrating the parameters of a generic prediction function that is semi-automatically generated from user-provided information about relevant properties and ranges, using linear regression. Our learning approach differs in that we require no assumptions or user hints about the terms that occur in the generic run-time prediction function.

STAPL [24] non-recursively applies dynamic algorithm selection for sorting and matrix computations. Three different learning algorithms are used: a Decision Tree learner based on Quinlan's ID3 algorithm with different pruning strategies, found to perform best in the experimental evaluation, a standard feed-forward neural network with back-propagation learning, and a Naive Bayes classifier found to be inferior in its classification accuracy.

Yu and Rauchwerger [25] take a similar approach for reductions. From measurements of the individual implementation variants they construct predictor functions in two steps. First, they select a small number of polynomial terms in the context and machine model parameters from a term pool to build a generic prediction function. Second, they calibrate the coefficients from the training data using general linear regression and Decision Tree learning. For each call, the calibrated run-time prediction functions are then evaluated and the decision is memorized so it can be reused if the same parameter configuration should occur again. This way, the overhead of the dispatch at each call is reduced.

Kessler and Löwe [26,27] consider optimized composition at the level of annotated user-defined components (i.e., not limited to closed libraries) together with scheduling, resource allocation and other optimizations, which allows for simultaneous optimization. For the off-line search and optimization phase, the approach uses an interleaved dynamic programming algorithm to construct a component variant Dispatch Table (V-table) for each component-provided functionality f and a resource allocation and schedule Dispatch Table (S-table) for independent calls. The tables are constructed simultaneously bottom-up for increasing problem sizes and resource assignments.

Olszewski and Voss [28] proposed a dynamic adaptive algorithm selection framework for divide-and-conquer sorting algorithms in a fork-join parallel setup. Their approach is divided into two phases. First, they use a dynamic programming algorithm to select the best sequential algorithm for different problem sizes. Then, they determine the threshold problem sizes for when to submit the subproblems to a shared work queue and execute in parallel rather than to execute sequentially. For the construction of a classifier, they use the C4.5 algorithm to generate a Decision Tree. While apparently sufficient prediction accuracy was achieved in the considered examples, the resulting sizes and overheads are not discussed. PetaBricks [29] applies a similar approach where, in the offline search phase, the variant choice functions for recursive components are not computed by dynamic programming but by a genetic algorithm, essentially applying heuristic cuts to the optimization space. There appears to be no further compression of the variant selection function. Schedules and resource allocation are not co-optimized with variant selection but delegated to a run-time system with a work-stealing dynamic scheduler. Numerical accuracy is considered as an additional algorithmic property in composition. The recent paper by Wernsing and Stitt [30] presents an approach that builds upon PetaBricks but targets multicore CPU systems with FPGA-based accelerators. Like PetaBricks, this approach relies on dynamic scheduling and the learning is done offline, and like the approach by Kessler and Löwe [26,27], the learned execution plan is stored in table form.

5   Conclusions and Future Work

This paper contributed with:

1. A framework for plugging classifiers into context-aware composition. It was instantiated with 5 classifier variants: Dispatch Tables (baseline), Decision Trees, Decision Diagrams, Naive Bayesian, and SVM-based classifiers.
2. A theoretical assessment of memory and decision overhead of the four alternative classification technologies.
3. A practical assessment on three different hardware platforms using Sorting as a running context-aware composition example.

It turns out that Decision Diagrams are the preferred learning technology: they reduce memory consumption (in our example by a factor of five) and increase the overall performance (in our example by a few percent). Future work needs to validate this observation in extended experiments.

Sorting is an extreme problem for context-aware composition in the sense that the ratio of dynamic decisions and payload operations is rather high. We need to extend our experimental basis to problems with a lower rate of decisions and payload, which possibly allows for a higher overhead in decision making. In these scenarios, speedups could be achieved using Bayesian and SVM-based classifiers benefiting from their higher decision accuracy despite their high decision overhead.

Also, composition based on more context attributes (e.g., including data-structure implementations of arguments and results) ought to be considered. This leads to larger Dispatch Tables and allows to validate the memory reduction of Decision Diagrams and their alternatives. Moreover, we need to reevaluate our findings in online learning scenarios as required in self-adaptive systems. Here, we would change the system environment, e.g., force energy saving mode or generate extra workload outside the program's control, which invalidates the learned best-fit variants. Execution of suboptimal variants detects such changed system environments. In these scenarios, learning time becomes crucial as it adds to the overhead of context-aware composition.

Finally, we used the different learning technology (almost) as black boxes. Adapting them to our specific application context could improve the overall speed-up (and the performance of the different technologies relative to each other) and further reduce the memory consumption. For instance, we could capture the Decision Diagram in a very compact array containing indices (inner nodes) and variants (leafs). Also, we could split the SVM classifier in several classification steps each possibly requiring a linear kernel function making them both faster and more compact and, hence, competitive again.

Acknowledgments. C. Kessler: EU FP7 project PEPPHER (#248481), www.peppher.eu.

References

1. Hirschfeld, R., Costanza, P., Nierstrasz, O.: Context-oriented programming. Journal of Obj. Tech. ETH Zurich 7(3), 125–151 (2008)
2. Costanza, P., Hirschfeld, R.: Language constructs for context-oriented programming: an overview of contextl. In: Proc. of the 2005 Symposium on Dynamic Lang, pp. 1–10. ACM, New York (2005)
3. Nilsson, N.J.: Introduction to machine learning: An early draft of proposed text book. Stanford University, Stanford (1996)
4. Han, J., Kamber, M.: Data Mining: Concepts and Techniques, 2nd edn. The Morgan Kaufmann Series in Data Management Systems. Morgan Kaufmann, San Francisco (2000)
5. Moshkov, M.: Algorithms for constructing of decision trees. In: Komorowski, J., Żytkow, J.M. (eds.) PKDD 1997. LNCS, vol. 1263, pp. 335–342. Springer, Heidelberg (1997)
6. Rokach, L., Maimon, O.: Data Mining with Decision Trees: Theory and Applications. World Scientific, Singapore (2008)
7. Bryant, R.E.: Symbolic boolean manipulation with ordered binary-decision diagrams. ACM Computing Surveys 24, 293–318 (1992)
8. Bryant, R.E.: Graph-based algorithms for boolean function manipulation. IEEE Transactions on Computers 35, 677–691 (1986)
9. Johnson, S.: Branching programs and binary decision diagrams: theory and applications by Ingo Wegener society for industrial and applied mathematics, vol. 41, pp. 36–38. ACM, New York (2010)
10. Mitchell, T.M.: Machine Learning. McGraw-Hill, New York (1997)
11. Keogh, E.J., Pazzani, M.J.: Learning augmented bayesian classifiers: A comparison of distribution-based and classification-based approaches (1999)
12. Cortes, C., Vapnik, V.: Support-vector networks. Mach. Learn. 20, 273–297 (1995)
13. Chang, C.-C., Lin, C.-J.: Libsvm – a library for support vector machines. National Taiwan University, Dep. of Comp. Science and Inf. Eng. (2001)
14. Hsu, C.-W., Chang, C.-C., Lin, C.-J.: A practical guide to support vector classification. National Taiwan University, Dep. of Comp. Science, Tech. Rep. (2003)
15. Kramer, K.A., Hall, L.O., Goldgof, D.B., Remsen, A., Luo, T.: Fast support vector machines for continuous data. Trans. Sys. Man Cyber. 39, 989–1001 (2009)
16. Cormen, T.H., Leiserson, C.E., Rivest, R.L., Stein, C.: Introduction to Algorithms. The MIT Press, New York (2001)
17. Quinlan, J.R.: C4.5: programs for machine learning. Morgan Kaufmann Publishers Inc., San Francisco, CA, USA (1993)
18. Andersson, J., Ericsson, M., Kessler, C.W., Löwe, W.: Profile-guided composition. In: Pautasso, C., Tanter, É. (eds.) SC 2008. LNCS, vol. 4954, pp. 157–164. Springer, Heidelberg (2008)
19. von Löwis, M., Denker, M., Nierstrasz, O.: Context-oriented programming: beyond layers. In: Proc. of the 2007 Int. Conf. on Dynamic lang.: in conjunction with the 15th Int. Smalltalk Joint Conf. 2007, pp. 143–156. ACM, New York (2007)
20. Moura, J.M.F., Johnson, J., Johnson, R.W., Padua, D., Prasanna, V.K., Püschel, M., Singer, B., Veloso, M., Xiong, J.: Generating platform-adapted DSP libraries using SPIRAL. In: High Performance Embedded Computing, HPEC (2001)
21. Moura, J.M.F., Johnson, J., Johnson, R.W., Padua, D., Prasanna, V.K., Püschel, M., Veloso, M.: SPIRAL: Automatic implementation of signal processing algorithms. In: High Performance Embedded Computing, HPEC (2000)
22. Li, X., Garzarán, M.J., Padua, D.: A dynamically tuned sorting library. In: Proc. CGO 2004, Palo Alto, CA, USA, pp. 111–124 (2004)

23. Brewer, E.A.: High-level optimization via automated statistical modeling. In: PPoPP 1995 (1995)
24. Thomas, N., Tanase, G., Tkachyshyn, O., Perdue, J., Amato, N.M., Rauchwerger, L.: A framework for adaptive algorithm selection in STAPL. In: Proc. ACM SIGPLAN Symp. on Princ. and Pract. of Parallel Programming, pp. 277–288. ACM, New York (2005)
25. Yu, H., Rauchwerger, L.: An adaptive algorithm selection framework for reduction parallelization. IEEE Trans. Par. Distr. Syst. 17, 1084–1096 (2006)
26. Kessler, C., Löwe, W.: A framework for performance-aware composition of explicitly parallel components. In: Bischof, C., et al. (eds.) ParCo-2007: Jülich/Aachen Parallel Computing: Architectures, Algorithms and Applications. Advances in Parallel Computing Series, vol. 15, pp. 227–234. IOS Press, Amsterdam (2008)
27. Kessler, C., Löwe, W.: Optimized composition of performance-aware parallel components. In: 15th Workshop on Compilers for Parallel Computing CPC, July 7-9. University of Technology, Vienna (2010)
28. Olszewski, M., Voss, M.: An install-time system for the automatic generation of optimized parallel sorting algorithms. In: Proc. PDPTA 2004, vol. 1 (June 2004)
29. Ansel, J., Chan, C.P., Wong, Y.L., Olszewski, M., Zhao, Q., Edelman, A., Amarasinghe, S.P.: PetaBricks: a language and compiler for algorithmic choice. In: Proc. ACM SIGPLAN Conf. on Progr. Language Design and Implem, pp. 38–49. ACM, New York (2009)
30. Wernsing, J.R., Stitt, G.: Elastic computing: a framework for transparent, portable, and adaptive multi-core heterogeneous computing. In: Proc. ACM Conf. on Lang, compilers, and tools for embedded systems (LCTES 2010), pp. 115–124. ACM, New York (2010)

An Implementation of Composable Memory Transactions in Haskell

André Rauber Du Bois

PPGC, UFPel, Brazil
dubois@inf.ufpel.edu.br

Abstract. This paper describes an implementation of STM Haskell [11] in Haskell using the Transactional Locking 2 (TL2) algorithm by Dice, Shalev, and Shavit. TL2 provides an important characteristic that makes it suitable for implementing transactions as a library: it efficiently avoids periods of unsafe execution, guaranteeing that transactions always see a consistent state of memory. Preliminary measurements suggest that our library performs reasonably well, and provides similar scalability to the original STM Haskell runtime system, that was implemented in C. The implementation presented in this paper could work as a testbed to experiment with new extensions for STM Haskell. As an example, we demonstrate how to modify the basic library to support the `unreadTVar` [20] construct.

1 Introduction

Transactional Memory is a concurrency control abstraction that is considered a promising approach to facilitate software development for multi-core processors. In this model, sequences of operations that modify memory are grouped into atomic actions. The runtime support for transactions must guarantee that these actions will appear to have been executed atomically to the rest of the system. STM Haskell [11] is a Haskell extension that provides *composable memory transactions*. The programmer defines *transactional actions* that are composable i.e., they can be combined to generate new transactions, and are first-class values. Haskell's type system forces threads to access shared variables only inside transactions. As transactions can not be executed outside a call to `atomically`, properties like *atomicity* (the effects of a transaction must be visible to all threads all at once) and *isolation* (during the execution of a transaction, it can not be affected by other transactions) are always maintained.

This paper describes an implementation of STM Haskell in Haskell, using the Transactional Locking 2 (LT2) algorithm by Dice, Shalev and Shavit [6]. The main reason to choose this algorithm is that, unlike most other lock-based Software Transactional Memory (STM) systems, it safely avoids periods of unsafe execution, meaning that transactions are guaranteed to always operate on consistent memory states. For example, in the current implementation of STM Haskell, threads can see an inconsistent view of memory that might lead to non-termination. The solution to the problem was to modify the scheduler of the

S. Apel and E. Jackson (Eds.): SC 2011, LNCS 6708, pp. 34–50, 2011.
© Springer-Verlag Berlin Heidelberg 2011

Haskell virtual machine, so that every time it is about to switch to a thread that is executing a transaction, it should validate its state to check if the transaction is not already doomed.

Since STM Haskell was first presented, many extensions to the basic primitives were proposed e.g., [20,21,12,5]. The STM library presented in this paper could work as a testbed to experiment with new extensions for STM Haskell. Using a high-level language like Haskell to implement STM delivers a more flexible and customizable implementation than the original system written in C. To demonstrate the flexibility of the TL2 library we show how unreadTVar [20], a new STM Haskell construct that improves execution time and memory usage when traversing linked data structures, can be implemented.

The paper is organized as follows: Section 2 introduces STM Haskell. Section 3 describes our implementation using the TL2 algorithm. Sections 3.9 and 3.10 describe how the basic TL2 algorithm can be extended to support higher level transactional primitives like retry and orElse. Preliminary performance measurements using the Haskell STM benchmark [2] are given in Section 4. Finally, Section 5 discusses related work, and Section 6 concludes.

2   STM Haskell: Composable Memory Transactions

STM Haskell [11], is a new concurrency model for Haskell based on *Software Memory Transactions* (STM) [9]. It provides the abstraction of *transactional variables*, or TVars: memory locations that can only be accessed inside transactions. TVars can be modified using two primitives:

```
readTVar  :: TVar a -> STM a
writeTVar :: TVar a -> a -> STM a
```

The readTVar primitive takes a TVar as an argument and returns an STM action that, when executed, returns the current value stored in the TVar. The writeTVar primitive is used to write a new value into a TVar. In STM Haskell, STM actions can be composed together using the same do notation used to compose IO actions and other monads. The only way to execute a transaction is by using the atomically primitive:

```
atomically :: STM a -> IO a
```

atomically takes a transaction and executes it atomically with respect to other concurrently executed transactions.

STM Haskell also provides two high level primitives to compose transaction: retry and orElse. retry aborts a transaction and executes it again when one of the TVars it read has changed. The orElse primitive is used to compose transactions as alternatives. orElse takes two transactions as arguments and returns a new transaction. The transaction

```
orElse t1 t2
```

will first execute t1; if it retries then t1 is discarded and t2 is executed. If t2 also retries then the whole transaction will retry.

3   Implementation

3.1   Transactional Locking 2 Algorithm

The TL2 algorithm, is basically similar to other lock based, deferred update transactional algorithms: threads execute reads and writes to objects, but no memory locations are actually modified. All writes and reads are recorded in write and read logs. When a transaction finishes, it validates its log to check if it has seen a consistent view of memory, and its changes are committed to memory.

The main difference of the TL2 algorithm is that conflicts are detected by using a global clock that is shared by all threads. When a transaction starts executing, it consults the global clock to get a *read stamp*. Every transacted memory location is associated with a write stamp and a lock (they can both be implemented as a single versioned lock, as described in Section 3.4). When opening an object for reading, a transaction checks if the write stamp of the memory address is not greater than the transaction's read stamp; in that case it means that the object was modified after the transaction started executing, hence the transaction must be aborted. If the memory passes the validation it means that the transaction has seen a consistent view of the memory. When committing, a transaction

 - Locks the objects in its write set
 - Increments the global clock getting its write-stamp
 - Validates the read set: checks if the memory locations in the read set are not locked and that their write stamp are still less then the transaction's read-stamp
 - Copies its changes into memory, updates the write stamp of each memory location with its own write stamp and released its locks.

By using a global clock, the TL2 algorithm guarantees that transactions observe only consistent memory states.

3.2   The STM Monad

The STM monad is defined as a state-passing monad that extends the IO monad, similar to the one described in [14]:

```
data STM a = STM (TState -> IO (TResult a))

data TResult a = Valid TState a | Retry TState | Invalid TState

instance Monad STM where
    (STM t1) >>= f = STM (\tState -> do
                            tRes <- t1 tState
                            case tRes of
                              Valid nTState v ->
                                    let (STM t2) = f v in
                                            t2 nTState
```

```
                              Retry nTState     -> return (Retry nTState)
                              Invalid nTState -> return (Invalid nTState)
                  )

    return x = STM (\tState -> return (Valid tState x))
```

An STM action is a function that takes the state of the current transaction and then executes a transactional action. The TResult describes the possible outcomes of executing an STM action. The bind (>>=) and return functions are implemented in a similar way to other state passing monads: return takes a value and does nothing with it, simply returning a Valid state. The bind function will execute its first argument and, if the outcome is a Valid state, it will continue executing the transaction, otherwise, if the outcome is a Retry of Invalid state, the transaction must be aborted and restarted.

3.3   TVars and TStates

TVars are represented by the following record:

```
data TVar a = TVar{
    lock :: Lock,
    id :: Integer,
    writeStamp :: IORef Integer,
    content :: IORef a,
    waitQueue :: IORef [MVar ()]
}
```

A TVar has a lock, that must be acquired during commit (see Section 3.7), an id that uniquely identifies it, a writeStamp that contains the write stamp of the last transaction to modify the TVar, its content, and a waitQueue that keeps the transactions waiting for an update on this TVar (see the implementation of retry in Section 3.9).

A transaction is represented by its state:

```
data TState = Tr {
    transId :: TId,
    readStamp :: Integer,
    readSet :: ReadSet,
    writeSet :: WriteSet
}
```

The TState record contains an id for the transaction, its read stamp and the write and read sets, i.e., the *logs* of the transaction.

3.4   Implementing Locks

Locks are implemented as IORefs:

```
type Lock = IORef Integer
```

To facilitate the validation of a transaction we use *versioned locks* (as in e.g., [13,11]). In this approach, when the lock is available, it contains the write stamp of the last transaction to modify the TVar, otherwise, it contains the id of the transaction that currently holds the lock. One way of implementing versioned locks is to use one bit of its content to represent the state of the lock (locked or unlocked) and the other bits to represent the content (transaction id or a write stamp). In our implementation we use a simpler scheme (inspired by [16,8]) where a transaction id is always an even number and the global clock is always an odd number. Hence, if the content of the lock is an even number, it means that the lock is locked and otherwise it is available. The content of a lock is changed using a CAS (*compare and swap*) operation. The CAS operation can be implemented using atomicModifyIORef, as in [21]:

```
atomCAS :: Eq a => IORef a -> a -> a -> IO Bool
atomCAS ptr old new = atomicModifyIORef ptr (\cur ->
                      if cur == old then (new, True) else (cur,False))
```

A transaction id is always the standard thread id, obtained using the concurrent Haskell's myThreadID function, multiplied by 2. The implementation of the global clock is described in Section 3.8.

3.5   Write Sets

The write set is represented as a hash table and the standard Data.Map library provided by the GHC compiler was used. Write sets map TVar ids to write set entries. These entries contain the new values that will be written into the TVars if the transaction commits. The main problem in implementing write sets in Haskell is that they are heterogeneous collections, i.e., as a transaction may write to TVars of different types, these values of different types must be collected in the write set. There are ways of implementing heterogeneous collection in Haskell (an overview on the subject is given in [1,15]) but these implementations impose some restrictions on the kind of values that can be stored in these collections (more details are provided in the related work section).

To avoid these restrictions we convert each write set entry into a pointer of type Ptr (). Hence write sets are maps from TVar ids to pointers representing entries. The implementation writeTVar is as follows:

```
writeTVar :: TVar a -> a -> STM ()
writeTVar (TVar lock id wstamp content queue) newValue =
  STM $ \tState -> do
    ptr <- castToPtr (WSE lock wsamp content queue newValue)
    putWS (writeSet tState) id ptr
    return (Valid tState ())
```

It first creates a write set entry (WSE) that contains the fields of the TVar needed to commit the transaction plus the new value to be stored in the TVar. It uses castToPtr to create a Ptr() from the write set entry and stores this pointer in the writeSet using the putWS function. Pointers are created using the Stable Pointers API [18]: castToPtr first creates a stable pointer for the read set entry and then `castStablePtrToPtr` is used to create a `Ptr ()`. The problem of using stable pointers is that they are not garbage collected and have to be manually freed. When a value is updated in the write set, the old stable pointer must be freed and after a transaction commits, the stable pointers in its write set must also be freed.

3.6 Read Sets

Read Sets are collections of read set entries and we use the `Data.Set` library provided by GHC to implement them. One advandage of the TL2 algorithm is that, to validate the read set, the content of the memory location is not needed. Hence, all read set entries have the same type and there is no need to use pointers. The `readTVar` function must first check the write set to see if there is an entry for the TVar. If so, the current content of the write set is returned:

```
readTVar :: TVar a -> STM a
readTVar tvar@(TVar lock id wstamp content queue) =
  STM $ \tState -> do
    mptr <- lookUpWS (writeSet tState) id
    case mptr of
        Just ptr -> do  (WSE _ _ _  _ v)<- castFromPtr ptr
                        return (Valid tState v)
                (...)
```

If there is no entry in the write set, `readTVar` must read the current content of the TVar and add an entry to the read set:

```
(...)
Nothing -> do
  lockVal <- readLock lock
  if (isLocked lockVal)
    then return (Invalid tState)
    else do
      result <- readIORef content
      lockVal2 <- readLock lock
      if ((lockVal/=lockVal2)||(lockVal > (readStamp tState)))
          then return (Invalid tState)
          else do
              putRS (readSet tState) (RSE id lock wstamp queue)
              return (Valid tState result)
```

First the content of the lock is read, and if the `TVar` is locked the transaction is aborted, i.e., it returns `Invalid`. Otherwise, the content of the TVar is read and the content of the lock is read again. These two consecutive reads of the lock guarantee the consistency of the TVar's content. If the lock is free, it contains the write stamp of the transaction that last modified the TVar. If the content of the lock has not changed between the two reads, it means that the value read from the TVar is consistent. Hence, to validate the transaction, `readTVar` must ensure that `lockVal` is equal to `lockVal2` and that the content of the lock (the write stamp) is not greater than the read stamp of the transaction. If the read was valid, an entry is added to the read set and the current content of the TVar is returned.

3.7   Executing a Transaction: atomically

The atomically function is responsible for executing a transaction:

```
atomically :: STM a -> IO a
atomically stmac@(STM ac) = do
   ts <- newTState
   r <- ac ts
   case r of
     Invalid nts ->do
                   clean nts
                   atomically stmac
(...)
```

It takes an STM action as an argument and executes it atomically with respect of other concurrently executed transactions. As an STM action is a function from a transaction state to a transaction result, atomically first creates a new transaction state that is passed to the STM action. If the TResult returned is Invalid, it means that a conflict occurred and the transaction must be executed again. First the transaction state is cleaned, i.e., all stable pointers in the write set are freed, and the transaction is re-executed by calling atomically again.

If the execution of the STM action was Valid, atomically tries to commit the transaction:

```
(...)
 Valid nts a -> do
     (ok,locks) <- getLocks transid writeset
     case ok of
              False -> do
                      unlock transid locks
                      clean nts
                      atomically stmac
```

To commit a transaction, first all locks in the write set must be acquired (getLocks). If getLocks can not acquire all locks, the transaction must be executed again. Otherwise, atomically proceeds by incrementing the global clock, validating the read set, and if the read set is valid, it must copy all modifications in the write set to memory:

```
(...)
  True -> do
     wstamp <- incrementGlobalClock
     valid <- validateRS readset readstamp transid
     if valid
        then do
```

```
        commitChangesToMemory wstamp writeset
        wakeUpBQ writeset
        unlock transid locks
        clean nts
        return a
    else do
        unlock transid locks
        clean nts
        atomically stmac
```

The call to `wakeUpBQ` is explained in Section 3.9.

Unlocking TVars The reader might have noticed in the definition of the `TVar` record, that every `TVar` has a `writeStamp` field that is not really necessary. As versioned locks are used, when the `lock` is available, it already contains the `TVar`'s write stamp. To unlock a `TVar` a transaction has to write into the lock the write stamp of the last transaction that modified it. If we are unlocking `TVars` after a successful commit, that is not a problem as the write stamp to be written into the locks is the transaction's write stamp. But if during commit, while locking the `TVars` of a write set, the transaction finds a `TVar` that is already locked, it must unlock the locks acquired so far. Hence the transaction must remember the values that were in the locks when they were available. A simple solution to that would be to make `getLocks` return, besides the locks acquired, also the values that were in the locks. But consider the following situation: in many cases a transaction reads a `TVar` and also writes to the same `TVar`. When this transaction is committing, it will first acquire the locks of the `TVars` in the write set (using `getLocks`), and then it validates the readset. During the validation of the readset, a transaction will find `TVars` that were locked by it when it called `getLocks`. To validate these `TVars` the transaction needs to know the `writeStamps` that were in the locks when they were available. In that case, the transaction would need to search for the write stamp in the list returned by `getLocks`. To simplify the implementation, we opted to add an extra `writeStamp` field to the `TVar` record.

The reader should notice that this field is thread safe: It is read when unlocking and during the validation of the read set (in the case explained above), and written during commit, and in all these cases the transaction already owns the lock of the `TVar`.

3.8 The Global Clock and TVar Ids

The global clock is an `IORef` containing an integer, and `unsafePerformIO` is used to turn it into a global reference:

```
globalClock :: IORef Integer
globalClock = unsafePerformIO (newIORef 1)
```

The global clock must be incremented using an atomic compare-and-swap operation:

```
incrementGlobalClock :: IO Integer
incrementGlobalClock = do
        ov <- readIORef globalClock
        changed <- atomCAS globalClock ov (ov+2)
        if changed then return (ov+2)
                   else incrementGlobalClock
```

The `incrementGlobalClock` function first reads the `globalClock` and then tries to change it using the `atomCAS` operation. The `globalClock` is always an odd number, it starts with 1 and is always incremented by 2. TVar ids are implemented in a similar way but they are incremented by 1.

3.9   Retry

The `retry` function has a simple implementation:

```
retry :: STM a
retry = STM $ \tState -> return (Retry tState)
```

When called, it will simply return the `Retry` transaction state thus suspending the execution of the transaction. One possible implementation of `retry` would be to automatically execute again this transaction as it is done with invalid transactions. But if it is executed right away, it will possibly call `retry` again for the same reason. To avoid this, a transaction that called `retry` should be executed again only when at least one of the TVars it has read is modified. When `atomically` detects that a transaction called `retry`, it takes the following steps:

```
(valid,locks) <- validateAndAcquireLocks readstamp transid readset
case valid of
        True -> do
                waitMVar <- newEmptyMVar
                addToWaitQueues waitMVar readset
                ulock transid locks
                clean nts
                takeMVar waitMVar
                atomically stmac
```

First, the transaction validates its read set to know if the call to `retry` is still valid. If so, the transaction must register itself in the `waitQueue`s of all the TVars it has read. When a TVar is updated, it awakes all transactions registered in its `waitQueue`. As in the parallel implementation of STM Haskell [10], we make the access to the wait queues thread-safe by re-using the per-TVar lock to protect the queues. The `validateAndAquireLocks` function tries to acquire the locks of all TVars in the read set and also validates these TVars, i.e., checks if the TVars' `writeStamps` are not greater than the transaction's `readstamp`. If `validateAndAquireLocks` was succesfull, the transaction creates a new empty MVar that is added to the `waitQueue`s, unlocks all locks, cleans its state, and tries to read from the MVar. The transaction will then block until a value is written into the MVar.

When a transaction commits, it must awake all transactions that are in the waitQueues of the TVars it has modified (see the call to wakeUpBQ in the implementation of atomically, Section 3.7). The wakeUpBQ function, tries to write () on each MVar in the waitQueues:

(...)

```
        mvarList <- readIORef waitQueue
        mapM_ (\mvar -> tryPutMVar mvar ()) mvarList
        writeIORef waitQueue []
```

The tryPutMvar function is non blocking: if the MVar is empty, the value is written and the transaction is awaken. If the MVar is full, meaning that the transaction was already awaken by an update on a different TVar, tryPutMVar has no effect.

3.10   OrElse

The orElse combinator takes two transactions as arguments (e.g., orElse t1 t2) and [11,9]:

- Executes t1. If it does not call retry, t2 will not be executed
- If t1 calls retry, the work done by t1 is discarded and t2 is executed
- If t2 completes, orElse will return the result of executing t2
- If t2 calls retry the whole transaction will retry.

The orElse combinator must provide proper nested transactions, i.e., if t1 called retry, the changes in memory it has done must be invisible while executing t2. We implement this behaviour by cloning the transaction's state:

```
orElse :: STM a -> STM a -> STM a
orElse (STM t1) (STM t2) = STM $ \tstate -> do
 tsCopy <- cloneTState tstate
 tRes1 <- t1 tstate
 case tRes1 of
     Retry nTSt1 -> do
             ok<-validateRS (readSet nTS1) (readStamp nTS1) (transId nTS1)
             case ok of
                 True -> do
                     tRes2 <- t2 tsCopy
                     case tRes2 of
                         Retry nTS2 -> do
                             fTState <- mergeTStates nTS1 nTS2
                             return (Retry fTState)
                         Valid nTState2 r ->  do
                             fTState <- mergeTStates nTS1 nTS2
                             return (Valid fTState r)
                         _  ->           return tRes2
                 False -> return (Invalid nTS1)
     _    -> return tRes1
```

orElse first creates an exact copy of the transaction's state (cloneTState) and then executes the first alternative (t1) using the original state. If t1 completes, i.e., it finishes execution with a Valid or Invalid state, orElse returns the same result returned by t1. If t1 retries, t2 must be executed, but it can not see the changes done by t1. Hence,t2 is executed using the copy of the original state (tsCopy). If both alternatives call retry, the retry must be propagated and the transaction must wait on the union on the sets of TVars they accessed [11]. The mergeTStates takes two transaction states (ts1 and ts2) and returns a new state where the read set is the union of the read sets of ts1 and ts2:

```
mergeTStates :: TState -> TState -> IO TState
mergeTStates ts1 ts2 = do
   rs1 <- readIORef (readSet ts1)
   rs2 <- readIORef (readSet ts2)
   let nrs = Set.union rs1 rs2
   writeIORef (readSet ts2) nrs
   return ts2
```

Notice that the merged state has the same write set as ts2. That does not matter in the case of a retry as all changes to memory will be discarded. If t2 is valid, the merged state is also returned. This covers a caveat in the original implementation that is described in [9]. In the original implementation of orElse, a call to orElse t1 t2 where t1 retries and t2 does not, the state of t1 would be discarded. But when the transaction commits, the view of memory that lead t1 to retry must still be valid. When both read sets are merged, we keep the TVars that t1 has read and they will be checked when the transaction commits.

4   Preliminary Results

Table 1 compares the mean run time (in **seconds**) of 8 programs from the *Haskell STM Benchmark* [17,2] using the original STM Haskell (**STM**) and the **TL2** implementation. The runtime presented is the average of 10 runs. The table also shows the slow down factor (**SD**) of **TL2** in comparison to **STM**. The experiments were executed on an Intel Core-2 Quad machine (with 4 processors), with 8 GB of RAM, and running Linux. The ghc version used was 6.12.1. Figures 1 and 2 show, respectively, the relative speed up of the original STM Haskell and the relative speed up of the TL2 implementation.

All programs but two give higher speedups with TL2 on all number of processors. However the speedups are relative, and the TL2 implementation in Haskell is 1 to 16 times slower than the original implementation in C, with factors of 2 and 3 being the most common. There is also one exception, SingleInt (SI), that is a corner case program in which threads continuously update a shared TVar and hence abort most of the time. This program presents the worst slow down in comparison to the original STM Haskell (40 times in 1 processor). But this

Table 1. Run times of the Haskell Benchmark suit using the original STM Haskell (**STM**), and the **TL2** version

Application	1 Proc			2 Proc			3 Proc			4 Proc		
	STM	TL2	SD	STM	TL2	SD	STM	TL2	SD	STM	TL2	SD
BT	0.13	1.63	12.80	0.09	1.12	11.85	0.08	0.90	11.01	0.08	0.83	10.58
HT	0.33	1.21	3.69	0.28	0.83	2.95	0.23	0.76	3.31	0.20	0.69	3.37
LL	0.66	4.85	7.33	0.45	4.13	9.14	0.39	4.47	11.36	0.35	5.17	14.91
SI	0.03	1.41	41.89	0.11	1.74	15.95	0.15	2.06	13.41	0.29	2.32	8.01
Blockworld	5.97	11.40	1.91	3.17	5.82	1.84	5.55	8.67	1.56	4.67	4.87	1.04
Prime	20.84	41.98	2.01	11.01	21.76	1.98	11.02	21.18	1.92	8.75	16.26	1.86
Sudoku	0.52	1.05	2.03	0.30	0.56	1.86	0.29	0.99	3.39	0.29	1.00	3.43
UnionFind	1.60	5.95	3.73	0.96	3.29	3.44	0.90	2.69	3.00	0.79	2.20	2.77

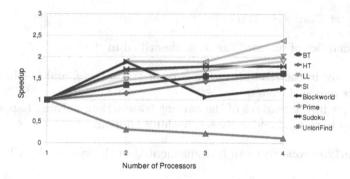

Fig. 1. Relative speedups of the original STM Haskell

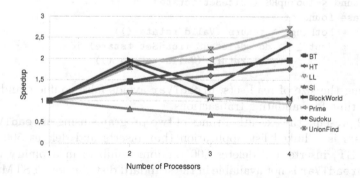

Fig. 2. Relative speedups of TL2

slow down decreases as the number of processors increases culminating to only 1.9 on 4 processors.

4.1 Unreadtvar

Transversing linked transactional data structures written in STM Haskell, involves reading as many transactional variables (Nodes) as needed to transverse the structure, which generates large read sets. Furthermore, transactions operating on different parts of a linked data structure may generate false conflicts. For example, suppose that two transactions are operating on a large linked list, t1 is trying to insert an element close to the beginning of the list and t2 is trying to delete an element close to the end. If t1 commits before t2, it will modify a node that is in t2's read set, thus causing t2 to abort when it tries to commit.

The unreadTVar [20] construct is an extension to the original STM Haskell interface that improves execution time and memory usage when traversing transactional linked structures. It is used to eliminate from the read set values that are far behind from the current position. unreadTVar has type

```
unreadTVar :: TVar a -> STM()
```

and the semantics of unreadTVar x, as described in [20], are:

- if x is only in the read set of the current transaction, and not in the write set, x is removed from it
- if x is not in the read set of the current transaction, nothing happens
- if x is in both read and write set, nothing happens

The unreadTVar construct can be implemented in the system described here as follows:

```
unreadTVar :: TVar a -> STM ()
unreadTVar tvar@(TVar _ id w c _) = STM  $ \tstate -> do
      found <-lookupRS (writeSet tstate) id
      case found of
            Nothing -> return (Valid tstate ())
            Just _ -> do  deleteRS (readSet tstate) id
                          return (Valid tstate ())
```

By reducing the size of read sets, ureadTVar avoids false conflicts and also reduces the time for validating transactions.

Table 2 presents the execution times of two programs using unreadTVar. The LL program is a linked list application that inserts and deletes 500 random numbers. BT, inserts and deletes 500 random numbers in a binary tree. Although unreadTVar is not available in the standard distribution of STM Haskell, the STM benchmark provides versions of the LL and BT programs that use unreadTVar to reduce the size of read sets. BTUn-1 and LLUn-1 use the implementation of unreadTVar described above. These programs perform worse than the version without unreadTVar. The reason for the bad performance is the call to lookupRS in the definition of unreadTVar. The hash tables provided by the standard Haskell distribution are known to perform very poorly. As both programs heavily use unreadTVar, it actually slows down execution time. The call

Table 2. Run times of programs using ureadTVar

Aplications	1 Proc		2 Proc		3 Proc		4 Proc	
	STM	TL2	STM	TL2	STM	TL2	STM	TL2
BT	0.13	1.63	0.09	1.12	0.08	0.90	0.08	0.83
BTUn-1		2.68		1.80		1.44		1.32
BTUn-2		1.13		0.79		0.63		0.54
LL	0.66	4.85	0.45	4.13	0.39	4.47	0.35	5.17
LLUn-1		5.04		4.28		4.73		5.50
LLUn-2		2.16		1.37		1.25		1.15

to lookupRS is only needed if we are not sure if the transaction has written into the TVar, e.g., when composing software from libraries. That is not the case in these benchmarks. If we reimplement unreadTVar without the write set check (BTUn-2 and LLUn-2), it improves execution time and scalability of programs.

5 Related Work

The TL2 algorithm and the GHC implementation of STM Haskell [11,10] use lock based, optimistic concurrency, where reads and writes to TVars are performed in logs and transaction validation occurs at commit time. However, in GHC validation is implemented by checking a per-TVar version number instead of a global clock. Version numbers are collected at every read, and at commit time the system checks if these versions numbers have not changed. This validation scheme can lead to *zombie transactions* i.e., inconsistent transactions that continue to execute even though they are doomed. As inconsistent transactions might not terminate, the GHC Scheduler, before switching to a thread executing a transaction, must validate its state. The TL2 algorithm guarantees that transactions always operate on consistant memory states, but it also introduces the possibility of contention on the global clock. Nevertheless, techniques to reduce updates in the global clock, and more scalable implementations of the global clock have been suggested in the literature. A survey of these techniques is provided in [9].

One of the challenges in implementing STM in Haskell using deferred update, is how to represent read and write sets. Huch and Kupke, in a paper presented at IFL 2005 [14], investigated two different approaches to represent transaction logs in Haskell. The first approach was to use an opposite referencing structure: instead of a write set, each TVar has a log where threads record their modifications to that TVar. As this log may be accessed by more than one transaction at the same time, it is protected by an MVar. This approach proved to be inefficient so the authors also present the *collecting approach*: writes are accumulated in one IO action that is executed when a transaction is committing, hence no logs are needed. The only problem with this approach is what to do if a transaction wants to read a TVar that it has written beforehand. In that case, a transaction acquires a global lock, calls the commit action so now all TVars have its view of memory, and then reads the `TVar`. The transaction must also accumulate an IO action that restores the original values in the `TVars`. The commit and restore actions must be protected by a validation check to ensure consistency. The use of a global lock limits the parallelism that can be obtained in this implementation and, although the collecting approach is very elegant, it hinders the implementation of extensions that modify the transaction's state, e.g., [20,5,21].

Twilight STM in Haskell [5] extends STM Haskell with safe embedding of I/O operations and a repair facility to resolve conflicts. Twilight splits the code of a transaction into two phases, a functional atomic phase (that behaves just like the original STM Haskell), and an imperative phase where Twilight code can be used. A prototype implementation of Twilight Haskell in Haskell is provided [3]. This implementation, that in many ways is similar to the one described here, also uses the TL2 algorithm to implement transactions. The main differences are on the representation of locks and write sets. The lock in each `TVar` is represented as an MVar of type `MVar ()`. With this simple implementation of locks, to avoid race conditions in the access of the write stamp field of each `TVar`, the lock of a `TVar` must be acquired when validating a read in `readTVar`. For the same reason, during commit, while validating each `TVar` in the read set, this lock must be acquired. The use of versioned locks, as in the system described in this paper, avoids excessive locking of `TVars`: with a single read of the content of a lock a transaction knows if it is unlocked and in that case it also knows the write stamp of the TVar at that moment. In the implementation of *Twilight* Haskell, the write set is a hash table that uses a *trick* with existential types to implement an heterogeneous collection, as described in [1]. Existential types provide a simple way of implementing heterogeneous collections in Haskell, but they restrict elements of the collection to certain types. For example, in the implementation of *Twilight* Haskell, the write set can contain only values of types that are instances of the `Show` class. Therefore, only values of such types can be written to a `TVar`, which is reflected in the type of `writeTVar`:

```
writeTVar :: Show a => TVar a -> a -> STM r p q a
```

A comparison between *Twilight* Haskell and the implementation described here using the Haskell STM benchmark is difficult as *Twilight* Haskell extends the type of STM actions with types related to the *Twilight* computations (as can be seen in the type of `writeTVar` shown above). This means that the programs of the benchmark would need to be changed to reflect this modification. Furthermore, *Twilight* Haskell provides a very simple implementation of `retry`, where transactions that retry are automatically restarted, and no implementation of `orElse` is provided.

6   Conclusions and Future Work

This paper presented a new implementation of STM Haskell using the *Transactional Locking 2 Algorithm*. Preliminary performance measurements of 8 programs from the Haskell STM Benchmark suite demonstrate the TL2 implementation in Haskell is usually 1 to 16 times slower than the original implementation in C, with one exception. The measurements also demonstrate that our library provides scalability similar to the standard STM Haskell.

For future work we would like to improve the implementation described here by providing support for exceptions, and by using a more scalable implementation of the global clock. Several techniques were developed which allow transactions to avoid incrementing the global clock (e.g., [22,6]) or which give a more distributed implementation of the clock (e.g., [19]). Techniques for handling clock and thread id overflow could also be implemented, e.g., [7].

The source code of TL2 STM Haskell can be downloaded from [4].

Acknowledgment. This work was partly supported by the CNPq/PRONEX/FAPERGS Green Grid project, and by a FAPERGS *Pesquisador Gaúcho* grant.

References

1. Heterogenous collections in Haskell (October 2010), http://www.haskell.org/haskellwiki/Hete\discretionary-rogenous_collections
2. The Haskell STM Benchmark. WWW page (October 2010), http://www.bscmsrc.eu/software/haskell-stm-benchmark
3. Twilight STM for Haskell. WWW page (October 2010), http://proglang.informatik.uni-freiburg.de/projects/twilight/
4. TL2 STM Haskell. WWW page (February 2011), https://sites.google.com/site/tl2stmhaskell/STM.hs
5. Bieniusa, A., Middelkoop, A., Thiermann, P.: Twilight in Haskell: Software Transactional Memory with Safe I/O and Typed Conflict Management. In: Preprocedings of IFL 2010 (September 2010)
6. Dice, D., Shalev, O., Shavit, N.N.: Transactional locking II. In: Dolev, S. (ed.) DISC 2006. LNCS, vol. 4167, pp. 194–208. Springer, Heidelberg (2006)
7. Felber, P., Fetzer, C., Riegel, T.: Dynamic performance tuning of word-based software transactional memory. In: PPoPP 2008, pp. 237–246. ACM, New York (2008)
8. Harris, T., Fraser, K.: Language support for lightweight transactions. SIGPLAN Not. 38(11), 388–402 (2003)
9. Harris, T., Larus, J.R., Rajwar, R.: Transactional Memory, 2nd edn. Morgan & Claypool Publishers, San Francisco (2010)
10. Harris, T., Marlow, S., Peyton Jones, S.: Haskell on a shared-memory multiprocessor. In: Haskell Workshop 2005, pp. 49–61. ACM, New York (2005)
11. Harris, T., Marlow, S., Peyton Jones, S., Herlihy, M.: Composable memory transactions. In: PPoPP 2005. ACM Press, New York (2005)
12. Harris, T., Peyton Jones, S.: Transactional memory with data invariants. In: TRANSACT 2006 (June 2006)
13. Harris, T., Plesko, M., Shinnar, A., Tarditi, D.: Optimizing memory transactions. SIGPLAN Not. 41(6), 14–25 (2006)
14. Huch, F., Kupke, F.: A high-level implementation of composable memory transactions in concurrent haskell. In: IFL, pp. 124–141 (2005)
15. Kiselyov, O., Lämmel, R., Schupke, K.: Strongly typed heterogeneous collections. In: Haskell Workshop 2004, pp. 96–107. ACM Press, New York (2004)
16. Lourenço, A., Cunha, G.: Testing patterns for software transactional memory engines. In: PADTAD 2007, pp. 36–42. ACM, New York (2007)

17. Perfumo, C., Sönmez, N., Stipic, S., Unsal, O., Cristal, A., Harris, T., Valero, M.: The limits of software transactional memory (STM): dissecting haskell stm applications on a many-core environment. In: CF 2008, pp. 67–78. ACM Press, New York (2008)
18. Peyton Jones, S., Marlow, S., Elliot, C.: Stretching the storage manager: weak pointers and stable names in haskell. In: Koopman, P., Clack, C. (eds.) IFL 1999. LNCS, vol. 1868, Springer, Heidelberg (2000)
19. Riegel, T., Felber, P., Fetzer, C.: A Lazy Snapshot Algorithm with Eager Validation, pp. 284–298 (2006)
20. Sonmez, N., Perfumo, C., Stipic, S., Cristal, A., Unsal, O.S., Valero, M.: Unreadtvar: Extending Haskell software transactional memory for performance. In: Trends in Functional Programming, vol. 8. Intellect Books (2008)
21. Sulzmann, M., Lam, E.S., Marlow, S.: Comparing the performance of concurrent linked-list implementations in Haskell. SIGPLAN Not. 44(5), 11–20 (2009)
22. Zhang, R., Budimlić, Z., Scherer III., W.N.: Commit phase in timestamp-based STM. In: SPAA 2008, pp. 326–335. ACM Press, New York (2008)

Synthesizing Glue Operators from Glue Constraints for the Construction of Component-Based Systems

Simon Bliudze[1] and Joseph Sifakis[2]

[1] CEA, LIST, Boîte Courrier 94, Gif-sur-Yvette, F-91191 France
Simon.Bliudze@cea.fr
[2] VERIMAG, Centre Équation, 2 av de Vignate, 38610, Gières, France
Joseph.Sifakis@imag.fr

Abstract. We study glue operators used in component-based frameworks to obtain systems as the composition of atomic components described as labeled transition systems (LTS). Glue operators map tuples of LTS into LTS. They restrict the behavior of their arguments by performing memoryless coordination. In a previous paper, we have proposed a simple format for SOS rules that captures, in particular, glue operators from known frameworks such as CCS, SCCS, CSP, and BIP.

This paper studies a new way for characterizing glue operators: as boolean *glue constraints* between interactions (sets of ports) and the state of the coordinated components. We provide an SOS format for glue, which allows a natural correspondence between glue operators and glue constraints. This correspondence is used for automated synthesis of glue operators implementing given glue constraints. By focusing on the properties that do not bear computation, we reduce a very hard (and, in general, undecidable) problem of synthesizing controllers to a tractable one. The examples in the paper show that such properties are natural and can be expressed as glue constraints in a straightforward manner. Finally, we compare expressiveness of the proposed formalisms with the glue used in the BIP framework and discuss possible applications.

1 Introduction

A central idea in systems engineering is that complex systems are built by assembling components. Large components are obtained by "gluing" together simpler ones. "Gluing" can be considered as a generalized composition operation on sets of components that allows building complex components from simpler ones.

Various component frameworks exist for developing hardware, software or mixed hardware/software systems. They all focus rather on the way components interact than on their internal behavior. They often use domain specific mechanisms for composing components, each mechanism implying specific approaches for organizing their interaction. For instance, hardware systems are built by using buses implementing usually synchronous multi-party interaction.

S. Apel and E. Jackson (Eds.): SC 2011, LNCS 6708, pp. 51–67, 2011.

Asynchronous message passing is very common in operating systems and middleware. For software the main paradigms are using lock/unlock operations or (blocking) function calls, although domain-specific design languages may rely on different mechanisms, e.g., broadcast for synchronous languages like Esterel and rendezvous in ADA. Such a heterogeneity is a main obstacle for

- comparing functionally equivalent designs integrating identical sets of components but using different types of "glue" for their coordination: How to evaluate the merits of different solutions by using theoretical tools and reasoning rather than experimental analysis of their implementations?
- composing systems based on different composition paradigms, often based on different models of computation that cannot be consistently combined.

In previous papers, we have advocated for component frameworks using rather families of composition operators than a single composition operator. This allows mastering complexity in designs and enhanced expressiveness. BIP (Behavior-Interaction-Priority) [1] is such a framework combining two families of composition operators: interactions and priorities. In [2], we formalized the concept of glue operator for behavior coordination by using SOS inference rules in a very simple restriction of the GSOS format [3]. Each operator gl composing behaviors $B_1, \ldots, B_n$ is defined by a set of inference rules of the form

$$\frac{\{B_i : q_i \xrightarrow{a_i} q_i'\}_{i \in I} \quad \{q_i = q_i'\}_{i \notin I} \quad \{B_j : q_j \xrightarrow{b_j^k} \}_{\substack{j \in J \\ k \in K_j}}}{gl(B_1, \ldots, B_n) : q_1 \ldots q_n \xrightarrow{a} q_1' \ldots q_n'} , \tag{1}$$

where a, in the conclusion, is the interaction obtained as the union of the interactions occurring in positive premises.

Example 1 (Mutual exclusion by preemption). Let T_1 and T_2 be two mutually preemptable tasks sharing a single processor for their computations. No interactions other than those needed for the preemption mechanism are possible. Tasks can be modeled by the generic behavior shown to the right. This behavior has three states: 1–the task is running, 2–the task is waiting to begin computation, and 3–the task has been preempted and is waiting to resume computation. The transitions are labeled b, f, p, and r for *begin, finish, preempt,* and *resume* respectively, and can be synchronized with external events through the corresponding ports of the behavior. Mutual preemption is described by two statements:

1. A running task is preempted, when the other one begins computation.
2. A preempted task resumes computation, when the other one finishes.

The glue operator gl ensuring this behavior in the composition of the two tasks is defined by the inference rules shown in Fig. 1 (for $i, j = 1, 2$ and $i \neq j$).

In [2], we have introduced a notion of expressiveness for component frameworks and have shown that BIP is as expressive as the family of the glue operators specified by (1).

$$\frac{B_i : q_i \xrightarrow{b_i} q_i' \quad B_j : q_j \xrightarrow{p_j}}{gl(B_1, B_2) : q_i q_j \xrightarrow{b_i} q_i' q_j} \qquad \frac{B_i : q_i \xrightarrow{b_i} q_i' \quad B_j : q_j \xrightarrow{p_j} q_j'}{gl(B_1, B_2) : q_i q_j \xrightarrow{b_i p_j} q_i' q_j'}$$

$$\frac{B_i : q_i \xrightarrow{f_i} q_i' \quad B_j : q_j \xrightarrow{r_j}}{gl(B_1, B_2) : q_i q_j \xrightarrow{f_i} q_i' q_j} \qquad \frac{B_i : q_i \xrightarrow{f_i} q_i' \quad B_j : q_j \xrightarrow{r_j} q_j'}{gl(B_1, B_2) : q_i q_j \xrightarrow{f_i r_j} q_i' q_j'}$$

Fig. 1. Inference rules for the mutual exclusion example

This paper studies a new way for characterizing glue operators for behavior coordination. We consider that a glue operator on a set of components is a *glue constraint*. This is a boolean constraint between interactions that can be fired and the state of the coordinated components. The state is characterized by the set of the ports through which interactions are possible. For each port of a component, the constraint has two variables—an activation variable p and a firing variable $\dot{p}$—connected by an additional axiom $\dot{p} \Rightarrow p$. For a given valuation of activation variables corresponding to some state of the interacting components, glue constraints characterize all the possible interactions. An interaction is possible from this state if the valuation setting to *true* only the firing variables corresponding to its ports satisfies the constraint. The axiom $\dot{p} \Rightarrow p$ expresses the fact that a port cannot participate in an interaction unless it is active.

Example 2. The two statements describing preemption in Ex. 1 are formalized by the following constraints (for $i, j = 1, 2$ and $i \neq j$):

- $\dot{p}_i \Rightarrow \dot{b}_j$, meaning that one task can be preempted only when the other one starts computation;
- $\dot{b}_i \wedge p_j \Rightarrow \dot{p}_j$, meaning that when one task begins computation, if the other one is computing (can be preempted) it must be preempted;
- $\dot{r}_i \Rightarrow \dot{f}_j$, meaning that a preempted task can resume only when the other one finishes computation;
- $\dot{f}_i \wedge r_j \Rightarrow \dot{r}_j$, meaning that when one task finishes computation, if the other one is preempted (can resume) it must resume.

In this paper, we define a new variation of the SOS format for glue operators proposed in [2]. In the new format, inference rules operators have three types of premises. The *firing* premises $q_i \xrightarrow{a_i} q_i'$ are the same as positive premises in (1). The two other types—*witness* premises $q_i \uparrow a_i$ and *negative* premises $q_i \not\uparrow a_i$—use a new predicate $\uparrow$. In an atomic behavior B_i, $q_i \uparrow a_i$ is satisfied iff, for every port $p \in a_i$, there is a transition $q_i \xrightarrow{b}$ such that $p \in b$. In other words, every port in a_i is *offered* by some transition in the state q_i of B_i. For a composed behavior B, $q \uparrow a$ signifies that each port in a is offered by some atomic component composing B. As in (1), the conclusion of a rule is labeled by the union of interactions labeling its firing premises, that is neither witness nor negative premises contribute to the resulting transition.

This new format has two advantages. Firstly, it is well adapted to formalizing hierarchical composition of behaviors, as the predicate $\uparrow$ allows to explicitly capture the notion of "atomic" component. Secondly, for each glue constraint there exists an equivalent glue operator defined by rules in the new SOS format. For any such glue operator, it is possible to find an equivalent glue constraint.

This paper is structured as follows. In Sect. 2, we define a new class of glue operators, which we call *universal glue*, as well as glue constraints. In Sect. 3, we show that glue constraints can encode universal glue in a way that allows to explicitly link glue operators to invariant properties of the composed systems. In particular, this allows the synthesis of glue operators enforcing such properties as illustrated in Sect. 4. In Sect. 5, we show that each type of premises in the proposed SOS format is essential for the expressiveness of universal glue. In Sect. 6, we compare this new universal glue with the glue used in BIP. In Sect. 7, we present a design methodology based on the introduced models and transformations. Finally, we discuss the related work in Sect. 8.

2   Modeling Behavior and Glue

2.1   Behavior

Definition 1. *A* labeled transition system *(LTS) is a triple* $(Q, P, \rightarrow)$, *where* Q *is a set of* states, P *is a set of* ports, *and* $\rightarrow \subseteq Q \times 2^P \times Q$ *is a set of* transitions, *each labeled by an* interaction. *For* $q, q' \in Q$ *and* $a \in 2^P$, *we write* $q \xrightarrow{a} q'$ *iff* $(q, a, q') \in \rightarrow$. *An interaction* $a \in 2^P$ *is* active *in a state* $q \in Q$ *(denoted* $q \xrightarrow{a}$*), iff there exists* $q' \in Q$ *such that* $q \xrightarrow{a} q'$. *We abbreviate* $q \xarrownot{a} \overset{def}{=} \neg(q \xrightarrow{a})$.

To simplify notation, we write, pq for the interaction $\{p, q\}$.

Definition 2. *A* behavior *is a pair* $B = (S, \uparrow)$ *consisting of an LTS* $S = (Q, P, \rightarrow)$ *and an offer* predicate $\uparrow$ *on* $Q \times P$ *such that* $q \uparrow p$ *holds (a port* $p \in P$ *is* offered *in a state* $q \in Q$*) whenever there is a transition from* q *containing* p, *that is* $(\exists a \in 2^P : p \in a \wedge q \xrightarrow{a}) \Rightarrow q \uparrow p$. *The set of ports* P *is the* interface *of* B.

The offer predicate extends to interactions: for $a \in 2^P$, $q \uparrow a \overset{def}{=} \bigwedge_{p \in a} q \uparrow p$. For $p \in P$, we have $q \uparrow p = q \uparrow \{p\}$. It is also important to observe that $\uparrow$ and $\rightarrow$ do not coincide: e.g., for a state q and ports p_1, p_2, if the only transitions possible from q are $q \xrightarrow{p_1}$ and $q \xrightarrow{p_2}$, one has $q \uparrow p_1 p_2$, but $q \xarrownot{p_1 p_2}$.

We write $B = (Q, P, \rightarrow, \uparrow)$ for $B = ((Q, P, \rightarrow), \uparrow)$.

Definition 3. *A* behavior $B = (Q, P, \rightarrow, \uparrow)$ *is* atomic *iff,* $\forall q \in Q, p \in P$, $(q \uparrow p \Leftrightarrow \exists a \in 2^P : p \in a \wedge q \xrightarrow{a})$. *A behavior is* composed *if it is not atomic.*

According to this definition, the same transition system S can define an atomic or a composed behavior $B = (S, \uparrow)$, depending on the offer predicate. Thus, the offer predicate allows to capture elements of the components in a composed behavior as illustrated by the following example.

Example 3. Consider the following transition systems:

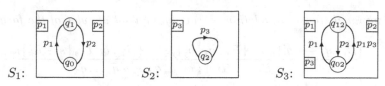

S_1: S_2: S_3:

S_3 can be considered as a composition of S_1 and S_2 with an operator that enforces for port p_3 a synchronization with port p_1, i.e. each of p_1 and p_2 can happen alone, but p_3 can happen only together with p_1. Thus, in the state q_{12} of S_3, there is no transition containing p_3, even though p_3 is active in the state 2 of S_2. This can be reflected by considering the behaviors $B_i = (S_i, \uparrow_i)$, for $i = 1, 2, 3$, with $\uparrow_i$ defined by the first three truth tables below.

B_1:
$\uparrow_1$	p_1	p_2
q_0	T	F
q_1	F	T

B_2:
$\uparrow_2$	p_3
q_2	T

B_3:
$\uparrow_3$	p_1	p_2	p_3
q_{02}	T	F	T
q_{12}	F	T	T

B_3':
$\uparrow_3'$	p_1	p_2	p_3
q_{02}	T	F	T
q_{12}	F	T	$\mathbf{F}$

Although, there is no interaction a such that $p_3 \in a$ and, in B_3, $q_{12} \xrightarrow{a}$, we have $q_{12} \uparrow p_3$, reflecting the fact that, in the behavior B_2 composing B_3, the port p_3 is active. On the other hand, S_3 can also be considered as "atomic", that is without any explicit information about its structure, by considering a behavior $B_3' = (S_3, \uparrow_3')$ with $\uparrow_3'$ defined by the fourth truth table above.

Note 1. In the rest of the paper, whenever we speak of a set of component behaviors $B_i = (Q_i, P_i, \rightarrow, \uparrow)$ with $i \in [1, n]$, we always assume that $\{P_i\}_{i=1}^n$ are pairwise disjoint (i.e. $i \neq j$ implies $P_i \cap P_j = \emptyset$) and $P \overset{def}{=} \bigcup_{i=1}^n P_i$.

Also, to avoid excessive notation, here and in the rest of the paper, we drop the indices on the transition relations $\rightarrow$ and offer predicates $\uparrow$, as they can always be unambiguously deduced from the state variables, e.g., $q_i \rightarrow$ always refers to the transition relation of the corresponding component B_i.

2.2 SOS Characterization of Glue

Structured Operational Semantics (SOS) [4] has been used to define the meaning of programs in terms of Labeled Transition Systems (LTS). A number of SOS formats have been developed, using various syntactic features [5].

In the context of component-based systems, definition of glue only requires the specification of parallel composition operators, as sequential and recursive computation can be represented by individual behaviors.

The SOS rules format below is a modification of the one defined in [2].

Definition 4. *An n-ary glue operator gl on a set of interfaces $\{P_i\}_{i=1}^n$ is defined as follows. The application of gl to behaviors $B_i = (Q_i, P_i, \rightarrow, \uparrow)$, for $i \in [1, n]$, is a behavior $gl(B_1, \ldots, B_n) = (Q, P, \rightarrow, \uparrow)$, with*

- *the set of states $Q = \prod_{i=1}^n Q_i$—the cartesian product of the sets of states Q_i,*
- *the set of ports $P = \bigcup_{i=1}^n P_i$,*
- *the minimal offer predicate $\uparrow$ satisfying, for $i \in [1, n]$, the inference rules*

$$\frac{B_i : q_i \uparrow p}{gl(B_1, \ldots, B_n) : q_1 \ldots q_n \uparrow p}, \qquad (2)$$

— *the minimal transition relation* $\rightarrow$ *satisfying a set of rules of the form*

$$r = \frac{\{B_i : q_i \xrightarrow{a_i} q_i'\}_{i \in I} \quad \{B_j : q_j \uparrow b_j\}_{j \in J} \quad \{B_k : q_k \,\not\uparrow\, c_s \mid s \in L_k\}_{k \in K}}{gl(B_1, \ldots, B_n) : q_1 \ldots q_n \xrightarrow{a} \widetilde{q}_1 \ldots \widetilde{q}_n} \quad (3)$$

where $I, J, K \subseteq [1, n]$ *and* $I \neq \emptyset$; $a = \bigcup_{i \in I} a_i$; *and* $\widetilde{q}_i$ *denotes* q_i', *for* $i \in I$, *and* q_i, *for* $i \in [1, n] \setminus I$. *In (3), we have three types of premises respectively called* firing, witness, *and* negative *premises. Firing and witness premises are collectively called* positive.

The condition $I \neq \emptyset$ means that r has at least one firing premise. Firing premises identify transitions that must actually be taken should the rule be applied; hence there is at most one firing premise per component behavior.

Notice that $q \uparrow b_1 \wedge q \uparrow b_2 = q \uparrow b_1 b_2$, i.e. several witness premises can always be merged into a single more complex one. Hence one witness premise per component behavior is sufficient to define any inference rule.

On the contrary, the conjunction of two negative premises $q \,\not\uparrow\, b_1 \wedge q \,\not\uparrow\, b_2 = \neg(q \uparrow b_1 \vee q \uparrow b_2)$ cannot be expressed as a primitive expression in terms of the transition relation $\rightarrow$ or offer predicate $\uparrow$. Hence, several negative premises for the same component behavior can be necessary to define an inference rule.

A rule is completely defined by its premises.

We identify the glue operator gl with its set of inference rules (3). A glue operator having no negative premises in any of its rules is called a *positive glue operator*. We call *glue* a set of glue operators and *universal glue* the glue consisting of all the glue operators in the sense of Def. 4. We denote the latter FWN (for Firing-Witness-Negative; see also Sect. 5).

2.3   Boolean Characterization of Glue

Let P be a set of ports, we denote $\dot{P} \stackrel{def}{=} \{\dot{p} \mid p \in P\}$.

Definition 5. *The* Algebra of Glue Constraints *on* P, *denoted* $\mathcal{GC}(P)$, *is the boolean algebra* $\mathbb{B}[P, \dot{P}]$ *on the set of variables* $P \cup \dot{P}$ *with an additional axiom* $\dot{p} \Rightarrow p$. *We call* $p \in P$ activation *variables and* $\dot{p} \in \dot{P}$ firing *variables.*

Activation variables indicate which ports are offered; firing variables indicate which ports will actually participate in a transition (interaction). Clearly, a port can participate in a transition only if it is offered; hence the axiom $\dot{p} \Rightarrow p$.

Note 2. Below, we overload the symbol P: depending on the context, it will denote the set of ports in a system or the set of the associated boolean variables.

We give the semantics of $\mathcal{GC}(P)$ by associating a glue operator (Def. 4) to each term of the algebra. For behaviors $\{B_i\}_{i=1}^n$, such that $P = \bigcup_{i=1}^n P_i$ where P_i is the set of the ports of B_i, and a glue constraint $\varphi \in \mathcal{GC}(P)$, the composed behavior $\varphi(B_1, \ldots, B_n)$ can be described intuitively as follows. For each $i \in [1, n]$, the current state of $q_i \in Q_i$ defines a valuation on the activation variables of φ:

for each variable $p \in P_i$, the valuation is $p = true$ iff $q_i \uparrow p$ (the underlying port is offered in the current state of the behavior). An interaction $a \subseteq P$ defines a valuation on the firing variables $\dot{P}$ by putting $\dot{p} = true$ iff $p \in a$. Finally, a is possible in the composite behavior $\varphi(B_1, \ldots, B_n)$ iff the valuation on $P \cup \dot{P}$ defined as above satisfies φ and the constituent interactions of a are possible in the corresponding component behaviors.

To formalize the above intuition, let us consider behaviors $B_i = (Q_i, P_i, \to, \uparrow)$ for $i \in [1, n]$ and a glue constraint $\varphi \in \mathcal{GC}(P)$. Denote $\nu_{B_i}^{q_i}(p) \stackrel{def}{=} q_i \uparrow p$ the valuation on the activation variables in P_i associated to the state $q_i \in Q_i$ of B_i. For an interaction $a \subseteq P$, denote $\mathbb{I}_a(\dot{p}) \stackrel{def}{=} (p \in a)$ the corresponding valuation on firing variables. The behavior obtained by composing $\{B_i\}_{i=1}^n$ with φ is defined by $\varphi(B_1, \ldots, B_n) = (Q, P, \to, \uparrow)$, with $Q = \prod_{i=1}^n Q_i$, the offer predicate $\uparrow$ defined by (2), and the transition relation $\to$ defined as follows. For any $q_1 \ldots q_n \in Q$ and $a \subseteq P$, and for all $q_i' \in Q_i$ such that $q_i \xrightarrow{a \cap P_i} q_i'$ for $i \in [1, n]$, we put

$$q_1 \ldots q_n \xrightarrow{a} q_1' \ldots q_n' \stackrel{def}{\Longleftrightarrow} (\nu_{B_1}^{q_1}, \ldots, \nu_{B_n}^{q_n}, \mathbb{I}_a) \models \varphi.$$

3 Transformations

3.1 From Glue Operators to Glue Constraints

Recall that a glue operator on a set of interfaces $\{P_i\}_{i=1}^n$ is identified with the set of its defining rules. Thus, we first present the translation into $\mathcal{GC}(P)$ of individual rules. Let r be a rule as in (3). Denoting $A = \bigcup_{i \in I} a_i$, $B = \bigcup_{j \in J} b_j$, we associate to r a formula $\varphi_r \in \mathcal{GC}(P)$ defined by

$$\varphi_r \stackrel{def}{=} \bigwedge_{p \in A} \dot{p} \wedge \bigwedge_{p \in P \setminus A} \overline{\dot{p}} \wedge \bigwedge_{p \in B} p \wedge \bigwedge_{k \in K} \bigwedge_{s \in L_k} \overline{c_s}, \tag{4}$$

where $\overline{c_s} = \bigvee_{p \in c_s} \overline{p}$. A formula $\varphi_{gl} \in \mathcal{GC}(P)$ associated to a glue operator gl is then defined by putting $\varphi_{gl} \stackrel{def}{=} \bigvee_{r \in gl} \varphi_r$.

Proposition 1. *Let $gl \in FWN$ be defined on interfaces $\{P_i\}_{i=1}^n$ and let $\varphi_{gl} \in \mathcal{GC}(P)$ be the glue constraint formula constructed as above. For any set of behaviors $B_i = (Q_i, P_i, \to, \uparrow)$, with $i \in [1, n]$, holds $gl(B_1, \ldots, B_n) = \varphi_{gl}(B_1, \ldots, B_n)$.*

3.2 From Glue Constraints to Glue Operators

Let again $\{P_i\}_{i=1}^n$ be a set of interfaces and $P = \bigcup_{i=1}^n P_i$. The transformation from $\mathcal{GC}(P)$ to FWN can be defined by giving, for a glue constraint formula $\varphi \in \mathcal{GC}(P)$, an equivalent operator $gl_\varphi \in FWN$ on $\{P_i\}_{i=1}^n$. In order to do so we have to rewrite φ as a disjunction of formulæ of the form (4).

Let $\varphi \in \mathcal{GC}(P)$ be a glue constraint formula. Observe first that φ has a unique representation in the *firing-full DNF*, i.e. a disjunctive normal form such that all firing variables $\dot{p} \in \dot{P}$ are explicitly present in each monomial. Thus $\varphi = \bigvee_{m \in M} \varphi_m$, with monomials (indexed by the set M) of the form

$$\varphi_m = \bigwedge_{p \in A_m} \dot{p} \wedge \bigwedge_{p \in P \setminus A_m} \overline{\dot{p}} \wedge \bigwedge_{p \in B_m} p \wedge \bigwedge_{i=1}^{n} \bigwedge_{p \in C_m \cap P_i} \overline{p}. \tag{5}$$

This formula has the same form as in (4). Denote, for $m \in M$ and $i \in [1,n]$, $a_i^m = A_m \cap P_i$ and $b_j^m = B_m \cap P_j$; $I_m = \{i \in [1,n] \,|\, a_i^m \neq \emptyset\}$ and $J_m = \{j \in [1,n] \,|\, b_j^m \neq \emptyset\}$. The glue operator gl_φ corresponding to the formula φ is defined by the set of inference rules, containing, for each $m \in M$, the rule (6), where $\widetilde{q}_i$ denotes q_i', for $i \in I_m$, and q_i, for $i \in [1,n] \setminus I_m$.

$$\frac{\{B_i : q_i \xrightarrow{a_i^m} q_i'\}_{i \in I_m} \quad \{B_j : q_j \uparrow b_j^m\}_{j \in J_m} \quad \{B_k : q_k \not\uparrow p \,|\, p \in C_m \cap P_k\}_{k=1}^{n}}{gl_\varphi(B_1, \ldots, B_n) : q_1 \ldots q_n \xrightarrow{A_m} \widetilde{q}_1 \ldots \widetilde{q}_n} \tag{6}$$

Example 4. Let $P_1 = \{p_1, p_2\}$ and $P_2 = \{p_3, p_4, p_5\}$, and consider an operator gl on these two interfaces that allows only transitions labelled p_1 (i.e. $\dot{p}_1 \overline{\dot{p}_2} \, \overline{\dot{p}_3} \, \overline{\dot{p}_4} \, \overline{\dot{p}_5}$) and, moreover, only when either $p_2 p_3$ is not active or neither is p_4 nor p_5 (i.e. $\dot{p}_1 \Rightarrow \overline{p_2 p_3} \vee \overline{p_4 p_5}$). Taking the firing-full DNF of the conjunction, we obtain $\dot{p}_1 \overline{\dot{p}_2} \, \overline{\dot{p}_3} \, \overline{\dot{p}_4} \, \overline{\dot{p}_5} \wedge (\dot{p}_1 \Rightarrow \overline{p_2 p_3} \vee \overline{p_4 p_5}) = \dot{p}_1 \overline{\dot{p}_2} \, \overline{\dot{p}_3} \, \overline{\dot{p}_4} \, \overline{\dot{p}_5} \wedge (\overline{p_2 p_3} \vee \overline{p_4 p_5}) = \dot{p}_1 \overline{\dot{p}_2} \, \overline{\dot{p}_3} \, \overline{\dot{p}_4} \, \overline{\dot{p}_5} \, \overline{p_2} \vee \dot{p}_1 \overline{\dot{p}_2} \, \overline{\dot{p}_3} \, \overline{\dot{p}_4} \, \overline{\dot{p}_5} \, \overline{p_3} \vee \dot{p}_1 \overline{\dot{p}_2} \, \overline{\dot{p}_3} \, \overline{\dot{p}_4} \, \overline{\dot{p}_5} \, \overline{p_4 p_5}$. The inference rules for the glue operator gl are shown below:

$$\frac{B_1 : q_1 \xrightarrow{p_1} q_1' \quad B_1 : q_1 \not\uparrow p_2}{gl(B_1, B_2) : q_1 q_2 \xrightarrow{p_1} q_1' q_2} \qquad \frac{B_1 : q_1 \xrightarrow{p_1} q_1' \quad B_1 : q_1 \not\uparrow p_3}{gl(B_1, B_2) : q_1 q_2 \xrightarrow{p_1} q_1' q_2}$$

$$\frac{B_1 : q_1 \xrightarrow{p_1} q_1' \quad B_2 : q_2 \not\uparrow p_4 \quad B_2 : q_2 \not\uparrow p_5}{gl(B_1, B_2) : q_1 q_2 \xrightarrow{p_1} q_1' q_2}$$

Lemma 1. *Let $\varphi \in \mathcal{GC}(P)$ be a glue constraint, $gl_\varphi \in FWN$ constructed as above, and $\varphi_{gl_\varphi} \in \mathcal{GC}(P)$ constructed as in Sect. 3.1 to gl_φ. Then $\varphi_{gl_\varphi} = \varphi$.*

Proposition 2. *Let $\{P_i\}_{i=1}^{n}$ be a set of interfaces, $\varphi \in \mathcal{GC}(P)$ a constraint formula, and $gl_\varphi \in FWN$ constructed as above. For any set of behaviors $B_i = (Q_i, P_i, \rightarrow, \uparrow)$, with $i \in [1, n]$, we have $\varphi(B_1, \ldots, B_n) = gl_\varphi(B_1, \ldots, B_n)$.*

4   Synthesis of Glue: A Rescue Robot Example

The following example was inspired by the hill-climbing robot discussed in [6]. Consider a robot R confined to a square paved region (Fig. 2(a)) and consisting of four modules: an engine E, a sensor S, a transmitter T, and a navigation system N. The engine can perform two actions: advance the robot one step forward and rotate 90°, controlled respectively through ports a (*advance*) and r (*rotate*). The sensor can measure the temperature in front of the robot and signal whether it is above a given threshold. The action of measuring is controlled through the port m (*measure*), whereas the produced signal can be observed on the port h (*hot*).

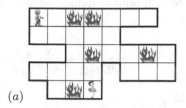   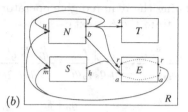

(a) $\qquad\qquad\qquad\qquad\qquad\qquad$ (b)

Fig. 2. (a) A rescue robot confined to a square paved region saving Betty Boop from fire; (b) architectural view of the robot.

The transmitter can send the robot's coordinates to the mission control. This action is controlled through the port s (*send*). Finally, the navigation system detects whether the robot is facing the border of the region and whether it has reached the objective. The navigation system data can be updated by an action controlled through the port u (*update*), the proximity of the border is signalled through the port b (*border*) and the objective through the port f (*finish*). Thus, the four interfaces are $P_E = \{a, r\}$, $P_S = \{m, h\}$, $P_T = \{s\}$, and $P_N = \{u, b, f\}$.

We want to synthesize the glue ensuring the following properties, which we encode by glue constraints. Notice, that the synthesized glue only has to ensure the safety of the robot and not that it reaches an objective.

1. The robot must not advance and rotate at the same time: $\bar{a}\,\bar{r}$;
2. The robot must not leave the region: $b \Rightarrow \bar{a}$;
3. The robot must not drive into hot areas: $h \Rightarrow \bar{a}$;
4. If the robot reaches the objective, it must stop and transmit its coordinates: $f \Rightarrow \bar{a}\,\bar{r}\,\bar{u}\,\bar{m}\,\dot{s}$;
5. The robot must only transmit its coordinates when it reaches the objective: $\dot{s} \Rightarrow f$;
6. Every time the robot moves (advances or rotates) the navigation system and the sensor must update their data: $\dot{a} \vee \dot{r} \Rightarrow \dot{u}\,\dot{m}$.

The architecture of the robot is illustrated in Fig. 2(b), with the controllable ports shown on the left-hand side of each component and the controlling ones on the right-hand side. The ports a and r of the engine are both controllable and controlling, so we duplicate them. The arrows indicate the control influence given by the constraints above.

In order to compute the required glue, we take the conjunction of the six constraints above and the *progress* constraint $(\dot{a} \vee \dot{r} \vee \dot{u} \vee \dot{m} \vee \dot{s}) \wedge \overline{\dot{h}}\,\overline{\dot{b}}\,\overline{\dot{f}}$—stating that some controllable action (a, r, u, m, or s) must be taken, but not the non-controllable actions h, b, and f—and apply the procedure described in Sect. 3.2. We rewrite the obtained glue constraint formula in the firing-full DNF: $\bar{a}\,\bar{r} \wedge (b \Rightarrow \bar{a}) \wedge (h \Rightarrow \bar{a}) \wedge (f \Rightarrow \bar{a}\,\bar{r}\,\bar{u}\,\bar{m}\,\dot{s}) \wedge (\dot{s} \Rightarrow f) \wedge (\dot{a} \vee \dot{r} \Rightarrow \dot{u}\,\dot{m}) \wedge (\dot{a} \vee \dot{r} \vee \dot{u} \vee \dot{m} \vee \dot{s}) \wedge \overline{\dot{h}}\,\overline{\dot{b}}\,\overline{\dot{f}} = (\bar{a}\,\bar{r}\,\dot{u}\,\bar{m}\,\dot{s}\,f \vee \bar{f}\,\bar{\dot{s}}\,\bar{a}\,\bar{r}\,\dot{u}\,\bar{m} \vee \bar{f}\,\bar{\dot{s}}\,\bar{a}\,\bar{r}\,\dot{u}\,\dot{m} \vee \bar{f}\,\bar{\dot{s}}\,\bar{a}\,\bar{r}\,\dot{u}\,\bar{m} \vee \bar{a}\,\dot{r}\,\bar{f}\,\bar{\dot{s}}\,\dot{u}\,\dot{m} \vee \dot{a}\,\bar{r}\,b\,\bar{h}\,\bar{f}\,\bar{\dot{s}}\,\dot{u}\,\dot{m}) \wedge \overline{\dot{h}}\,\overline{\dot{b}}\,\overline{\dot{f}}$
Positive parts of all the monomials in this formula are distinct. Therefore no further transformations are necessary, and we directly obtain the following rules

defining the required glue operator (we drop the component names, as they are clear from the context):

$$\frac{q_n \xrightarrow{u} q'_n \quad q_n \not\upharpoonright f}{q_e q_s q_n q_t \xrightarrow{u} q_e q_s q'_n q_t}, \quad \frac{q_s \xrightarrow{m} q'_s \quad q_n \xrightarrow{u} q'_n \quad q_n \not\upharpoonright f}{q_e q_s q_n q_t \xrightarrow{mu} q_e q'_s q'_n q_t}, \quad \frac{q_s \xrightarrow{m} q'_s \quad q_n \not\upharpoonright f}{q_e q_s q_n q_t \xrightarrow{m} q_e q'_s q_n q_t},$$

$$\frac{q_t \xrightarrow{s} q'_t \quad q_n \upharpoonright f}{q_e q_s q_n q_t \xrightarrow{s} q_e q_s q_n q'_t}, \quad \frac{q_e \xrightarrow{r} q'_e \quad q_s \xrightarrow{m} q'_s \quad q_n \xrightarrow{u} q'_n \quad q_n \not\upharpoonright f}{q_e q_s q_n q_t \xrightarrow{rmu} q'_e q'_s q'_n q_t},$$

$$\frac{q_e \xrightarrow{a} q'_e \quad q_s \xrightarrow{m} q'_s \quad q_n \xrightarrow{u} q'_n \quad q_s \not\upharpoonright h \quad q_n \not\upharpoonright b \quad q_n \not\upharpoonright f}{q_e q_s q_n q_t \xrightarrow{amu} q'_e q'_s q'_n q_t}.$$

It is important to observe here that this glue operator ensures the required safety properties independently of the specific implementation of the behaviors of the atomic components (Engine, Sensor, Navigation system and Transmitter), as long as this implementation respects the specified interfaces.

5   The Glue Expressiveness Hierarchy

The rule format for defining glue operators that we introduced in Sect. 2.2 allows three types of premises: firing, witness, and negative. In this section, we use the notion of glue expressiveness [2] to show that all three types are essential for the expressiveness of the glue that can be defined with these rules. To do so, we compare the following four classes of glue operators:

F: the class of glue operators obtained by using rules with only firing premises (of the form $q \xrightarrow{a} q'$). Classical composition operators, e.g., parallel composition in CCS or CSP belong to this class;

FW: the class of glue operators obtained by using rules with only positive premises (firing premises, as above, and witness premises of the form $q \upharpoonright a$);

FN: the class of glue operators obtained by using rules with only firing and negative (of the form $q \not\upharpoonright a$) premises;

FWN: the universal glue obtained by using rules with all three types of premises.

Let $\mathcal{B}$ be a set of behaviors with a fixed equivalence relation $\mathcal{R} \subseteq \mathcal{B} \times \mathcal{B}$. A glue is a set G of operators on $\mathcal{B}$. We denote by $\mathcal{G}lue$ the set of all glues on $\mathcal{B}$. We denote $G^{(n)} \subseteq G$ the set of all n-ary operators in G. Thus, $G = \bigcup_{n \geq 1} G^{(n)}$.

To determine whether one glue is more expressive than another, we compare their respective sets of behaviors *composable* from the same *atomic* ones. This consists in exhibiting for each operator of one glue an equivalent operator in the other one. We only consider *strong expressiveness* [2], i.e. , where the exhibited glue operator must be applied to the same set of behaviors as the original one.

Although the results we present can also be extended to *weak expressiveness* [2], where the exhibited glue operator must be applied to the same set of behaviors as the original one with an addition of some fixed set of *coordination behaviors*, we do not present these extensions to avoid overcharging the paper.

Definition 6. *For a given set* $\mathcal{B}$ *and an equivalence* $\mathcal{R}$ *on* $\mathcal{B}$, *the* expressiveness preorder $\preccurlyeq \subseteq \mathcal{G}lue \times \mathcal{G}lue$ *w.r.t.* $\mathcal{R}$ *is defined by putting, for* G_1, $G_2 \in \mathcal{G}lue$, $G_1 \preccurlyeq G_2$ *if, for any* $n \geq 1$ *and* $B_1, \ldots, B_n \in \mathcal{B}$, *holds* $\forall gl_1 \in G_1^{(n)} \exists gl_2 \in G_2^{(n)} :$ $gl_1(B_1, \ldots, B_n) \mathcal{R} gl_2(B_1, \ldots, B_n)$.

We consider the partial order induced by $\preccurlyeq$, that is we say that G_1 is *less expressive* than G_2 if $G_1 \preccurlyeq G_2$ and $G_2 \not\preccurlyeq G_1$.

Definition 7. *Let* $B_1 = (Q_1, P_1, \rightarrow, \uparrow)$, $B_2 = (Q_2, P_2, \rightarrow, \uparrow)$. *A binary relation* $\sqsubseteq \subseteq Q_1 \times Q_2$ *is a* simulation *iff, for all* $q_1 \sqsubseteq q_2$ *and* $a \subseteq P$, $q_1 \uparrow a$ *implies* $q_2 \uparrow a$ *and* $q_1 \xrightarrow{a} q_1'$ *implies* $q_2 \xrightarrow{a} q_2'$, *for some* $q_2' \in Q_2$ *such that* $q_1' \sqsubseteq q_2'$.
We write $B_1 \sqsubseteq B_2$ *if there exists a simulation relating each state of* B_1 *to some state of* B_2. $\sqsubseteq$ *is the* simulation preorder *on behaviors. The relation* $\simeq = \sqsubseteq \cap \sqsubseteq^{-1}$ *is the* simulation equivalence *on behaviors.*

Proposition 3. *With respect to the simulation equivalence, F is less expressive than FW and FN, which are both less expressive than FWN.*

6   Glue Constraints, FWN, and BIP

BIP [1,7] is a component framework for constructing systems by superposing three layers of modeling: Behavior, Interaction, and Priorities. The lower layer consists of a set of atomic components modeled by transition systems. The second layer models interactions between components. Priorities are used to enforce scheduling policies applied to interactions of the second layer. Below, we provide a succinct formalization of the BIP component model.

Contrary to Def. 2, a behavior in BIP is an LTS (cf. Def. 1). Let $B_i = (Q_i, P_i, \rightarrow)$, for $i \in [1, n]$, be a set of transition systems and $P = \bigcup_{i=1}^n P_i$. The *composition* of $\{B_i\}_{i=1}^n$, parameterized by a set of interactions $\gamma \subseteq 2^P$, is the transition system $\gamma(B_1, \ldots, B_n) = (Q, P, \rightarrow)$, where $Q = \prod_{i=1}^n Q_i$ and $\rightarrow$ is the minimal relation defined by the following set of rules:

$$\left\{ \frac{\{B_i : q_i \xrightarrow{a \cap P_i} q_i' \mid i \in I_a\} \quad \{q_i = q_i' \mid i \notin I_a\}}{\gamma(B_1, \ldots, B_n) : q_1 \ldots q_n \xrightarrow{a} q_1' \ldots q_n'} \;\middle|\; a \in \gamma \right\}, \tag{7}$$

where, for $a \in \gamma$, $I_a = \{i \in [1, n] \mid a \cap P_i \neq \emptyset\}$. We call γ an *interaction model*.

Given a transition system $\gamma(B_1, \ldots, B_n)$, a *priority model* π is a strict partial order on 2^P. For $a, a' \in 2^P$, we write $a \prec a'$ iff $(a, a') \in \pi$, meaning that interaction a has less priority than interaction a'. The system obtained by applying the priority model π to $\gamma(B_1, \ldots, B_n)$ is the transition system $\pi\gamma(B_1, \ldots, B_n) = (Q, P, \rightarrow)$, where Q and P are the same as above, while $\rightarrow$ is the minimal set of transitions satisfying the set of inference rules

$$\pi\gamma = \left\{ \frac{\gamma(B_1, \ldots, B_n) : q \xrightarrow{a} q' \quad \{\{a'\}(B_1, \ldots, B_n) : q \xrightarrow{a'} \mid a \prec a'\}}{\pi\gamma(B_1, \ldots, B_n) : q \xrightarrow{a} q'} \;\middle|\; a \in \gamma \right\}$$

Intuitively, the premises of a rule for $a \in \gamma$ mean that, in the state $q \in Q$, a is possible in $\gamma(B_1, \ldots, B_n)$, and, for each interaction a' having higher priority than a, there is at least one component B_i such that the constituent interaction $a' \cap P_i$ is not possible in B_i. It is not required that a' belong to γ. In [2], we have shown that the glue of BIP is as expressive as the most general glue defined by inference rules of the form (1).

Example 5. The glue operator for the mutual preemption (Ex. 1) is expressed in BIP by considering the interaction model $\gamma = \{b_i, f_i, b_i p_j, f_i r_j | i, j = 1, 2, i \neq j\}$ and a priority model given by $b_i \prec b_i p_j$ and $f_i \prec f_i r_j$, for $i, j = 1, 2$ and $i \neq j$.

Proposition 4. *With respect to the simulation equivalence, FN is less expressive than the glue in BIP; FWN and the glue in BIP are not comparable.*

An important advantage of BIP is that it allows mastering the complexity of designs by developers: separating glue into two layers corresponding to interactions and priorities drastically simplifies readability of specifications. By redefining the semantics of priority models in terms of the predicate $\uparrow$, it can be shown that this separation can be achieved for the glue operators of Def. 4.

Separation of the coordination level defined by the glue operators into interactions and priorities allows the application of our previous results presented in [7,8]. By comparing (1) and (3), one can observe that both Interaction layer of BIP and positive glue operators of this paper are uniquely characterized by the *interactions* appearing in their premises. For the former, interactions are subsets of 2^P; for the latter, they are subsets of $2^{P \cup \dot{P}}$. The sets P and $\dot{P}$ being disjoint, all the results from the two papers cited above can be applied to connectors of the algebra $\mathcal{AC}(P \cup \dot{P})$. This allows considering structured hierarchical connectors instead of exponential sets of interactions (in BIP) or rules (for glue operators of this paper). Connectors are well suited for compositional design and can be manipulated by symbolic techniques [7]. Furthermore, connectors can be synthesized directly from *causal rules*, which are boolean constraints (implications) on port variables similar to the constraints found in the examples of Sect. 4.

7   Design Methodology

Synthesis of reactive systems has been initiated by Pnueli and Rosner. They have shown that synthesis of *distributed* systems is hard and, sometimes, undecidable [9]. Lustig and Vardi have obtained similar hardness results for synthesis, where reusable components must be selected from component *libraries* [10].

This paper lays ground to a less ambitious, but more tractable design methodology relying on the observation that one of the main difficulties of systems design resides in the concurrent nature of modern software (particularly due to the state space explosion). This methodology can be summarized by the following steps:

1. Choice of the functionalities to be realized by sequential atomic components. This step *does not involve* specifying coordination among these atomic components. It is usually driven by the functional requirements (e.g., functionalities that must be provided by the system) or target platform hardware

specifications. Tools and techniques needed for this design step are, in general, well mastered by software engineers.

2. Independent design of sequential atomic components of the system. As mentioned above, development of sequential programs is much less complex than that of concurrent ones and can also be successfully realized by engineers.

3. Specification of state safety properties to be satisfied by the system. The general case complexity of this design step has yet to be investigated. All the properties that we have encountered are obtained as *causal rules* in a manner similar to that of the example in Sect. 4 (cf. [8]).

4. Automatic glue operator and connector synthesis. This implies that the underlying state safety properties are satisfied *by construction*.

For safety properties other than state properties, compositional deadlock analysis can be performed by adding (sequential) observer components to the synthesized model.

8   Related Work

A number of paradigms for unifying interaction in heterogeneous systems have been studied [12,13,14]. In these works, unification is achieved by reduction to a common low-level semantic model. Coordination mechanisms and their properties are not studied independently of behavior. Our approach is closest to that of [15], where an algebra of connectors is developed that allows one to construct *stateless* connectors from a number of basic ones.

This paper combines several notions that already exist in the literature. We use *boolean constraints* expressed in terms of *activation and firing variables* in order to *synthesize* glue operators expressed in terms of *SOS rules*.

In concurrency, the term *constraints* appears primarily in connection with the constraint automata [16,17], where constraints are used to restrict transition non-determinism. These automata are now widely referred to as having guarded transitions. We speak of *interaction constraints* that characterize mechanisms used in architectures such as connectors, channels, synchronization primitives and result from the composition of actions [18]. Architectural mechanisms are used to constrain the interaction among parallel communicating components.

Few authors have considered the approach by constraints in this context, e.g., [19]. The approach used in [20] is close to the one we adopted in our previous paper [8]. The important difference is that, following the separation of concerns principle, we distinguish coordination and data flow among components.

Separating the coordination layer allows to express coordination constraints as boolean formulæ. In [8], we consider *causal rules*, which are boolean constraints on port variables. Causal rules are used to synthesize connectors to describe interactions among components in BIP. In the present paper, we extend this methodology to the complete Coordination layer (Interactions and Priorities), which requires a more sophisticated notion of boolean constraints on *activation* and *firing* port variables, where firing variables are exactly the port variables we refer to in [8].

To the best of our knowledge, few authors in the domain of component-based design use activation or firing variables as we do in this paper, and we are not aware of any work making a combined use of both. The techniques closest to ours can be found in [20] and in the use of clocks in synchronous languages such as Lustre [21], Esterel [22], and Signal [23].

Several methodologies for synthesis of component coordination have been proposed in the literature, e.g., connector synthesis in [24,25,26]. In [24], connectors are synthesized in order to ensure deadlock freedom of systems that follow a given architectural style. The proposed methodology is seriously limited by two factors. Firstly, the proposed architectural style is very restrictive: components can only be connected in a specific way and communicate by passing two types of messages (notifications and requests). Secondly, in order to ensure deadlock freedom, the authors rely on the analysis that requires computing the product automaton representing the complete system, which is impractical for large systems.

In [25], Reo circuits are generated from constraint automata. This approach is limited, in the first place, by the complexity of building the automaton specification of interactions. An attempt to overcome this limitation is made in [26] by generating constraint automata from UML sequence diagrams. A commonly accepted problem of using UML, in general, and sequence diagrams, in particular, is the absence of formal semantics. Although the Reo approach effectively provides such semantics, there is no guarantee that this semantics can be understood by the designer, as the synthesized constraint automata can be rather complex. More importantly, synthesized Reo connectors (with the constraint automaton semantics) have state. Hence, they contribute to the state space explosion hampering verification of the final system properties.

Our approach allows one to directly synthesize stateless glue from safety requirements in a generic setting and circumvents the difficulty of behavior synthesis by applying the separation of concerns principle; it develops the line of [8] and has similarities with the synthesis of circuits from boolean specifications.

Finally, following the common practice, we use SOS rules to define composition (glue) operators. Since their introduction in [4], numerous formats for SOS rules have been proposed and extensively studied in order to provide generic properties of objects defined by SOS rules. The rule formats that we use in this paper represent two very simple special cases of the existing SOS formats. In particular, the format given by (1) is a special case of GSOS [3].

9   Conclusion

We proposed and studied a general framework for component-based construction of systems. The framework is based on an SOS-style characterization of composition operators, called glue operators. The presented boolean characterization of glue operators allows moving from heavy SOS-style definition to a lightweight boolean representation. The representation distinguishes between firing and activation variables. This distinction is essential for expressing priorities and, in general, situations where the state of one component influences enabledness of an interaction without participating in it. The use of the offer predicate ↑ is essential for taking into account offers of the composed individual behaviors. This leads to a concept of transition system richer than usual transition systems, which allows to distinguish between composite and atomic behavior.

The equivalence between glue constraints and universal glue can drastically simplify component-based design. We have shown through examples that glue constraints can be used to express given safety requirements. The synthesis of an implementation from such requirements can be automated by computing the firing-full DNF and the corresponding operational semantics rules. This provides means for deriving executable models from declarative safety requirements opening the way for an automated synthesis paradigm similar to hardware synthesis.

Contrary to the algebra presented in [2], the Algebra of Glue Constraints, is very general and intuitive. Indeed, the only axiom different from the standard Boolean ones is, basically, a sanity check: a port cannot participate if it is not active. Any formula in this algebra gives rise to a valid glue operator.

Furthermore, we have shown that, by focusing on the properties (expressed as glue constraints) that do not bear computation, we reduce a very hard and, in general, undecidable problem of synthesizing controllers to a tractable one. The Rescue Robot example shows that such properties are quite natural and can be expressed as glue constraints in a straightforward manner.

Amongst the formalisms discussed in the paper, BIP presents the advantage of being more appropriate for mastering the complexity of designs by developers. The principle of separating glue into two layers corresponding to interactions (glue with positive premises) and priorities (glue with negative premises and a single positive premise) drastically simplifies readability of specifications. The presented results suggest an evolution of BIP semantics to encompass the universal glue defined in this paper.

This work is part of a broader research project around BIP, including the development of the BIP language and associated tool-set for component-based design. The tool-set includes compilers as well as compositional verification tools. It has been successfully applied to modeling and validation of heterogeneous systems [11,27]. We will continue our study to further explore relations between three identified approaches: SOS-based, constraint-based, and layered.

References

1. Basu, A., Bozga, M., Sifakis, J.: Modeling heterogeneous real-time components in BIP. In: 4th IEEE Int. Conf. on Software Engineering and Formal Methods (SEFM 2006), pp. 3–12 (2006) Invited talk
2. Bliudze, S., Sifakis, J.: A notion of glue expressiveness for component-based systems. In: van Breugel, F., Chechik, M. (eds.) CONCUR 2008. LNCS, vol. 5201, pp. 508–522. Springer, Heidelberg (2008)

3. Bloom, B.: Ready Simulation, Bisimulation, and the Semantics of CCS-Like Languages. PhD thesis, Massachusetts Institute of Technology (1989)
4. Plotkin, G.D.: A structural approach to operational semantics. Technical Report DAIMI FN-19, University of Aarhus (1981)
5. Mousavi, M., Reniers, M.A., Groote, J.F.: SOS formats and meta-theory: 20 years after. Theoretical Computer Science 373(3), 238–272 (2007)
6. Cheng, C.P., Fristoe, T., Lee, E.A.: Applied verification: The Ptolemy approach. Technical Report UCB/EECS-2008-41, University of California at Berkeley (2008)
7. Bliudze, S., Sifakis, J.: The algebra of connectors — Structuring interaction in BIP. In: Proc. of the EMSOFT 2007, pp. 11–20. ACM SigBED, New York (2007)
8. Bliudze, S., Sifakis, J.: Causal semantics for the algebra of connectors. Formal Methods in System Design 36(2), 167–194 (2010)
9. Pnueli, A., Rosner, R.: Distributed reactive systems are hard to synthesize. In: Annual IEEE Symposium on Foundations of Computer Science, vol. 2, pp. 746–757 (1990)
10. Lustig, Y., Vardi, M.Y.: Synthesis from component libraries. In: de Alfaro, L. (ed.) FOSSACS 2009. LNCS, vol. 5504, pp. 395–409. Springer, Heidelberg (2009)
11. Bensalem, S., Bozga, M., Nguyen, T.-H., Sifakis, J.: D-Finder: A tool for compositional deadlock detection and verification. In: Bouajjani, A., Maler, O. (eds.) CAV 2009. LNCS, vol. 5643, pp. 614–619. Springer, Heidelberg (2009)
12. Balarin, F., et al.: Metropolis: An integrated electronic system design environment. IEEE Computer 36(4), 45–52 (2003)
13. Balasubramanian, K., et al.: Developing applications using model-driven design environments. IEEE Computer 39(2), 33–40 (2006)
14. Eker, J., et al.: Taming heterogeneity: The Ptolemy approach. Proc. of the IEEE 91(1), 127–144 (2003)
15. Bruni, R., Lanese, I., Montanari, U.: A basic algebra of stateless connectors. Theor. Comput. Sci. 366(1), 98–120 (2006)
16. Fribourg, L., Peixoto, M.V.: Concurrent constraint automata. In: ILPS 1993: Proc. of the 1993 International Symposium on Logic Programming, vol. 656. MIT Press, Cambridge (1993)
17. Baier, C., et al.: Modeling component connectors in Reo by constraint automata. Sci. Comput. Program. 61(2), 75–113 (2006)
18. Gößler, G., Sifakis, J.: Composition for component-based modeling. Sci. Comput. Program. 55(1–3), 161–183 (2005)
19. Montanari, U., Rossi, F.: Graph rewriting and constraint solving for modelling distributed systems with synchronization (extended abstract). In: Hankin, C., Ciancarini, P. (eds.) COORDINATION 1996. LNCS, vol. 1061, pp. 12–27. Springer, Heidelberg (1996)
20. Clarke, D., et al.: Deconstructing Reo. In: FOCLASA 2008. ENTCS (2008)
21. Halbwachs, N., et al.: The synchronous dataflow programming language LUSTRE. Proc. of the IEEE 79, 1305–1320 (1991)
22. Berry, G., Gonthier, G.: The ESTEREL synchronous programming language: Design, semantics implementation. Sci. Comput. Program. 19(2), 87–152 (1992)
23. Benveniste, A., Guernic, P.L., Jacquemot, C.: Synchronous programming with events and relations: the SIGNAL language and its semantics. Sci. Comput. Program. 16(2), 103–149 (1991)
24. Inverardi, P., Scriboni, S.: Connectors synthesis for deadlock-free component-based architectures. In: ASE 2001, pp. 174–181. IEEE Computer Society, Los Alamitos (2001)

25. Arbab, F., Baier, C., de Boer, F.S., Rutten, J., Sirjani, M.: Synthesis of Reo Circuits for Implementation of Component-Connector Automata Specifications. In: Jacquet, J.-M., Picco, G.P. (eds.) COORDINATION 2005. LNCS, vol. 3454, pp. 236–251. Springer, Heidelberg (2005)
26. Arbab, F., Meng, S.: Synthesis of connectors from scenario-based interaction specifications. In: Chaudron, M.R.V., Ren, X.-M., Reussner, R. (eds.) CBSE 2008. LNCS, vol. 5282, pp. 114–129. Springer, Heidelberg (2008)
27. Basu, A., et al.: Incremental component-based construction and verification of a robotic system. In: ECAI, pp. 631–635 (2008)

A Sequence of Patterns for Reusable Aspect Libraries with Easy Configuration

Maarten Bynens, Eddy Truyen, and Wouter Joosen

DistriNet, K.U.Leuven
Maarten.Bynens@cs.kuleuven.be
http://distrinet.cs.kuleuven.be

Abstract. Using well-known AspectJ idioms has been shown to increase the reusability of aspect libraries. Availability of such reusable libraries is an important motivating factor to drive the further adoption of AspectJ in industry and aspect-oriented-programming in general. Existing work, however, mostly presents the existing AspectJ idioms as relatively independent solutions. As experience grows in using these idioms, it is possible to increasingly combine related idioms to form patterns and subsequently, pattern languages. A pattern language provides a structured process on how to apply a family of related patterns and idioms that cover a particular domain or discipline. This paper presents a first step towards a pattern language for building reusable aspect libraries in the form of a sequence of aspect-oriented patterns that each combine a set of idioms to achieve (i) a configurable core design of the aspect library, (ii) library-controlled mediation of the interactions between the different aspects in the library and (iii) flexible configuration by providing multiple alternative modes for binding the aspect library to an application. An initial evaluation of the pattern sequence in the context of a pricing library shows improved reusability and ease-of-configuration in comparison to an existing idiom-based implementation of the pricing library.

1 Introduction

The availability of qualitative aspect libraries is an important driver to improve mainstream adoption of aspect-oriented (AO) technology [34]. Concrete examples of reusable aspect libraries exist [16, 5, 27], typically providing stable functionality with regard to a specific concern (transactions, persistence, etc.). Also typical is that configuration of such libraries can become complex and requires use of AO constructs.

Developing qualitative aspect libraries has been shown to be difficult in real-world software. As aspect-oriented programming (AOP) is a very powerful technology, programmers are often unaware of what interactions will happen between different program elements at run-time. Apart from being reliable in performing the correct behavior [32, 4, 18], qualitative aspect libraries should exhibit stability [33, 17, 14], versatility and ease-of-configuration. In a previous study [2] we have shown that applying AspectJ idioms has a positive impact on versatility

S. Apel and E. Jackson (Eds.): SC 2011, LNCS 6708, pp. 68–83, 2011.

and stability of aspect libraries. An idiom is a pattern specific to a programming language or programming environment. An idiom describes how to implement particular behavior or structures in code using the features of the given language or environment [1]. One example idiom is the use of a marker interface in the definition of pointcuts and inter-type declarations (ITD) instead of concrete types from the base application. Many examples of idioms for AOP are available in the literature [12, 15, 19, 25, 25].

The use of these idioms, however, has not significantly reduced the configuration complexity of aspect libraries. We believe that the underlying reason for this lack of improvement is the absence of the necessary guidance on how to combine the different idioms. In existing work, aspect-oriented idioms are mostly presented as relatively independent solutions. However, as experience grows in using these idioms, it is possible to increasingly combine related idioms to form patterns and subsequently, pattern languages. This paper explores the benefits of defining a pattern language that will provide the necessary guidance on how to combine the different idioms in order to achieve easy configuration while preserving versatility and stability of aspect libraries. In practice, configuration of aspect libraries is often achieved using annotations [31]. However, because of their inherent limitations, annotations alone are insufficient to realize configuration of aspect libraries in general. Annotations perform well in identifying the relevant join points, but are troublesome for specifying behavior and handling of interactions between different aspects.

The goal of this paper is to present a first step towards a pattern language by describing by example a sequence of patterns for building reusable aspect libraries. A pattern sequence represents a process made up of smaller processes– its constituent patterns– arranged in an order that achieves a particular architecture, architectural feature, or change of environment with desired properties [1]. The resulting libraries should be applicable to a wide range of applications without the need for complex configuration. This paper presents the creation of the aspect-oriented architecture and design of a pricing library in terms of the pattern sequence. Although the patterns are valuable for AO composition in general, we focus on AspectJ for the example and its implementation. AspectJ has a workable implementation and is the most mature AO language available. We believe that AspectJ will remain the future mainstream AO language as research on AO languages will lead to changes to AspectJ instead of new languages replacing AspectJ as mainstream. The process for adding changes into AspectJ is actively taken up by some of the leaders in AOP research[1].

Our methodology for exploring the benefits of a pattern language is as follows. First, we collected, classified and described the idioms for developing aspect libraries [2]. Second, we let students design reusable aspect libraries based on this collection. Third, we listed the remaining problems of the resulting library with respect to ease-of-configuration. Finally, we improved the design of the libraries and distilled the pattern sequence from this experience.

---

[1] http://www.aosd.net/wiki/index.php?title=Getting_Changes_into_AspectJ

Our pattern sequence contributes by promoting a step-wise process to develop reusable aspect libraries that employs existing idioms. In subsequent steps it results in an extensible and configurable core design with library-controlled mediation of the internal aspect interactions and by providing multiple alternative configuration modes.

The structure of the paper is as follows: in section 2 we give an overview of the patterns in the sequence, their consistent idioms and the requirements they aim to solve. Section 3 presents the running example of a pricing library. Section 4 applies the pattern sequence to the pricing library and evaluates the benefits. We discuss related work in section 5 and conclude in section 6.

2   Pattern Sequence Overview

This section presents the required qualities for the aspect libraries built using the pattern sequence and gives an overview of the patterns and idioms used.

2.1   Qualities

The one top-level design problem our pattern sequence aims to solve is the design of reusable aspect libraries with easy configuration. We focus on three qualities related to this general problem: versatility, ease-of-configuration and stability.

Versatility. Versatile aspect libraries are applicable to a wide range of applications. To achieve versatility the aspect should make as little assumptions as possible about the structure or behavior of the base code it interacts with.

This is a challenge for most AO technologies, as they need a mechanism to refer to properties of the base code (e.g. element names, code structure) to realize their crosscutting nature. An alternative is to use abstractions exposed by the base code [9], like annotations, explicit join points [13] or events [26]. The challenge is then shifted to bridging the possible mismatch between the abstractions exposed by the base code and the abstractions expected by the aspect library.

Ease-of-configuration. The composition of an aspect with a concrete application is specified in a configuration. When the configuration itself consists of relatively complex AO constructs, using the aspect library is not easy for non-AOP experts and might not be beneficial in the long term.

Configuration of aspects not only involves identifying the relevant join points. Specifying the crosscutting functionality and fine-tuning how different aspects should work together, is just as important. Libraries will consist of multiple different aspects, each acting independently. As a result it is necessary to specify configuration rules to regulate the interaction between the different aspects (e.g. in AspectJ, precedence declarations can resolve simple interactions).

Stability. Stable aspects reduce the effort and risk of extending the system. When the functionality of either the base code or the library is extended or refined, correctness of the configuration is no longer guaranteed [33]. For instance, the fragile pointcut problem is a well-known threat to the stability of AO systems [17, 14].

The relative importance of each of these qualities depends on the choice of AO technology. For AspectJ, which is the focus for this paper, all three qualities are essential to achieve reusability of aspect libraries.

2.2 Overview of Pattern Sequence

The pattern sequence consists of three patterns in the following order:

1. **Specify the core of the library.** The core consists of a behavioral part (what the aspect does) and a binding part (when it does it). This step ensures versatility and makes explicit the core abstractions to increase extensibility.
2. **Specify the mediation between resulting aspects.** In this step we control the internal interactions of the different aspects in the library through aspect mediation.
3. **Enable flexible composition.** To reduce complexity of configuration, we provide multiple alternatives to bind the library. Each alternative partially specifies the relevant join points using more structured abstractions like annotations or type parameters.

Each pattern in the sequence will employ a combination of idioms. These idioms have been documented before by several authors. We refer the reader to our earlier work [2] for a comprehensive overview of these idioms. Here, we briefly introduce them.

- Join point abstraction idioms:
  - Abstract pointcut: Use an abstract pointcut to abstract from any cross-cutting behavior [12, 11]
  - Marker interface: A (usually) empty interface that can be used as a type abstraction [12, 23]
  - Type parameter: Abstract from type information using type parameters in a generic aspect
  - Annotation introduction: Use an annotation to abstract from certain locations in the base code
- Decomposition idioms:
  - Template pointcut: Decompose a pointcut into hook pointcuts, separating stable and variable parts [20, 29]
  - Pointcut method: Encapsulate a dynamic condition in a method to be called from advice [12]
  - Template advice: Decompose advice into hook methods, separating stable and variable parts [12]
- Mediation idioms:
  - Chained advice: Let the cooperating aspects interact at the same join point and specify an order between their pieces of advice [12, 10]
  - Mediation data introduction: Introduce mediation-specific data members into base objects and mediate the cooperating aspects using these data members.

3   Case Study Pricing Library

This section first presents the design of a pricing library as it resulted from a master thesis. The students were given a collection of patterns and idioms [2], but without any guidance on how to use them. Secondly, this section analyses the shortcomings of the resulting design with respect to the reusability qualities.

Core functionality of the library is to realize pricing rules according to certain promotions, taxes, service costs, etc. The library will apply modifications to the price of certain items as defined by the pricing rules. Additionally, the library enables conflict resolution between different pricing rules, e.g. a general promotion should not be applied to book items when a more specific promotion for books is applicable.

The case study is meant as a pedagogical example as pricing is understandable, but still sufficiently complex to illustrate the problems we wish to address. Also, pricing is an interesting case for reusable libraries as it is relevant in multiple domains. For instance, in the master thesis the pricing library is also used as part of a real-time strategy game, where it is responsible for movement of units. Speed of movement depends on multiple factors, such as terrain type, proximity of enemy units, etc. Pricing (or business rules in general) has been used before as a target concern for AOSD [3, 6].

3.1   Original Design of the Pricing Library

Figure 1 shows the design. Central to the design is `AbstractPriceAspect`, giving an abstract definition of pricing rules. It advises executions of `getPrice` on objects of type `PricedItem` (pointcut `allPricedItem`) in the control flow of a `@ModifiedPrice` annotation (pointcut `scope`) by means of the idioms *annotation*

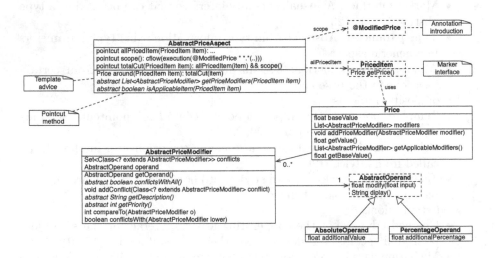

Fig. 1. Design of the pricing library based pattern collection

introduction and *marker interface*. Also *template advice* is used to abstract from the modifications (instances of `AbstractPriceModifier`) that need to occur (`getPriceModifiers`). The method `isApplicableItem` is a *pointcut method* to check if the pricing rule is applicable to the intercepted item.

The advice also employs a variant of *mediation data introduction* to control the combined behavior of the pricing aspects[2]. `AbstractPriceAspect` will add the `AbstractPriceModifier` instances from `getPriceModifiers` to the returned price object. Only when the resulting price is needed (by calling `getValue`) the different price modifications will take effect, taking priorities and conflicts into account (`getPriority` and `conflictsWith`).

To connect the pricing library to a concrete application, the user needs to do the following

1. provide a sub-aspect of `AbstractPriceAspect`
   (a) connect the marker interface `PricedItem` to base code elements
   (b) override `isApplicableItem`
   (c) override `getPriceModifiers`
       i. define a price modifier (sub-class of `AbstractPriceModifier`)
       ii. specify conflicts between certain price modifiers
       iii. specify priorities

An example configuration of the pricing library for a small web-shop example is depicted in Fig. 2. It defines three price modifications: a general promotion of 10%, a specific promotion for books of 20% and a fixed shipping cost. It also connects the type `Item` from the base code to the `PricedItem` type of the pricing library and connects the `@ModifiedPrice` annotation to activate the price modification in the necessary scope. In the next subsection we will discuss the difficulties of this configuration and list the underlying problems of the pricing library

3.2   Limitations of Original Design

Despite the fact that the library is designed with an extensive list of well-documented idioms for reusable aspects, there are still important limitations. The design is not optimal in terms of versatility and easy configuration. The main problems that lead to difficult configuration are as follows:

– Binding of the aspects to the relevant join points is difficult
   • Using a marker interface with a signature complicates its binding (a combination of an inheritance declaration, an introduction and a redirecting around advice is needed, see yellow elements in Fig. 2)
   • Using only a marker interface prohibits diversification of intercepted items (all sub-aspects of `AbstractPriceAspect` will interact with the same items, leading to an extensive need of pointcut methods, see green elements in Fig. 2)

---

[2] Instead of using the base object itself to store mediation data it uses a separate and specific Price object.

- Suboptimal use of annotations (to bind annotation @ModifiedPrice to a constructor, a workaround is needed, see orange elements in Fig. 2).
– Mediation is cumbersome and error-prone
  - Resolving conflicts and handling priorities between pricing rules is scattered over the different pricing rules (see red and blue elements in Fig. 2).

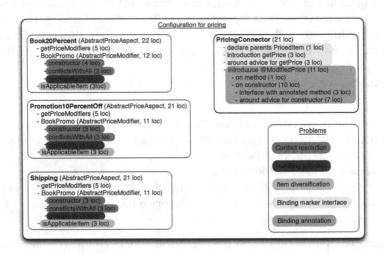

Fig. 2. Example configuration for the original design of the pricing library

4   Applying the Pattern Sequence to Build Reusable Aspect Libraries with Easy Configuration

In this section we apply the pattern sequence to the pricing library to improve its versatility and reduce complexity of configuration.

4.1   Core

Context. The design of a versatile and extensible library that provides crosscutting functionality.

Problem. How to define the core abstractions without tight coupling with the base code?

Solution. Specify the behavior (what the aspect does) and the binding (when the aspect does it) in abstract terms. In AspectJ this can be achieved using a combination of *abstract pointcut*, *template advice* and *pointcut method*.

Figure 3 depicts the core design of the pricing library using these idioms.

It provides the core functionality in the most abstract way. `AbstractPricing` defines an abstract method (`modify`) that executes at the join points selected by an abstract pointcut, `pricing`, using the *template advice* idiom. `CheckedPricing`

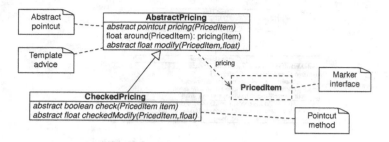

Fig. 3. Core design of the pricing library

extends this basic functionality by introducing a *pointcut method*. Different sub-aspects of either `AbstractPricing` and `CheckedPricing` represent different price modifications.

To connect the core of the pricing library, the user needs to

- provide a sub-aspect of either `AbstractPricing` or `CheckedPricing` for each pricing rule
- give a definition for the `pricing` pointcut
- implement method `modify` (or `checkedModify`)
- optionally implement pointcut method `check`

The core design of the pricing library is extensible and versatile, but as a consequence, the user needs to define his own pointcuts, which shifts some of the complexity to the configuration. Also, it is not easy to control the interaction between the different price modifications. It can be done through the pointcut methods, but that solution doesn't scale to non-trivial interactions. Therefore, the next step deals with support for mediation between the sub-aspects.

4.2 Mediation

Context. Design of a reusable aspect library consisting of a group of interacting aspects.

Problem. It is difficult to control the resulting behavior of this group of aspects.

Solution. Separate the effect an aspect has from its intention. Instead of each aspect having an effect immediately, we encapsulate its effect (similar to *command* pattern [7]) and control the combined behavior through a mediator. Figure 4 presents the resulting design, showing new elements in grey. Each pricing aspect will add itself as a modification to the base object (`modifications` in `PricedItem`). The `Mediator` aspect will introduce mediation data (`MediationData`) to the individual pricing aspects at the appropriate time, which, in this case, is when a price modifier that overrules another price modifier or might be overruled, is added to a `PricedItem` object (pointcuts `conflictAdded` and `conflictedAdded`). For pricing the mediation meta-data is concerned with possible conflicts. After all pricing aspects have made their

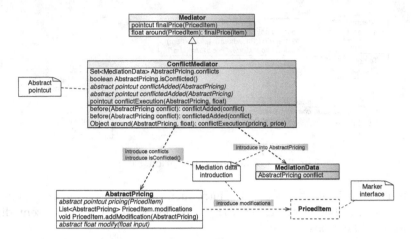

Fig. 4. Design of the pricing library with support for mediation

intentions clear, the mediator can apply the correct changes based on mediation meta-data (advice on pointcut `finalPrice` and `conflictExecution`).

The aspect user can now specify pricing interactions as follows:

- define pointcuts `conflictAdded` and `conflictedAdded`, e.g.
  `execution(void PricedItem.addModification(..)) && args(conflict) && args(Book20Percent)` for `conflictAdded`.
- declare precedence between the different price modifiers to control the order in which they will be added to an item and also will be executed

Complex mediation is now feasible in the library, but still configuration requires complex (aspect) definitions. We will deal with this in the third step.

4.3   Flexible Composition

Context. An aspect is versatile through the use of abstract pointcuts.

Problem. Binding the aspect means defining the pointcut descriptors, introducing complex and risky constructions in the configuration. How to ease aspect configuration?

Solution. Decompose abstract pointcuts to more fine-grained pointcuts and provide partial definitions.

In AspectJ this can be achieved with repeated use of *template pointcut* complemented with the use of structured abstractions like annotations, type parameters or marker interfaces. As a result, the aspect library remains flexible in how it can be configured. Figure 5 presents the complete design for the pricing library[3]. *Template pointcut* is not necessary here, the pointcuts

---

[3] Some details already represented in Fig. 4 are left out for clarity.

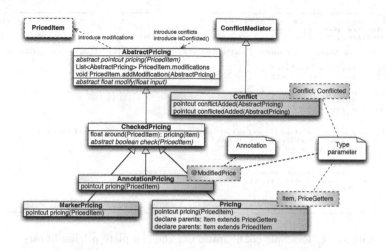

Fig. 5. Design of the pricing library with flexible configuration

`pricing`, `conflictAdded` and `conflictedAdded` are sufficiently fine-grained and can be represented directly using structured abstractions. Conflicts between price modifiers only really need the types behind the two conflicting price rules, so `conflictAdded` and `conflictedAdded` are implemented with *type parameters* in sub-aspect `Conflict`. For the `pricing` pointcut, more options are provided: via a marker interface (`MarkerPricing`), via annotations (`AnnotationPricing`) and via type parameters (`Pricing`).

To connect the resulting design of the pricing library, the aspect user needs to do the following:

- provide a sub-aspect of `Conflict` for each conflict between price modifiers
- provide a sub-aspect of either `Pricing`, `AnnotationPricing` or `MarkerPricing` for each price modifier
- provide a precedence declaration to control the order of price modifications

4.4   Connecting the Aspect Library to an Application

Now that we have our complete design of the pricing library, we can have a deeper look at the configuration. Listing 1 gives the complete configuration of the pricing library for the same small web-shop example – general promotion (lines 15-19), specific promotion for books (lines 10-14), fixed shipping cost (lines 20-24). It also connects the type `Item` from the base code to the `PricedItem` type of the pricing library (line 2). One conflict is specified: when the promotion for books is activated, the general promotion is not valid (line 5). The precedence declaration specifies that shipping costs are added after promotions are dealt with (line 3). This configuration is very concise compared to the necessary code to configure the original design (less than half in terms of lines of code). If we compare this configuration with Fig. 2, we can note that handling of conflicts is now

```
1   public aspect PricingConfiguration {
2       declare parents: Item implements PricedItem;
3       declare precedence: Promotion10PercentOff, Book20Percent, Shipping;
4   }
5   aspect BookConflict extends Conflict<Book20Percent, Promotion10PercentOff>{}
6
7   public interface GetPrice {
8     public float getPrice();
9   }
10  public aspect Book20Percent extends Pricing<Book, GetPrice>{
11    public float modify(float input) {
12        return input*0.8f;
13    }
14  }
15  public aspect Promotion10PercentOff extends Pricing<Item, GetPrice> {
16      public float modify(float input) {
17          return input*0.9f;
18      }
19  }
20  public aspect Shipping extends Pricing<Item, GetPrice> {
21      public float modify(float input) {
22          return input+10f;
23      }
24  }
```

Listing 1. Example configuration of the complete pricing library

centralized; specification of priorities is achieved with 1 precedence declaration; binding of the marker interface is done with 1 inheritance declaration; and price items are diversified through type parameters. In the following section we will present a more proper evaluation of the benefits of our pattern sequence.

4.5   Evaluating the Contribution of the Pattern Sequence

In this section we present an initial explorative evaluation of the benefits of our pattern sequence with respect to the reusability qualities. We compare the discussed original design of the pricing library with our own design that resulted from using the pattern sequence based on the same idioms. To put the results in perspective we also compare it to a naive implementation of the pricing library without explicit knowledge of the idioms or the pattern sequence (taken from an earlier study [2]).

We evaluate the designs in the context of USell, a prototype sales application[4]. We add pricing strategies to the application by means of 7 change requests (CR), e.g. providing a change log to visualize all price factors, extra costs for delivery, products involved in a couple promotion are not subject to other promotions, etc.

Stability. To give an idea of the impact on stability we compared the number of changed and added pointcuts for each change request of the USell application.

Figure 6 shows that using our pattern sequence, less pointcuts are needed and thus also less pointcuts will need to be changed. This is the result of using structured abstractions, taking away the need for the user to define pointcuts. As a result, the configuration is more robust.

---

[4] The source code of the aspects and the USell applications are available at http://distrinet.cs.kuleuven.be/software/aodesignpatterns

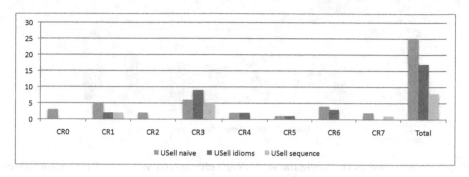

Fig. 6. Added and changed pointcuts for each change request in the USell application

Versatility. To measure versatility we compare the degree of library use for the three different implementations of the pricing library. We show the trend in library use by giving the value after the first change request and the value after all change requests. The degree of library use is defined as the lines of code (LOC) that are actually used divided by total LOC of the library. We would expect that as more change requests have been performed, more functionality of the aspect library will be used. Table 1 shows that both the use of idioms and the pattern sequence lead to an increased reuse of library functionality. Initial reuse of the library developed using the pattern sequence is lower because not all modules need to be configured for trivial cases.

Table 1. Degree of library use for the pricing aspect after 1 change request and after all change requests

Pricing version	naive	idioms	sequence
Degree of library use (%)	63→35	89→99	62→ 95

4.5.1   Ease-of-Configuration

To measures the effort of integrating the aspect library with a certain application we analyze the configuration for each change request in terms of conciseness. We use lines of code as the metric for conciseness.

Figure 7 shows significant improvement. Providing structured abstractions really helps in managing the complexity of the configuration by encapsulating this complexity in the library as much as possible.

4.5.2   Threats to Validity

Although this minimal evaluation is not meant to be conclusive, we believe that these results give a good impression on the applicability of the pattern sequence and the benefits of applying it. To assess the real value of these results we analyze the threats to the validity.

Stability, reusability and ease-of-configuration are attributes that are difficult to measure. The metrics used for stability have been used before [8]. The metric

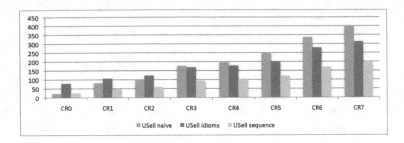

Fig. 7. Conciseness of the configuration for each change request in the USell application (in LOC)

used for ease-of-configuration is less established, but size is always an important indicator for effort [21]. The most important threat to internal validity is the difference in experience in using AOP between the master students and the authors of this paper. The size of the application and aspect used is not sufficient to make general conclusions about the benefits of the pattern sequence in a real-world context. Also, all code in the study was written in AspectJ, which limits the portability of the results to other AOP technologies.

5   Related Work

Many sources exist that present good practices, idioms or patterns for AOP. Far less common are integrated solutions consisting of multiple elements that define a process towards a specific goal. Hanenberg et al. have describes many idioms and patterns [12] and also an initial process on how to combine good practices [11]. Kiczales and Mezini discuss and compare some practices for separating concerns [15]. Other sources of patterns include Laddad [19], Noble [25] and Schmidmeier [30]. Santos and Koskimies describe an actual pattern language that employs AO patterns and idioms for the reuse of OO frameworks [29].

Other AO languages deal with the problems in this paper by providing alternative means to bind aspects [26, 28]. Although these alternatives cause different problems with respect to the qualities discussed, we believe they would also benefit from our patterns on an abstract level. Also related are techniques that increase aspect awareness of base code. We gave an overview of such techniques in earlier work [2].

The complexity of aspect mediation has been discussed before. Schmidmeier [30] describes two core patterns for aspects interacting and cooperating with other aspects. Marot and Wuyts introduce some new AO language constructs to more easily compose aspects with other aspects [22].

The limitations we discussed with respect to the original design of the pricing library are related to code smells that give rise to refactorings [24] and implicit design assumptions [35] that limit the reusability of aspect code.

D'Hondt and Cibran have described how AO technology can be used to handle business rules (e.g. pricing) [3, 6]. A comparison with their results is future work.

6   Conclusions

In this paper we have presented a sequence of patterns aimed at the development of reusable aspect libraries with easy configuration. Our contribution is the presentation of a sequence of patterns that each combines a set of idioms to achieve (i) a configurable core design of the aspect library, (ii) library-controlled mediation of the internal aspect interactions and (iii) flexible configuration by providing multiple alternative modes for binding the aspect library to an application.

Initial evaluation shows improved reusability and configurability in the context of a pricing example. The results give a first impression on the applicability of the pattern sequence and the benefits of applying it and shows that the way different patterns and idioms are combined has a big impact on the reusability properties of an aspect library.

The pattern sequence we present are based AspectJ idioms. Other AO languages, and also more advanced OO composition mechanisms, need to be studied in order to evaluate their potential to provide reusable solutions for the separation of crosscutting concerns.

By adding more knowledge on the relations between the patterns and idioms, the definition of a real pattern language is a logical next step. Additionally, other qualities can be taken into account requiring the need of other pattern sequences. New patterns and idioms will become relevant and other forces will drive pattern selection.

References

[1] Buschmann, F., Henney, K., Schmidt, D.: Pattern Oriented Software Architecture: On Patterns and Pattern Languages. Wiley Software Patterns Series. John Wiley & Sons, Chichester (2007)

[2] Bynens, M., Truyen, E., Joosen, W.: A system of patterns for reusable aspect libraries. Transactions on Aspect-Oriented Software Development VIII (2011) (accepted), http://distrinet.cs.kuleuven.be/software/aodesignpatterns

[3] Cibrán, M.A., D'Hondt, M.: A slice of MDE with AOP: Transforming high-level business rules to aspects. In: Wang, J., Whittle, J., Harel, D., Reggio, G. (eds.) MoDELS 2006. LNCS, vol. 4199, pp. 170–184. Springer, Heidelberg (2006)

[4] Clifton, C., Leavens, G.T., Aumann, Y.: MAO: Ownership and effects for more effective reasoning about aspects. In: Bateni, M. (ed.) ECOOP 2007. LNCS, vol. 4609, pp. 451–475. Springer, Heidelberg (2007)

[5] Cunha, C.A., Sobral, J.L., Monteiro, M.P.: Reusable aspectoriented implementations of concurrency patterns and mechanisms. In: AOSD, pp. 134–145. ACM, New York (2006)

[6] DHondt, M., Jonckers, V.: Hybrid aspects for weaving object-oriented functionality and rule-based knowledge. In: AOSD, pp. 132–140 (2004)

[7] Gamma, E., Helm, R., Johnson, R., Vlissides, J.: Design Patterns, Elements of Reusable Object-Oriented Software. Addison-Wesley, Reading (1995)

[8] Greenwood, P., Bartolomei, T., Figueiredo, E., Dosea, M., Garcia, A., Cacho, N., Sant'Anna, C., Soares, S., Borba, P., Kulesza, U., Rashid, A.: On the impact of aspectual decompositions on design stability: An empirical study. In: Bateni, M. (ed.) ECOOP 2007. LNCS, vol. 4609, pp. 176–200. Springer, Heidelberg (2007)

[9] Griswold, W.G., Sullivan, K., Song, Y., Shonle, M., Tewari, N., Cai, Y., Rajan, H.: Modular software design with crosscutting interfaces. IEEE Softw. 23(1), 51–60 (2006)

[10] Hanenberg, S., Schmidmeier, A.: Idioms for building software frameworks in aspectj. In: AOSD Workshop on Aspects, Components, and Patterns for Infrastructure Software (2003)

[11] Hanenberg, S., Unland, R.: Using and Reusing Aspects in AspectJ. In: Workshop on Advanced Separation of Concerns, OOPSLA (2001)

[12] Hanenberg, S., Unland, R., Schmidmeier, A.: AspectJ Idioms for Aspect- Oriented Software Construction. In: Proceedings of EuroPLoP, pp. 617–644 (2003)

[13] Hoffman, K., Eugster, P.: Towards reusable components with aspects: an empirical study on modularity and obliviousness. In: ICSE, pp. 91–100. ACM, New York (2008)

[14] Kellens, A., Mens, K., Brichau, J., Gybels, K.: Managing the evolution of aspect-oriented software with model-based pointcuts. In: Hu, Q. (ed.) ECOOP 2006. LNCS, vol. 4067, pp. 501–525. Springer, Heidelberg (2006)

[15] Kiczales, G., Mezini, M.: Separation of concerns with procedures, annotations, advice and pointcuts. In: Black, A. (ed.) ECOOP 2005. LNCS, vol. 3586, pp. 195–213. Springer, Heidelberg (2005)

[16] Kienzle, J., Gélineau, S.: Ao challenge - implementing the acid properties for transactional objects. In: AOSD, pp. 202–213. ACM, New York (2006)

[17] Koppen, C., Stoerzer, M.: Pcdiff: Attacking the fragile pointcut problem. In: First European Interactive Workshop on Aspects in Software, EIWAS (2004)

[18] Kuhlemann, M., Kästner, C.: Reducing the complexity of AspectJ mechanisms for recurring extensions. In: Proc. GPCE Workshop on Aspect- Oriented Product Line Engineering, AOPLE (2007)

[19] Laddad, R.: AspectJ in Action: Practical Aspect-Oriented Programming. Manning Publications Co, Greenwich (2003)

[20] Lagaisse, B., Joosen, W.: Decomposition into elementary pointcuts: A design principle for improved aspect reusability. In: SPLAT (2006)

[21] Li, W., Henry, S.M.: Object-oriented metrics that predict maintainability. Journal of Systems and Software 23(2), 111–122 (1993)

[22] Marot, A., Wuyts, R.: Composing aspects with aspects. In: AOSD, pp. 157–168. ACM, New York (2010)

[23] Miles, R.: AspectJ Cookbook. O'Reilly Media, Inc, Sebastopol (2004)

[24] Monteiro, M.P., Fernandes, J.M.: Towards a catalogue of refactorings and code smells for aspectj. T. Aspect-Oriented Software Development, 1, 214–258 (2006)

[25] Noble, J., Schmidmeier, A., Pearce, D.J., Black, A.P.: Patterns of aspect-oriented design. In: In Proceedings of European Conference on Pattern Languages of Programs (2007)

[26] Rajan, H., Leavens, G.T.: Ptolemy: A language with quantified, typed events. In: Ryan, M. (ed.) ECOOP 2008. LNCS, vol. 5142, pp. 155–179. Springer, Heidelberg (2008)

[27] Rashid, A., Chitchyan, R.: Persistence as an aspect. In: AOSD, pp. 120–129. ACM, New York (2003)

[28] Rho, T., Kniesel, G., Appeltauer Fine-grained, M.: generic aspects. In: Foundations of Aspect-Oriented Languages (2006)

[29] Santos, A.L., Koskimies, K.: Modular hot spots: A pattern language for developing high-level framework reuse interfaces. In: In Proceedings of European Conference on Pattern Languages of Programs (2008)

[30] Schmidmeier, A.: Cooperatingaspects. In: Proceedings of EuroPLoP (2005)

[31] SpringSource. Spring roo, http://www.springsource.org/roo

[32] Steimann, F.: The paradoxical success of aspect-oriented programming. SIGPLAN Not., 41(10), 481–497 (2006)

[33] Tourwe, T., Brichau, J., Gybels, K.: On the Existence of the AOSD-Evolution Paradox. In: SPLAT Workshop, Boston, AOSD (2003)

[34] Wiese, D., Meunier, R., Hohenstein, U.: How to convince industry of aop. In: AOSD, Industry Track (2007)

[35] Zschaler, S., Rashid, A.: Aspect assumptions: a retrospective study of aspectj developers assumptions about aspect usage. In: AOSD, pp. 93–104. ACM, New York (2011)

Pluggable Aspect Instantiation Models*

David H. Lorenz and Victor Trakhtenberg

Dept. of Mathematics and Computer Science,
Open University of Israel, Raanana 43107 Israel
`lorenz@openu.ac.il`, `victortr75@gmail.com`

Abstract. An aspect encapsulates not only crosscutting behavior, but also cross-cutting state. When aspects are stateful, there is a need to specify and control their instantiation. Unfortunately, aspect instantiation is a hard-wired feature in AS-PECTJ. This feature cannot be customized by the application programmer. Specifically, there are six pre-defined instantiation models to choose from, each designated by a keyword: `issingleton`, `perthis`, `pertarget`, `percflow`, `percflowbelow`, `pertypewithin`. In this work, we introduce a new language mechanism and keyword '`perscope`' that lets third-parties define custom aspect instantiation models. This new keyword replaces the six existing keywords in ASPECTJ, and may eliminate the need for introducing future ones.

1 Introduction

A *stateful aspect* is a unit of modular definition of a crosscutting concern that encapsulates not only crosscutting behavior, but also *crosscutting state*. An *aspect instantiation model (AIM)* is a policy that defines the manner in which stateful aspects are to be instantiated and managed [12]. This work is concerned with third-party customization of AIMs.

The need for custom AIMs has historically influenced the evolution of the ASPECTJ language [5]. Initially, ASPECTJ assumed only singleton aspects. A *singleton aspect* is instantiated exactly once (i.e., a single aspect instance for each aspect declaration). Singleton aspects are useful for implementing concerns that have system-wide behaviors.

Gradually, ASPECTJ was extended to include finer-grained AIMs. A *per-object aspect* (`perthis` and `pertarget`) associates a unique aspect instance with each advised object. A *per-flow aspect* (`percflow` and `percflowbelow`) associates a unique aspect instance with each flow of control that is matched by a specified pointcut argument. These per-clauses were added in early versions of ASPECTJ. A later version of AS-PECTJ introduced a new *per-type* clause (`pertypewithin`) for associating a unique aspect instance with each type matched by a specified type pattern.

This evolution begs the question: what other sorts of per-clause may be needed, and how can the authority and responsibility for defining such AIMs be decoupled from the evolution of the aspect language?

---

* This research was supported in part by the *Israel Science Foundation (ISF)* under grant No. 926/08.

S. Apel and E. Jackson (Eds.): SC 2011, LNCS 6708, pp. 84–99, 2011.

1.1 Background

In ASPECTJ, aspect instantiation is a hard-wired feature of the aspect language. This feature cannot be customized or extended. ASPECTJ does give the application programmer some control over the instantiation of aspects, but only through a limited set of pre-defined AIMs. For example, one cannot associate a thread-local aspect instance with each execution thread (i.e., a **perthread** aspect). Consequently, the aspect state has to be managed manually in, e.g., a JVM ThreadLocal control. Another example is dealing with user state. In J2EE applications it is often useful to define a **persession** aspect. Unfortunately, ASPECTJ does not support this (yet). The developer must therefore manage the aspect state manually using J2EE controls, namely an HTTP session and HTTP filters.

When the pre-defined AIMs do not meet the need, the programmer may either manage the aspect state within the application code, or introduce a new AIM into ASPECTJ by modifying the compiler code (e.g., ajc). The first option results in code tangling, increasing code complexity, diminishing maintainability and robustness. The second option is a tedious task even for an experienced compiler developer. The code fragments implementing the built-in AIMs in ajc are scattered, tangled, and strongly coupled with the implementation of other features of the language. This also requires a change to the ASPECTJ language, i.e., new syntax to let the application code refer to the new AIM. Both changes to the language and changes to the compiler need to be redone whenever a new version of ASPECTJ or ajc is released.

1.2 Contribution

This work contributes a framework for enabling the definition and use of third-party AIMs in ASPECTJ. All the built-in AIMs in ASPECTJ can be defined in this framework. New AIMs not currently part of ASPECTJ can also be defined. From the application programmer perspective, the framework provides a way to define and use AIMs that are required in the application design but currently not available in ASPECTJ. From the compiler developer perspective, extending the language with new AIMs, whether implemented in-house or supplied by third-party vendors, can be accomplished in a modular way without modifying the ASPECTJ compiler code.

The framework provides the ability to realize an AIM as either a pluggable static mechanism that is invoked during compilation, or as a pluggable dynamic mechanism that is invoked at runtime. This flexibility has the advantage of supporting the implementation of built-in AIMs with static mechanisms that produce woven code identical to the code generated today by the ASPECTJ compiler, while permitting new AIMs to be quickly implemented and tested as dynamic mechanisms.

We extended the ASPECTJ language with a new language feature for supporting custom AIMs. Syntactically, the feature subsumes all of the six ASPECTJ built-in aspect instantiation keywords into a single new keyword: **perscope**. Semantically, this feature allows the programmer to use custom third-party AIMs. We implemented the framework by refactoring the ajc compiler. Obviously, should this refactoring be adopted by the ASPECTJ development team and become a part of future ajc releases, refactoring will not be necessary for using this framework.

2 Approach

In ASPECTJ, aspects are instantiated implicitly according to the AIM specified in the aspect declaration. The application programmer expresses declaratively which AIM is required. The ASPECTJ compiler weaves the specified AIM into the aspect class, producing efficient woven code. However, the set of available AIMs in ASPECTJ is fixed, and the main drawback of ASPECTJ is the inability to define new ones.

This work enables the definition and use of third-party AIMs in ASPECTJ. We present a pluggable framework for AIMs. The framework is:

- *Extensible:* new AIMs can be introduced, and pre-defined AIMs can be refined. Generic AIMs can be offered by third-party providers independent of the ASPECTJ language evolution, or implemented and customized by ASPECTJ developers.
- *Declarative:* use of AIMs can be specified in a declarative manner similar to the way AIMs are specified in ASPECTJ today, allowing their implementation to vary independently of their use.
- *Expressive:* realistically complex AIMs can be defined. For the very least, it is possible to implement third-party AIMs that provide the same semantics as the six AIMs available in ASPECTJ today.
- *Efficient:* implementation of custom AIMs can be optimized to produce as efficient woven bytecode as their hard-wired counterparts implementation in ASPECTJ. In particular, it is possible to implement the six standard AIMs of ASPECTJ and generate the same bytecode as ASPECTJ does, thus providing not only identical functionality, but also the same runtime performance.
- *Flexible:* the framework supports both static and dynamic AIM mechanisms. An AIM can be initially implemented via a dynamic mechanism that is invoked at runtime, possibly surrendering some performance for simplicity. The implementation can later be replaced with a more efficient static mechanism that is invoked during compilation, without altering code that already uses the AIM.

Providing support for both static and dynamic mechanisms promotes not only adoption, but also experimentation with new AIMs. A dynamic AIM mechanism is often simpler to implement than a static mechanism, because programming is done directly in terms of the runtime elements. The programmer that is unfamiliar with the internals of bytecode manipulation may initially implement the dynamic version, and migrate to a static implementation when performance becomes crucial.

2.1 Language Extension

To support pluggable AIMs we introduce a new **perscope** keyword to ASPECTJ. This single keyword subsumes the existing six ASPECTJ keywords (and hopefully eliminates the need to introduce future AIM keywords). The changes to the ASPECTJ grammar are listed in Figure 1.

perscope is a parametrized keyword. The first argument is mandatory. It is a name of the class that implements the AIM mechanism. The additional arguments are optional and depend on the specific AIM definition. For example, in case of **perthis**, a

```
<aspect_decl> ::= [<modifiers>]
                  "aspect" <identifier>
                  [<super>][<interfaces>]
                  [<perclause>]
                  <aspect_body>
  <perclause> ::= "perscope" "(" <identifier> {"," <perparam>}* ")"
   <perparam> ::= <pointcut> | <identifier>
```

Fig. 1. Changes to the ASPECTJ grammar

```
public aspect IndividualClientCaching
   extends SimpleCaching //an abstract aspect defined elsewhere
   perscope(Perthis, cachedOperation(Object)) {
}
```

Listing 1. Example of a client-specific cache

second argument is needed to represent the pointcut. In case of **pertypewithin**, the second argument represents a type. When the **perscope** clause is omitted, the default **issingleton** AIM is assumed, as is the case in ASPECTJ.

Listing 1 illustrates the use of the **perscope** keyword for a client-specific cache. In the listing, *SimpleCaching* is an abstract aspect defined elsewhere [3]. Perthis is the name of a class that implements the **perthis** AIM, and cachedOperation is a pointcut defined in *SimpleCaching*. Perthis can be implemented either as a static or as a dynamic mechanism. For this purpose two new interfaces are introduced: *StaticPerscope* and *DynamicPerscope*. Only a class that implements one of these interfaces is permissible as the first argument to the **perscope** keyword. With these interfaces in place, there is no need to modify the compiler code intrusively whenever a new AIM is needed. The compiler developer can implement a new AIM by implementing either *StaticPerscope* or *DynamicPerscope* and ship the AIM with a new version of the compiler or provide it as a library.

2.2 Pluggable Framework

The **perscope** keyword together with the *StaticPerscope* and *DynamicPerscope* interfaces provide a pluggable and flexible mechanism for defining and using AIMs in ASPECTJ. With these interfaces, language designers are able to implement new AIMs. Programmers are able to implement custom AIMs. Libraries may offer generic AIMs. The AIMs can be invoked during compilation, dealing with bytecode manipulations, producing efficient code. The AIMs can be implemented as runtime plug-ins and later optimized to run during compilation, as needed. Whatever the implementation choice may be, the end-user is able to use the AIMs in a declarative way.

In order to implement a custom AIM, the implementer specifies what should happen when an aspect instance is handled (during compilation or at runtime). This is done as a part of the process of implementing the *StaticPerscope* interface (Section 3.1) or the *DynamicPerscope* interface (Section 3.3).

```
public interface DynamicPerscope {
    void bindAspect(Object aspekt,Object object);
    Object aspectOf(Class<?> aspectType, Object object);
    boolean hasAspect(Class<?> aspectType, Object object);
}
```

Listing 2. *DynamicPerscope* interface

```
public class Perthread implements DynamicPerscope {
    private static ThreadLocal<Object> theAspect = new ThreadLocal<Object>();
    public Object aspectOf(Class<?> aspectType, Object object) {
        return theAspect.get();
    }
    public void bindAspect(Object aspekt, Object object) {
        if (theAspect.get() == null) {
            theAspect.set(aspekt);
        }
    }
    public boolean hasAspect(Class<?> aspectType, Object object) {
        return theAspect.get() != null;
    }
}
```

Listing 3. Perthread definition

```
public aspect PerThreadCaching
    extends SimpleCaching //an abstract aspect defined elsewhere
    perscope(Perthread, cachedOperation(Object)) {
}
```

Listing 4. Perthread use

An implementation of the *StaticPerscope* interface requires to deal with byte-code manipulation and as such it is harder to implement than *DynamicPerscope* but capable of producing efficient code. We expect this interface to be implemented mostly by third-party infrastructure programmers who wish to provide novel generic AIMs. The org.aspectj.ajdt.internal.compiler.ast.perscope.Perobject class is an example of a *StaticPerscope* implementation [1]. In order to invoke static AIM mechanisms during compilation, calls to the *StaticPerscope* interface were inserted into ajc, replacing the hard-wired weaving code, thus allowing the class specified in the **perscope** clause to override the default weaving.

Alternatively, a dynamic AIM mechanism may be realized by implementing the *DynamicPerscope* interface to specify how the aspect instance should be bound and retrieved. A *DynamicPerscope* implementation is invoked at runtime. Thus, it does not need to deal with bytecode manipulation, but rather can be expressed in plain JAVA. We expect this interface to be implemented mostly by application programmers who wish to non-intrusively customize the compiler with AIMs that are needed but not available. For example, if a **perthread** AIM is needed for caching, and if that AIM is not available in ASPECTJ, then it can still be defined and used via a Perthread class (Listing 3) that implements the *DynamicPerscope* interface (Listing 2), and then used with **perscope** (Listing 4). A third-party vendor can develop this way an independent set of AIMs and provide them as a library.

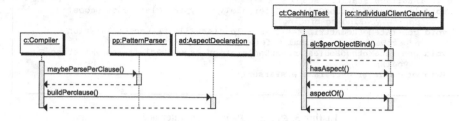

Fig. 2. Compilation of aspects   **Fig. 3.** Runtime behavior of aspects

2.3 Limitations

Obviously, we cannot predict all future needs, so there could certainly be AIMs that cannot be easily implemented with **perscope** (i.e., without modifying the compiler code). Another limitation is the difficulty that application programmers may have in implementing the *StaticPerscope* interface themselves. Bytecode manipulation is a job for the more experienced infrastructure programmers. However, even infrastructure programmers can benefit from having the option to implement the *StaticPerscope* interface instead of performing intrusive modifications to the compiler code.

3   Implementation

The **perscope** framework was implemented by refactoring the ASPECTJ ajc compiler (version 1.6.5). The compiler reads class and aspect declarations as input, and generates Java bytecode as output. We first briefly review how ajc generates code for regular aspects. We then explain how our implementation generates code for **perscope** aspects.

The ASPECTJ compiler translates an aspect declaration into a class, and places the advice body into a method of that class. To ensure that the advice gets executed, method calls are inserted into locations where the pointcut of the advice statically matches [8]. First (Figure 2), the Compiler (an ajc internal class) checks whether any of the six per-clause keywords are specified, by invoking maybeParsePerClause on the PatternParser (another ajc internal class). When a per-clause is detected, the parser runs special code for handling that keyword by invoking buildPerclause in the AspectDeclaration class.

For this purpose, there are a number of *if-then-else* blocks that are spread all over the compiler code (AspectDeclaration). These blocks control the generation of synthetic methods. Synthetic methods are methods not derived directly from the user specified code. The aspect instantiation synthetic methods for a **perthis** aspect are: hasAspect, aspectOf and ajc$perObjectBind (Figure 3). There are also methods responsible for creating the ajc objects used for synthetic method generation. Finally, there is the code that actually generates the bodies of these synthetic methods.

```
public interface StaticPerscope {
    void instantiateMethodObjects(ReferenceType typeX, ClassScope scope,
        SourceTypeBinding binding);
    void generateMethodAttributes(ClassFile classFile, AspectDeclaration
        aspectDeclaration, final ReferenceType typeX);
    void generateMethodBodies(AspectDeclaration aspectDeclaration, ReferenceType
        typeX);
    ParametersParser getParametersParser();
}
```

Listing 5. *StaticPerscope* interface

```
public interface ParametersParser {
    PerClause parseParameters();
}
```

Listing 6. *ParametersParser* interface

3.1 The StaticPerscope Interface

Since AIM-related code is scattered all over the AspectDeclaration class, it is difficult to override and extend it. The purpose of the *StaticPerscope* (Listing 5) interface is first and foremost to provide the abstraction necessary for customizing AIM-related code.

perscope aspects are compiled into Java classes in a similar manner as regular aspects. The compiler code was modified to delegate the code generation to the appropriate *StaticPerscope* interface method. The compilation flow of **perscope** aspects is depicted as sequence diagrams in Figures 4(a) and 4(b). In phase 1, the ajc Compiler invokes the maybeParsePerClause method of PatternParser. The modified behavior of the PatternParser is to create a new instance of the user specified implementation of the *StaticPerscope* interface, and then to fetch the *ParametersParser* implementation in order to parse the **perscope** parameters. This parsing process produces a concrete instance of PerClause, which is then used to store the created *StaticPerscope* instance. In phase 2, the Compiler invokes the buildPerclause method of the AspectDeclaration, which holds the reference to the PerClause instance that was created in phase 1. The synthetic method generation is then delegated to the fetched *StaticPerscope* instance.

The six built-in ASPECTJ AIMs are provided as classes (Figure 6) that implement the *StaticPerscope* interface and execute the original AspectDeclaration code. Since the original code was moved "as is" into these implementing classes, they produce the same bytecode as the built-in AIMs. Other implementations may realize custom AIMs. All *StaticPerscope* implementations are executed during parsing according to the aspect declaration.

StaticPerscope is open for extension. A **perscope** AIM may have as many parameters as needed. In order to support this ability, the *ParametersParser* interface should be implemented (Listing 6). Two default implementations are provided. One parses the name of a pointcut (PointcutParametersParser). The other parses the

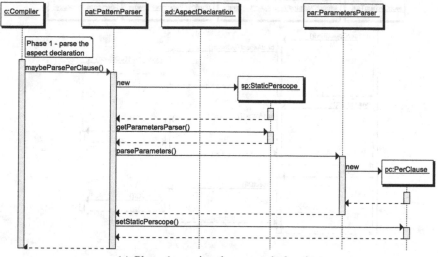

(a) Phase 1: parsing the aspect declaration

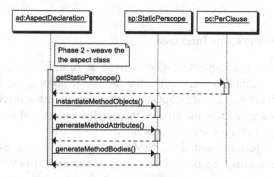

(b) Phase 2: weaving the aspect class

Fig. 4. Compilation of **perscope** aspects

name of a Java type (TypeParametersParser). The parseParameters method re-turns the PerClause instance, which is the ajc built-in type that is used later in the compilation process.

3.2 PerscopeDelegator

A special default PerscopeDelegator implementation of the *StaticPerscope* in-terface is provided with the framework, in order to make the implementation of dy-namic AIM mechanisms easier. This implementation weaves into the aspect code special hooks that delegate at runtime to the user specified *DynamicPerscope* implementation.

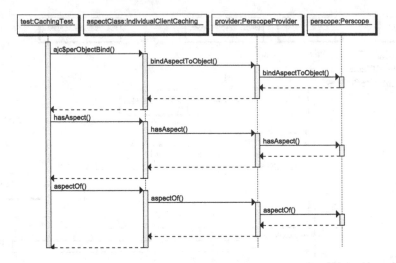

Fig. 5. Runtime behavior of **perscope** aspects

3.3 The DynamicPerscope Interface

The *DynamicPerscope* implementation is used at runtime for aspect instantiation. The bindAspect method is responsible for the registration of an aspect. It takes as arguments an aspect instance and an optional object instance that is related to this aspect instance. The first argument is the type of the needed aspect and the second argument is the concrete object that the aspect is bound to.

The concrete object is needed in AIMs like **perthis** and **pertarget**. Other AIMs may ignore the object parameter, e.g., **perthread**. It is worth noting that for **perthis** a **this** object is essential and for **pertarget** a **target** object is essential, but they are never both needed. Therefore, a single argument is sufficient.

For the aspectOf method, the object argument is optional as well. Sophisticated AIMs may use this object argument to implement AIMs that depend on the state of an object, such as the value of a certain field of the object. The hasAspect method is similar to aspectOf, but it queries whether the aspect instance exists.

The compiler uses the utility class PerscopeProvider (Listing 7) for delegating the invocations of the hasAspect, aspectOf, and all binding methods to the programmer's specified class. Invocations of aspectOf, hasAspect, and binding methods are delegated to the PerscopeProvider class. For example, Listing 8 presents the decompiled bytecode generated for the PerThreadCaching class (Listing 4). The user-defined Perthread class name is provided as an argument to PerscopeProvider (lines 8, 12, and 16 in Listing 8). Also, the class object of the aspect class itself (class1) and the actual object in use (obj) are arguments in these calls.

```
class PerscopeProvider {
    private static DynamicPerscope aspectInstantiation;
    private PerscopeProvider() {}
    public static DynamicPerscope getStaticPerscope(String implName) {
        if(aspectInstantiation) == null) {
            try {
                Class<?> clazz = Class.forName(implName);
                Object object = clazz.newInstance();
                aspectInstantiation = (DynamicPerscope) object;
            }catch (Exception e) {
                throw new RuntimeException("Failed to instantiate the aspects
                    instantiation implementation");
            }
        }
        return aspectInstantiation;
    }
    public static void bindAspect(String implName,Object aspekt,Object object) {
        getStaticPerscope(implName).bindAspect(aspekt, object);
    }
    public static Object aspectOf(String implName,Class<?> type,Object object) {
        return getStaticPerscope(implName).aspectOf(type, object);
    }
    public static boolean hasAspect(String implName,Class<?> type,Object object)
    {
        return getStaticPerscope(implName).hasAspect(type, object);
    }
}
```

Listing 7. `PerscopeProvider` class

```
public class PerThreadCaching extends SimpleCaching {
    public static PerThreadCaching aspectOf(Object obj) {
        // load aspect class
4       Class class1 = Class.forName("PerThreadCaching");
        // delegate to PerscopeProvider aspectOf()
        // with the user specified DynamicPerscope
        // implementation class name
8       return (PerThreadCaching)PerscopeProvider.aspectOf("Perthread", class1,
            obj);
    }
    public static boolean hasAspect(Object obj) {
        Class class1 = Class.forName("PerThreadCaching");
12      return PerscopeProvider.hasAspect("Perthread", class1, obj);
    }
    public static void perObjectBind(Object obj) {
        PerThreadCaching threadCaching = new PerThreadCaching();
16      PerscopeProvider.bindAspect("Perthread", threadCaching, obj);
    }
}
```

Listing 8. Code generated for `PerThreadCaching` (Listing 4)

3.4   Summary

The implementer of a **perscope** AIM has two options: (1) to implement a static custom AIM by implementing the *StaticPerscope* interface; or (2) to implement a dynamic custom AIM by implementing the *DynamicPerscope* interface. In the first case, the implementation is usually more complex as it involves bytecode manipulation, but it is also more efficient. The *StaticPerscope* interface is intended for the more advanced infrastructure programmer. The *DynamicPerscope* interface is intended for regular infrastructure programmers.

These implementation trade-offs are transparent to the end user of the AIM. As soon as the AIM is implemented (as either *DynamicPerscope* or *StaticPerscope*) all the end user needs to do is to provide the name of the class implementing the AIM as an argument to the **perscope** keyword.

4   Evaluation

In this section we discuss and summarize various experiments that we ran to validate our approach. First, we verified that with **perscope** aspects we can implement all of ASPECTJ built-in AIMs (Section 4.1). Second, we implemented additional AIMs that do not exist in ASPECTJ (Section 4.2). We conclude that **perscope** enables third-party providers to easily add new AIMs in a modular and extensible way, to be invoked during compilation or at runtime. The implementation and test code can be found at: http://aop.cslab.openu.ac.il/research/perscope/.

4.1   Implementing ASPECTJ Built-In Aspect Instantiation Models

Using the special *StaticPerscope* interface, we have implemented AIMs corresponding to all six existing ASPECTJ keywords [7]. On a set of tested aspect examples, our *StaticPerscope* implementation generates exactly the same bytecode as the original ASPECTJ implementation. As explained in Section 3.1, this is a result of the refactoring, which merely moved aspect instantiation related code from hard-wired *if-then-else* blocks to the appropriate *StaticPerscope* implementations. As depicted in Figure 6, the classes that implement the six existing ASPECTJ keywords are: Perthis, Pertarget, Percflow, Percflowbelow, Pertypewithin and Persingleton.

To test the **perscope** static implementation we implemented and ran a caching example [3] using **perscope**. Both ajc and our **perscope** implementation produced the same bytecode and therefore exhibit the same behavior and performance.

We also ran the benchmark implementation of the Law of Demeter [6], which is part of the AspectBench abc compiler distribution [2]. The Law of Demeter example uses both **pertarget** and **percflow** intensively. We compared the implementation that uses ASPECTJ 1.6.5 with an implementation that uses the **perscope** framework and observed the same functionality and performance in both.

4.2   Implementing Non-ASPECTJ Aspect Instantiation Models

The **perscope** aspects allow the application programmer to implement AIMs that do not exist in ASPECTJ.

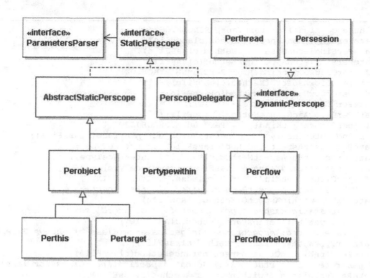

Fig. 6. AIM class hierarchy

Aspect instantiation models found in other AOP languages: ASPECTS [4], an aspect language for SMALLTALK (SQUEAK), supports certain cflow advice activations that are not available in ASPECTJ. The *Class First* and *Class all-but-first* cflow advice trigger activation on an object-recursion *first* and *other than first* method invocation, respectively. Similarly, *Instance First* and *Instance all-but-first* cflow advice will trigger activation on a method-recursion *first* and *other than first* method invocation, respectively. With **perscope**, it is possible for the application programmer to implement similar AIMs without modifying the compiler code.

With **perscope** it is possible to implement the **perthread** AIM, i.e., specifying that there should be a dedicated aspect instance per execution thread, as provided in the JASCO [13] language. If we wish to have a **perthread** caching, we can declare the aspect exactly as it appears in Listing 4. Perthread is the class that implements the **perthread** AIM (Listing 3). The Perthread class implements the *DynamicPerscope* interface (Figure 6).

Novel aspect instantiation models not found in other languages: With **perscope**, it is also possible to define and use a **persession** AIM. This AIM creates a dedicated aspect instance per specific user session, for example in a web application. The Persession class also implements the *DynamicPerscope* interface (Figure 6). The implementation of Persession is available elsewhere [1].

4.3   Code Complexity

With the **perscope** framework the complexity of AIM implementation is reduced significantly compared to what would have been required for modifying ajc directly. The framework is modular and extensible. We refactored the ASPECTJ compiler code found

```
if (perClause.getKind() == PerClause.SINGLETON) {
    generatePerSingletonAspectOfMethod(classFile);
    generatePerSingletonHasAspectMethod(classFile);
    generatePerSingletonAjcClinitMethod(classFile);
} else if (perClause.getKind() == PerClause.PERCFLOW) {
    generatePerCflowAspectOfMethod(classFile);
    generatePerCflowHasAspectMethod(classFile);
    generatePerCflowPushMethod(classFile);
    generatePerCflowAjcClinitMethod(classFile);
} else if (perClause.getKind() == PerClause.PEROBJECT) {
    TypeBinding interfaceType = generatePerObjectInterface(classFile);
    generatePerObjectAspectOfMethod(classFile, interfaceType);
    generatePerObjectHasAspectMethod(classFile, interfaceType);
    generatePerObjectBindMethod(classFile, interfaceType);
} else if (perClause.getKind() == PerClause.PERTYPEWITHIN) {
    // PTWIMPL Generate the methods required *in the aspect*
    generatePerTypeWithinAspectOfMethod(classFile);
        // public static <aspecttype> aspectOf(java.lang.Class)
    generatePerTypeWithinGetInstanceMethod(classFile);
        // private static <aspecttype> ajc$getInstance(Class c) throws Exception
    generatePerTypeWithinHasAspectMethod(classFile);
    generatePerTypeWithinCreateAspectInstanceMethod(classFile);
        // generate public static X ajc$createAspectInstance(Class forClass)
    generatePerTypeWithinGetWithinTypeNameMethod(classFile);
}
```

Listing 9. `AspectDeclaration` implementation in ajc

```
StaticPerscope staticPerscope = perClause.getStaticPerscope();
staticPerscope.generateMethodAttributes(classFile, this, typeX);
```

Listing 10. `AspectDeclaration` with **perscope**

in the `AspectDeclaration` class (Listing 9), which is responsible for generating aspect instantiation methods. Instead of handling the aspect instantiation method generation directly via *if-then-else* blocks, the refactored code delegates the task to the proper user defined class, which implements the `StaticPerscope` interface (Listing 10). If the user supplied as the **perscope** argument a class that implements the `DynamicPerscope`, a special built-in `StaticPerscope` implementation called `PerscopeDelegator` is used to weave the code in a way that postpones the aspect instance binding or retrieval until runtime.

There are three places in the `AspectDeclaration` class with such *if-then-else* statements. All of them were replaced by a two-line API call to the **perscope** interface. The total size of the `AspectDeclaration` class in ASPECTJ version 1.6.5 is 1102 lines of code. The refactored **perscope** implementation code size was reduced to 648 lines of code. The ASPECTJ compiler developer can extend the language with new AIMs easily, just by implementing one of the interfaces, without changing the complex `AspectDeclaration` class.

4.4 Threats to Validity

The **perscope** feature was successfully implemented only for the ajc compiler. It was not tested with other ASPECTJ language implementations, such as abc. However, since the feature is language-specific (rather than implementation-specific), it should be equally possible to implement **perscope** in other implementations.

The ASPECTJ six built-in AIMs were implemented using **perscope** aspects and this implementation was tested on the caching example and on the Law of Demeter benchmark example. While two examples are not proof of correctness, the fact that the bytecode generated for these examples was identical to the bytecode generated by ajc version 1.6.5 on the same examples is a strong indication that the refactoring and *StaticPerscope* implementations for the six AIMs were behavior preserving.

Various AIMs were demonstrated in this paper and all of them were implemented using **perscope** AIMs. There may be other AIMs that cannot be implemented with **perscope** (without compiler modifications). However, while **perscope** may be imperfect, it nonetheless presents a significant improvement over the current ASPECTJ implementation, which does not support the implementation of customized AIMs at all.

5 Related Work

The closest related work to ours are aspect factories in the JASCO language [13]. There are five built-in aspect factories: **perobject, permethod, perall, perclass** and **perthread**. It is also possible to implement custom AIM by implementing an IAspectFactory interface. As with **perscope**, the usage of aspect factories is declarative. One of the pre-defined keywords may be specified in the connector code, or the **per** keyword may be used when a custom AIM is needed. The IAspectFactory implementation is used at runtime for aspect instantiation management. With **perscope** the user has a choice: either implement the *DynamicPerscope* interface to get a behavior similar to the JASCO IAspectFactory, or implement the *StaticPerscope* interface and specify how the AIM should be implemented during compilation, gaining more efficient code in most cases.

Tanter et al. [14,15] discuss the need for dynamic deployment of aspects. They propose *deployment strategies* for parametrized dynamic aspect deployment. To a certain extent, AIMs could be viewed as a special case of deployment strategies. However, dynamic deployment of aspects is not supported in ASPECTJ. In our work, we focus on decoupling the AIMs that are supported, rather than extending ASPECTJ to support dynamic deployment of aspects.

There are certain similarities between **perscope** and CAESAR [9] wrappers. The ASPECTJ built-in AIMs can be implemented with wrapper instances in CAESAR. Wrapper instances roughly correspond to aspect instances in ASPECTJ, but they can be manually instantiated and associated with objects. In addition, the wrapper recycling mechanism helps to retrieve associated wrappers from objects. Other AIMs can be implemented as well. There is no need to introduce a new keyword for each new AIMs, making the language simpler. One can introduce AIM semantics that cannot be easily expressed in ASPECTJ. There are also clear differences between the **perscope** framework and CAESAR. In CAESAR the aspects are instantiated explicitly, while with **perscope**, aspects are instantiated implicitly according to the aspect declaration, just as in ASPECTJ.

Association aspects [11] is a mechanism for associating an aspect instance with a group of objects. This mechanism introduces a **new** keyword, which allows to instantiate an aspect. The aspect instantiation is explicit. In comparison, a dedicated aspect instance per a pair of objects or per a group of objects can also be achieved with **perscope**. A class that manages the logic of such aspect instantiation can be implemented and used as an argument to the **perscope** keyword.

EOS [10] is an AOP language that has support for instance-level aspect weaving. Instance-level aspect weaving is the ability to differentiate between two instances of a class and to weave them differently if needed. It allows the developer to differentiate between instances. Their work characterizes the AOP languages with respect to the pointcut language richness and the instance-level aspect weaving support. This differs from AIMs, which is the focus of our **perscope** framework.

Skotiniotis et al. [12] claim that aspect instantiation is an essential feature in AOSD languages. They show that the program's complexity increases in situations where multiple instances of aspects are present. They contrast ASPECTJ with the approach of aspect instantiation taken by ASPECTS [4]. ASPECTS permits the instantiation of an aspect and the activation and deactivation of an aspect. Obtaining a reference to an aspect instance in ASPECTS is a matter of a simple assignment during instantiation, and deployment of the aspect is as simple as calling its activation method. In comparison, the use of **perscope** is declarative.

6   Conclusion

Various AOP languages take different approaches regarding aspect instantiation. Some languages grant the programmer explicit control over when and where aspects are instantiated. In these languages, the aspect instantiation mechanism is extensible.

ASPECTJ hides the instantiation details from the programmer and permits the programmer to specify the instantiation model only in a declarative way. In ASPECTJ there are six built-in AIMs. Their usage is simple; the programmer just needs to declare the aspect and specify the AIM by using the appropriate keyword. However, the aspect instantiation mechanism in ASPECTJ is not extensible. It is not possible to specify AIMs other than those built-in to the language.

This work contributes a framework for enabling the definition and use of third-party pluggable AIMs in ASPECTJ. To support pluggable AIMs we introduce a new **perscope** keyword to ASPECTJ. **perscope** is both declarative and extensible. It lets one define and implement various AIMs that are not part of the ASPECTJ language. These AIMs may be provided by third-parties. Once a new AIM is implemented, it can be immediately used by programmers in a declarative way, in the spirit of ASPECTJ.

References

1. The Perscope project (2011),
   http://aop.cslab.openu.ac.il/research/perscope/
2. Avgustinov, P., Christensen, A.S., Hendren, L., Kuzins, S., Lhoták, J., Lhoták, O., de Moor, O., Sereni, D., Sittampalam, G., Tibble, J.: abc: an extensible AspectJ compiler. In: Proceedings of the 4th International Conference on Aspect-Oriented Software Development (AOSD 2005), March 14-18, pp. 87–98. ACM, New York (2005)

3. Colyer, A. Implementing caching with AspectJ (blog). The Aspect Blog (June 2004), http://www.aspectprogrammer.org/blogs/adrian/2004/06/
4. Hirschfeld, R.: AspectS - aspect-oriented programming with squeak. In: Aksit, M., Mezini, M., Unland, R. (eds.) NODe 2002. LNCS, vol. 2591, pp. 216–232. Springer, Heidelberg (2003)
5. Kiczales, G., Hilsdale, E., Hugunin, J., Kersten, M., Palm, J., Griswold, W.G.: An overview of AspectJ. In: Lee, S.H. (ed.) ECOOP 2001. LNCS, vol. 2072, pp. 327–353. Springer, Heidelberg (2001)
6. Lieberherr, K., Lorenz, D.H., Wu, P.: A case for statically executable advice: Checking the Law of Demeter with AspectJ. In: Proceedings of the 2nd International Conference on Aspect-Oriented Software Development (AOSD 2003), March 17-21, pp. 40–49. ACM, New York (2003)
7. Lorenz, D.H., Trakhtenberg, V.: Perscope aspects: Decoupling aspect instantiation interface and implementation (poster). In: IBM Programming Languages and Development Environments Seminar, Haifa, Israel, April 14, IBM Research (2010)
8. Hansen, K.A., Kiczales, G., Dutchyn, C.: A compilation and optimization model for aspect-oriented programs. In: Hedin, G. (ed.) CC 2003. LNCS, vol. 2622, pp. 46–60. Springer, Heidelberg (2003)
9. Mezini, M., Ostermann, K.: Conquering aspects with Caesar. In: Proceedings of the 2nd International Conference on Aspect-Oriented Software Development (AOSD 2003), March 17-21, pp. 90–99. ACM, New York (2003)
10. Rajan, H., Sullivan, K.: Eos: instance-level aspects for integrated system design. In: ESEC/FSE-11: Proceedings of the 9th European software engineering conference held jointly with 11th ACM SIGSOFT international symposium on Foundations of software engineering, pp. 297–306. ACM Press, New York (2003)
11. Sakurai, K., Masuhara, H., Ubayashi, N., Matsuura, S., Komiya, S.: Association aspects. In: Proceedings of the 3rd International Conference on Aspect-Oriented Software Development (AOSD 2004), March 17-21, pp. 16–25. ACM, New York (2004)
12. Skotiniotis, T., Lieberherr, K., Lorenz, D.H.: Aspect instances and their interactions. In: Proceedings of the AOSD'03 Workshop on Software-engineering Properties of Languages for Aspect Technologies (SPLAT 2003), March 18. ACM, New York (2003)
13. Suvée, D., Vanderperren, W., Jonckers, V.: JAsCo: an aspect-oriented approach tailored for component based software development. In: Proceedings of the 2nd International Conference on Aspect-Oriented Software Development (AOSD 2003), March 17-21, pp. 21–29. ACM, New York (2003)
14. Tanter, E.: Expressive scoping of dynamically-deployed aspects. In: Proceedings of the 7th International Conference on Aspect-Oriented Software Development (AOSD 2008), pp. 168–179. ACM, New York (2008)
15. Tanter, E., Fabry, J., Douence, R., Noyé, J., Südholt, M.: Expressive scoping of distributed aspects. In: Proceedings of the 8th International Conference on Aspect-Oriented Software Development (AOSD 2009), pp. 27–38. ACM, New York (2009)

Composing Event-B Specifications - Case-Study Experience

Ali Gondal, Michael Poppleton, and Michael Butler

School of Electronics and Computer Science
University of Southampton, Southampton, SO17 1BJ, UK
{aag07r,mrp,mjb}@ecs.soton.ac.uk

Abstract. Event-B is a formal method, based on set theory and first-order logic, for specification and verification of reactive systems supported by the Rodin tool kit. Feature modelling is a well-known technique for managing variability and configuring products within software product lines (SPLs). Our objective is to explore whether we can use existing Event-B composition techniques and tooling for feature-based product line development. If case-study experiments reveal these mechanisms to be inadequate, then they also should suggest further research directions. The main objective is to maximise the amount of reuse. This includes avoiding as far as possible having to reprove a composed specification when the models being composed have already been proven. We have modelled two case-studies in Event-B using both horizontal and vertical refinements. This work contributes by analysing existing tools and techniques in Event-B for feature-based development, exploring composition related issues by modelling example case-studies and suggesting further tooling requirements.

1 Introduction

Event-B [1] is a formal modelling language, a successor of Abrial's classical B [2]. It was developed as part of the RODIN[1] and earlier EU projects. The DEPLOY[2] project, along with industrial partners, is currently focused on deploying this work into industry. Event-B, a state-based language, is based on set theory and first-order logic and allows the specification and verification of reactive systems. The correctness of a model is defined by invariant properties on its state which must be preserved by all transitions in a system, called *events*. An event is enabled when certain pre-conditions on the event, called *guards*, become true. Verification conditions (known as proof obligations or *PO*s), concerned with model consistency, i.e., invariant preservation, are generated and discharged by proof support tools. Event-B is further supported by the integrated Rodin toolkit comprising editors, theorem provers, animator and model checker.

A Software Product Line (*SPL*) refers to a set of related products built from a shared set of resources with a common base while having significant variability

---

[1] RODIN: EU Project IST-511599. http://rodin.cs.ncl.ac.uk
[2] DEPLOY: EU Project IST-214158. http://www.deploy-project.eu

S. Apel and E. Jackson (Eds.): SC 2011, LNCS 6708, pp. 100–115, 2011.
© Springer-Verlag Berlin Heidelberg 2011

to meet the user requirements [3]. SPLs provide the benefits of reusability in reducing the time to market, lower cost and reduce effort involved in product development. Feature modelling [4] is a well-known technique for building SPLs. The *feature* has been defined as "a logical unit of behaviour specified by a set of functional and non-functional requirements"[5] and usually referred as a property of the system that is of some value to the stakeholders. A feature model is drawn using tree structured feature diagrams to describe variability among the product line members, and the valid ways in which these features can be instantiated to generate various products.

Our objective is to explore how we can devise a feature-oriented approach for reuse, and ultimately for modelling product lines in Event-B. This will allow the reuse of existing specifications for a product line to build further products of the family without redoing all the modelling and proof effort. In the feature-oriented software development (*FOSD*) community, a feature is in general made up of different modules or classes. In Event-B, a feature is a well-formed model, the basic modular unit in the Rodin tool. Eventually, we will consider a feature to be a partial Event-B model; this will require further research and tooling development. In a state-machine semantics, a feature can add or remove states and transformations. Also, we are specifying features in the problem space (abstract requirements) compared to the features in solution space (concrete implementation, e.g., java classes) as considered by the FOSD community. In order to build a product, we must compose various features and that brings us to the core issue of composing specifications. The real benefit of the product line modelling can not be achieved without automatically proving composed specifications. At present, there are three types of composition for Event-B which guarantee refinement preservation.

We present two case-studies to investigate whether the existing composition techniques are adequate for feature-oriented modelling in Event-B and suggest further tooling requirements for such development. We call this formal modelling of a system to produce reusable specifications "Domain Modelling" which corresponds to domain engineering activity within SPL engineering. Also, we seek to find some composition patterns that can be applied to automate the composition process to save time and effort. This work can be encouraging for SPL community to use formal methods as we have adapted and extended existing feature modelling notations. This paper focuses on the application of our feature modelling and composition methodologies to the case-study work. This work builds on the methodology of Snook et al. [6] for the formal verification of product lines. We want to explore how their methodology can be developed by experimenting with the case-studies using Event-B and suggesting further research.

Section 2 gives a brief introduction of the Event-B language and the (de)composition techniques for Event-B are presented in Section 3. Section 4 summarises our feature-oriented modelling support for Event-B. Section 5 describes the two case-studies we have modelled using Event-B. Related work is given in Section 6. Section 7 concludes the paper and suggests directions for the future work.

2   Event-B Introduction

An Event-B model consists of a *machine* and multiple *contexts*. The machine specifies the behavioural or dynamic part of the system and the context contains static data which includes *sets*, *constants*, *axioms* and *theorems*. The sets define types whereas the axioms give properties of the constants such as typing etc. Theorems must be proved to follow from axioms. The machine *sees* context(s). State is expressed by machine *variables*. *Invariant* predicates provide the typing for the variables and also specify correctness properties that must always hold. The state transition mechanism is accomplished through *events* which modify the variables. An event can have conditions known as event *guards* which must be true in order for the event to take place. It can also have *parameters* (also known as local variables). The variables are initialized using a special event called `Initialization` which is unguarded. An event has the following syntax:

$$e = \text{Any } t \text{ where } G(t,v) \text{ then } A(v,t) \text{ end}$$

An event e having parameters t can perform actions A on variables v if the guards G on t and v are true. A model is said to be consistent if all events preserve the invariants. These invariant preservation properties, called proof obligations (POs), are the verification conditions automatically generated by the tool and then discharged using theorem provers to verify correctness of the model. Figure 1 shows an example of a complete Event-B model with a machine and its seen context. It has a variable *bal*, typed by the invariant inv1 and initialized in the `Initialization` event. The set ACCOUNT is given in the context. There are two events, i.e., *transfer* and *deposit*, which update the variable *bal* when their respective guards become true. This example is taken from our ATM case-study which is explained in Section 5.2.

Refinement is a top-down development method and is at the core of Event-B modelling. We start by specifying the system at an abstract level and gradually refine by adding further details in each refinement step until the concrete model is achieved. A refinement is a development step guaranteeing every behaviour in the concrete model is one specified in the abstract model. It usually reduces non-determinism and each refinement step must be proved to be the correct refinement of the abstract model by discharging suitable refinement POs. Typically, we classify the refinement into horizontal and vertical refinements [1]. In horizontal refinement, we add more details to the abstract model to elaborate the existing specification or introduce further requirements of the system being modelled. In vertical refinement (also known as data refinement), the focus is on design decisions, i.e., transforming and enriching data types and the elaboration of algorithms. In vertical refinement, the state of a concrete model is linked to the abstract model using *gluing invariants*. It is usually harder to prove vertical refinements compared to horizontal refinements since the gluing invariants increase PO complexity. A model is vertically refined after the horizontal refinement has been performed to introduce all the requirements of the system.

MACHINE IntegralATM_0
SEES IntegralATM_CO
VARIABLES
    bal
INVARIANTS
    inv1 : $bal \in ACCOUNT \nrightarrow \mathbb{N}$
EVENTS
Initialisation
    begin
        act1 : $bal := \varnothing$
    end
Event *transfer* $\hat{=}$
    any
        $src\_ac, dest\_ac, am$
    where
        grd1 : $src\_ac \in ACCOUNT$
        grd2 : $dest\_ac \in ACCOUNT$
        grd3 : $src\_ac \neq dest\_ac$
        grd4 : $am < bal(src\_ac)$
    then
    act1 : $bal := bal \lessdot \{dest\_ac \mapsto (bal(dest\_ac) + am), src\_ac \mapsto (bal(src\_ac) - am)\}$
    end

CONTEXT IntegralATM_CO
SETS
    ACCOUNT
END

Event *deposit* $\hat{=}$
    any
        acc, am
    where
        grd1 : $acc \in ACCOUNT$
        grd2 : $acc \in dom(bal)$
        grd3 : $am \in \mathbb{N}$
    then
        act1 : $bal(acc) := bal(acc) + am$
    end
END

Fig. 1. Integral ATM abstract model

3   Decomposition and Composition in Event-B

Decomposition: When a model becomes too big to be easily refined, we need to decompose it into various sub-models (components) which can then be refined independently. In effect, this is complexity management by reducing the size of models, which keeps them understandable and reduces the number of POs to be proved for each model. This also allows the refinement of components in parallel by different teams. There are two types of decomposition in Event-B known as *shared-variable* decomposition (*SVD*) [7] and *shared-event* [8] decomposition (*SED*). Like Event-B language, these techniques are influenced by earlier formalizms such as CSP [9] and Action Systems [10]. The refinement preserving nature of these decomposition techniques differentiates these from the feature-based decomposition with in the FOSD community.

In *shared-variable* style, shared variables are kept in all the components, and events are partitioned between components. Each shared variable v in each component C is affected by - i.e. has possible transitions defined by - every event E in every other component acting on that variable. To model this, for each such E, an *external event* E_{ext} is added to C. When a component is refined, shared variables and external events must not be refined. This type of decomposition corresponds to asynchronous shared-memory communication between components. Figure 2 (left) is an example of SVD where machine M is decomposed, with shared variable v2, by partitioning events into machines M1 and M2. Thus event E3', a new external event in M1, models the effect on v2 of E3 in M2. Similarly, E2' is an external event in M2 modelling the effect on v2 in M2 of E2.

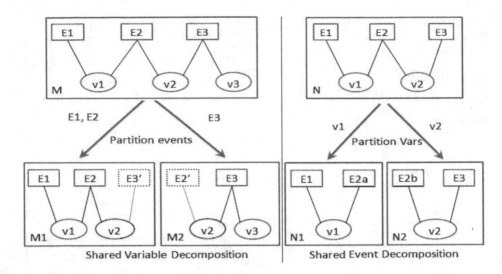

Fig. 2. Decomposition types in Event-B

The *shared-event* style is based on shared events rather than shared variables. During the decomposition, the independent events are kept in each decomposed component and the shared events are split. Figure 2 (right) is an example of SED where machine N is decomposed by partitioning variables into machines N1 (with v1) and N2 (with v2). Since event E2 works on variables v1 and v2, it will be split between N1 and N2. So, part of event E2 (E2a) that deals with variable v1 becomes an event of N1 and its other part (E2b) that deals with v2 becomes event of N2. Event splitting is achieved by decomposing its parameters, guards and actions into two. This type of decomposition is considered appropriate for systems based on synchronous message passing.

Both the SVD and SED approaches have semantic support for modular refinement. This means that it has been shown for both approaches that decomposition preserves refinement: if we were to recompose components, even after further refinement steps, the composite would refine the single abstract model.

In practice the designer might choose to recompose - e.g. all code to run on a single processor - or might not - e.g. where component models are deployed on separate physical devices. The key point is that the final model is 'correct by construction'. A decomposition plug-in [11] has been developed for the Rodin tool which can be used to demonstrate both styles of decomposition.

Composition: Since we are interested in composition, we would like to use the decomposition styles discussed above by inverting the decomposition method. For the shared-event style this is straightforward, whether one is composing all, or just a subset of components, provided these do not have any shared state. For shared variable, composition is straightforward provided *all* components are included; if not, remaining external events are a problem. So, this brings up a tooling requirement to automatically generate external events for the components being composed. We could manually do this but it will be cumbersome and even more difficult when composing large number of components with many events. We will discuss this further in our example case-studies later.

Fusion [12] is another style of composition which allows the fusion of events when composing Event-B models having shared variables. During the fusion of two events, guards are conjoined and actions are concatenated. This style of composition, inspired by the above two decomposition styles, promises the support for reuse of models through composition as envisaged in feature-based development. The refinement preservation is also guaranteed as each of the abstract input feature events is refined by the concrete fused event. A prototype feature composition tool [13] has been developed which allows the composition of models using this style. Since the tool is not restrictive, it does not enforce the correct fusion style composition. This means that the user needs to make sure that the composition is performed correctly. Also, the tool does not automatically discharge proof obligations for the composite model at the moment but our case-study results will provide some directions to deal with proof reuse as mentioned in future work (Section 7).

4   Feature-Orientation for Reuse with Event-B

We have adapted and extended the cardinality-based feature modelling notations [15]. Apart from our prototype tool (discussed below), there are no feature modelling tools specifically for Event-B. Tooling specific to Event-B is required because standard feature modelling tools are not enough to provide Event-B semantics and all the modelling, proving, animation and model checking facilities provided by the Rodin toolkit.

We define an Event-B *feature* as an Event-B model which consists of a machine and one or more contexts. An Event-B feature model - except for its leaf nodes - supports all the usual feature modelling constructs and constraints [15], subject to some syntactic customization [14]. The leaf level nodes in the tree denote Event-B features. So, a leaf feature could be a whole Event-B development modelling various refinement levels[3]. We have also developed a prototype feature modelling tool [14] that can be used to build feature models of product lines. These feature models can be configured by selecting a set of features, resolving any conflicts and composing these to model an instance of the product line.

5   Approach to Experimental Case-Study Work

We have modelled two well-known case-studies in Event-B using different modelling styles to explore composition related issues that may arise when we try to model product lines in Event-B. Our focus has been the feature-oriented development approach while modelling these systems and to maximise the amount of reuse that can be achieved. We have used the different types of decompositions available in Event-B (see Section 3) to decompose each system into a number of

---

[3] This notion of feature has evolved over the time and is slightly different to what we have published previously.

features which can be independently refined. These features can then be composed later to build a particular product of the product line. So, we have used the top-down methodology of Event-B in order to build an asset of reusable features to experiment with. This case-study work should also suggest further guidelines for feature modelling, should one needs to do so using the existing techniques and tool. Following is a brief overview of each of the case-studies.

5.1   Production Cell Case-Study

The Production Cell (*PC*) [16] is an example of a reactive system, which has been specified in a number of formal modelling languages. The PC is a metal processing plant where metal blanks enter into the system through the feed belt and are dropped on to the elevating-rotary table. The table elevates and rotates to a position so that the first robot arm can pick up the blanks. The robot rotates anti-clockwise to drop the blanks in the press. The press forges the blanks which are then picked up by the second robot arm dropping on to the deposit belt. A moving crane then picks the blanks from the deposit belt, that have not been forged properly, and brings them back to the feed belt for reprocessing. Figure 3 shows the top view of the production cell plant.

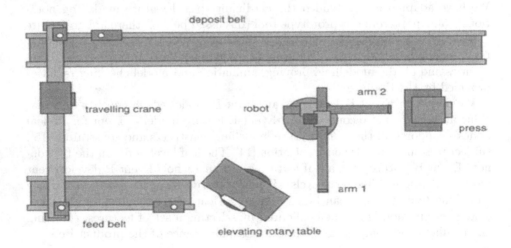

Fig. 3. Production Cell Plant [16]

The production cell was modelled in two ways, (i) based on the physical components and (ii) the controllers of the system. We will refer to these as component or control based modelling of PC. This allows us to use two different methods of modelling the same system in Event-B and analysing our methodologies for the feature-based modelling framework using existing tools and techniques in Event-B.

PC Component-based: We started with an abstract model of the production cell where we only model the processing of metal blanks from unforged to forged state. We then introduced further requirements in the next three levels of refinements. These were all horizontal refinements. At this stage we found it reasonable to decompose this integral model into separate models for each of the physical components of the PC. Each of these components can then be refined vertically to include sensors and actuators bringing it closer to implementation. We tried both the shared-event (*SED*) and shared-variable decomposition (*SVD*). Since there were shared-variables in the model (e.g. *blanks* shared by all components), it was not possible to use the SED technique without further refinement. The decomposition of the integral model using SVD resulted in six sub-models (components), i.e., feed belt, table, robot, press, deposit belt and crane. We could then refine each of these sub-models of PC independently while maintaining the restrictions of the SVD style, i.e., not to refine shared state and the external events. For example, we vertically refined the 'press' component up to three refinement levels by introducing actuators and sensors for handling the press using the refinement patterns for control systems [17].

We can build more variants of PC by selecting a different configuration of these reusable physical components. For example, if we need to increase productivity, we can model a production cell with two press components for forging the blanks and two robots. We can build another product of PC by modelling a different kind of press and reusing existing models where a second robot picks a blank processed by press1 to be processed differently by press2.

PC Controller-based: The control-based modelling of Production Cell was done by grouping the requirements for various controllers of the system. Each group of requirements was modelled as a controller. This was not just decomposing the PC system into controllers but also generalized these controllers so that these can be specialized and reused for modelling various PC components. Hence, the control-based modelling of PC was a result of decomposition plus generalization. The control-based PC models consisted of loader, movement, rotation and magnet controllers. These models were generic so that these can be used later on for modelling a particular physical component of PC. A complete PC model could also be modelled by instantiating and composing these control-based reusable features. We only discuss the magnet and movement controllers here. We refined these using the sensing and actuation patterns for refining control systems as suggested in [17]. Following is the detail of modelling and refining the magnet and movement features respectively.

Magnet Controller: At the abstract level, we have events for picking and dropping of blanks by a component. A component which has not already picked a blank can do so and a component which has picked a blank can drop it. The feature will be instantiated to a specific component such as a crane or a robot arm. The model is quite abstract and the details are added later in the refinements and during specialization. In the first refinement, we added sensor for magnet which informs the controller whether a blank has been picked up or dropped off. An electromagnet switch acts as an actuator for the magnet which performs the pick and drop of blanks. We have events for starting and stopping the magnet and switching the sensor on and off. In the second refinement, we differentiate between the actual and sensed values of the sensors. This is done to model the system closer to reality, as the actual value of the sensors at some point in time will be different from the sensed values. Similarly, in the third refinement, we refine the actuation where controller sets the actuation of the motor before the motor can be actuated. Here we split the actuation events into two, i.e., an event for setting the actuation of magnet by the controller and the event for magnet to actuate accordingly.

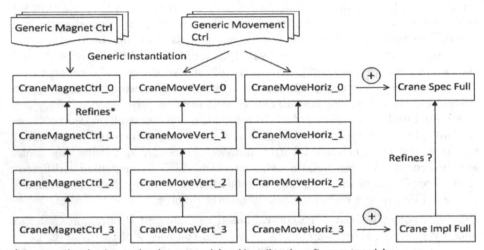

* An arrow head points to the abstract model and its tail to the refinement model.

Fig. 4. Crane Instantiation

Movement Controller: At the abstract level, we have events for moving a physical component forward and backward between two positions. The feature will be instantiated to a specific component such as a press or a crane. During the first refinement, we added sensors for the two positions and a motor for moving backward and forward. Events were added for starting and stopping the motor at different positions and switching the sensors on and off. In the second refinement, we differentiate between the actual and sensed values of the sensors as discussed earlier. Using the same refinement style, at third level of refinement, we differentiate between setting the motor's actuation by the controller from its actual movement.

Instantation & Composition: The Magnet and Movement controllers provide us refinement chains of generic Event-B models for the two features. In order to model any component of the PC, we need to instantiate and compose these chains of models. For example, if we want to model the crane component, we have to specialize one instance of the magnet controller to pick and drop blanks and two instances of movement controllers for moving the crane horizontally and vertically, as shown in Figure 4. Figure 5 shows a simple example where event *PickBlank* of Magnet controller is specialized for the crane component. Here the generic model parameter X_comp_X is replaced by *crane* provided both of these are of the same type. For now, we use $X\_\ldots\_X$ as a syntactic convention to model a generic parameter, given that current Rodin tool does not support generics.

event PickBlank (before)	event CranePickBlank (after)

any *b*
 where
    @grd1 X_comp_X ∉ ran(position)
    @grd2 *b* ∈ dom(position)
 then
    @act1 position(*b*) := X_comp_X
 end
	any *b*
	 where
	    @grd1 **crane** ∉ ran(position)
	    @grd2 *b* ∈ dom(position)
	 then
	    @act1 position(*b*) := crane
	 end

Fig. 5. Event Specialization for Crane

The composition of abstract level models from each refinement chain would give us an abstract specification for the crane. We also had to do some guard strengthening and add some invariants during the composition. The composition of implementation level models for each refinement would provide us with the implementation of the crane. Again extra guards for events and invariants were needed. Figure 6 shows two events from crane and movement controllers for picking up blanks by crane and the movement of crane to feed belt (before composition). Figure 7 (after composition) shows these events with extra guards added during the composition. For example, grd3 of *CranePickBlank* event specifies that the crane can only pick a blank when it is positioned on the deposit belt. Similarly, grd2 of *moveToFB* event in Figure 7 specifies that the crane can only move to feed belt if it has picked up a blank. The guard grd2 of *CranePickBlank* event means it can pick any blank in the system. When we finally model the entire PC model, we will need to strengthen this guard to say that the crane can only pick a blank from the deposit belt.

We call this style of composition 'feature composition' which extends the fusion composition where additional predicates can be added during the composition. As of yet, this style of composition does not guarantee refinement preservation between the composed abstract and implementation models. In order to deal with this kind of composition, we need support for proof reuse. By this we mean to find a way of automatically discharging composite POs with the help of already discharged POs of the components being composed. This requires further work. In comparison to the component-based approach discussed earlier, this style of modelling SPLs in Event-B seems more appropriate because it provides more reuse opportunities.

The shared-event composition could not be applied here due to the shared state between the components being composed. The shared-variable composition approach is too constraining and could only be used here if we start with an abstract model containing the functionality of both the Magnet and Movement features. We could then decompose these into two, refine each of these, instantiate for the crane and compose to build the crane model. The ATM case-study

```
event CranePickBlank    (before)      event moveToFB           (before)
  any b                                 where
  where                                   @grd1 cranePosHorz=posDB
    @grd1 crane∈ran(position)           then
    @grd2 b∈dom(position)                 @act1 cranePosHorz = posFB
  then                                  end
    @act1 position(b) = crane
end
```

Fig. 6. Events of Magnet and Movement Controllers

```
event CranePickBlank    (after)       event moveToFB            (after)
  any b                                 where
  where                                   @grd1 cranePosHorz=posDB
    @grd1 crane∈ran(position)             @grd2 crane∈ran(position)
    @grd2 b∈dom(position)               then
    @grd3 cranePosHorz = posDB            @act1 cranePosHorz = posFB
  then                                  end
    @act1 position(b) = crane
end
```

Fig. 7. Guard strengthening of events during composition

discussed in Section 5.2 further explores these issues and suggests the modelling style through which we could use existing techniques of Event-B to achieve partial reuse of existing specifications, when modelling variants of a product line.

Evaluation: By modelling the PC in two different ways, we can argue that the amount of reusable assets can be increased by modelling the system from a reuse perspective. If we model features by generalizing, as in control-based modelling, then this increases the amount of reuse. For example, a PC model can be built by composing six physical components. If we want to model the same PC model using control-based features, we need to specialize and compose many generic features, e.g., a crane component would require the instantiation and composition of three features. In fact, we are modelling coarse-grained features in component-based PC where as the features in control-based PC are fine-grained. The top-down development of component-based PC resulting in coarse-grained features provides the communication between various physical components. Where as the bottom-up development of control-based PC resulting in fine-grained features provides more reuse opportunities. We could only utilise the potential benefits of reuse if we can automate this process of specialization and composition.

We could further explore reusability of component-based features by modelling them completely independent of each other, unlike we did for the component-based PC by decomposing horizontally refined integral model to get these. Then again there will be a question of how these components will communicate for passing blanks to each other when composing these to build a PC? Another option is to decompose horizontally refined integral model using SED where the components would communicate by synchronising their shared-events. This means that the individual components are not completely independent of each other and their reuse must be constrained by the topology of the PC. We could also have generic predicates in each component which must be specialized during the composition. For example, the table receives a blank from the feed belt (fb). So, a predicate $position(b) = XinputCompX$ could be used which must be specialized to $position(b) = fb$. In this way we can model the static variability represented by the connection topology of the physical components of PC. For instance, the input component for table is feed belt and the output component is robot which picks blanks from the table. It would be useful to have a tool that reads product configuration from a file to instantiate a product line, i.e., the $XinputCompX$ is instantiated to fb in the above example. So, our objective is to prototype some mechanism (e.g., syntactic definitions or patterns) that could be used for generic instantiation and composition of Event-B specifications.

We also found that the process of vertically refining the features to include sensors and actuators is quite similar in both the modelling styles. This is because we used the patterns for refining control systems [17]. This refinement process can also be automated where features can be refined vertically to model actuators and sensors. This requires further work.

5.2   ATM Case-Study

The auto teller machine (ATM) provides services to bank customers using their ATM cards issued by the bank. There are some basic services provided by an ATM such as cash withdrawal, view account balance and card pin related services. Other services can also be provided by ATMs which vary for different banks and ATM locations, e.g., mobile top up and cash deposit etc. In this Section, we will only discuss balance transfer, deposit and withdrawal features of the ATM.

We can build a product line of ATMs to manage variability and benefit from reuse while building various ATMs providing different features from a shared set of available features. A different configuration of features will result in a variant of an ATM. We have modelled some ATM features in Event-B to see if existing tools and techniques are capable enough for our feature-oriented modelling in Event-B or whether we can find other patterns where these existing approaches fall short. Hence, we can propose ways to handle those situations and suggest any requirements for the tools and techniques to be built in the future to compliment the feature-based development in Event-B.

We started with an integral model of the ATM that allows cash deposit and balance transfer between two accounts. This abstract model is shown in Figure 1. We then decomposed this model into deposit and balance transfer features using shared-variable decomposition (SVD). The event $deposit$ goes into the deposit feature and the $transfer$ event goes to the transfer feature - see Figure 8. Both features will have shared variable bal and external events, e.g., deposit feature will have $transfer$ event as external event which must not be refined along with the shared variable. These features were then refined horizontally and vertically.

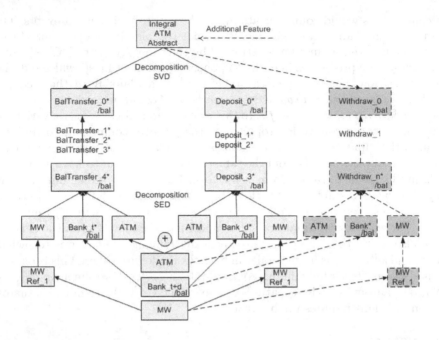

Fig. 8. Refinement & (de)composition architecture for ATM features

The first refinement of the balance transfer feature refines the *transfer* event for a successful transfer of money and another event is introduced when the transfer fails due to the account balance being less than the transfer amount. The second level of refinement introduce request and response mechanism between the ATM and the Bank. Here the ATM sends a balance transfer request to the bank, which responds after a successful or failed transfer event takes place and then the ATM displays the transfer status. The third level of refinement further refines the request and response mechanisms by partitioning the request event for sending and receiving the request and similarly for the response event. The fourth refinement introduces the middleware (*MW*) between the ATM and the Bank. This allow us to make an architectural decomposition of the balance transfer feature into ATM, MW and the Bank where MW is used for communicating between the two. The recomposition of these (ATM, MW, Bank) would refine the feature being decomposed (fourth refinement).

An ATM sends a balance transfer request through the MW which is received by the bank. The bank then sends a response for a successful or failed transfer through the middleware. The ATM finally displays the transfer status accordingly. We used SED here and the components synchronise using the shared-events. Each of these three components can be further refined. Similarly, we refined the deposit feature resulting in three components, i.e., ATM, MW and the Bank. Figure 8 shows the development and composition structure for the deposit and balance transfer features of the ATM. In the figure, asterisk (*) denotes a model with external events, and */bal* indicates the model's shared variable. Note that in this case study, the shared variable bal and its corresponding external events are localized in the Bank component.

Now that we have the same architectural decomposition (ATM, MW, Bank) for each feature, we would like to compose these models pairwise (i.e $Bank_{t+d} = Bank_t + Bank_d$, etc.) for implementation purposes. In general, the task would of course be more complex, involving more than two features. In our case, where the shared variable bal is localized into the two architectural Bank components, intuition suggests that these can be composed, with the composite Bank refining each component Bank. This is because each Bank's external events are exactly "cancelled out", or implemented, by the other Bank's actual events. This assertion remains to be proved in general for this pattern of mixed decomposition-recomposition. There is to date no shared-variable composition (SVC) tool support.

Evaluation: Consider generalizing the above approach. For example, after building an ATM with two features, we want another ATM product having a cash withdrawal feature as well (as shown by dotted lines in Figure 8). We elaborate the top-level integral model to include withdrawal feature and decompose it into three components (i.e., deposit, balance transfer and withdrawal). Provided the new feature is *separable* - in the sense that in the SVD refinement the other two feature models remain unchanged - then all we have to do is refine the withdrawal component. Since the deposit and balance transfer components have already been proven, new POs will only be generated for the newly added external events corresponding to events of the withdrawal component acting on bal. Hence, we will only have to discharge these small number of POs when reusing existing models. So, If we can have a tool for analysing and automatically generating external events in the existing components for the newly added components, then we could reduce the amount of POs needed to be discharged.

Recall that in SVD the shared-variable (SV) may not be refined - this is very restrictive, and further investigation is required to establish whether after architectural recomposition, it is possible to then refine the SV for implementation purposes.

We have examined a specific pattern of mixed decomposition-recomposition - SVD followed by SED and then SVC in a single development. It appears possible to do this provided shared variables and their associated external events become localized in one of the shared-event components. Should this pattern be validated theoretically, other architectural possibilities should emerge: e.g., an ATM-specific shared variable as well as a Bank-specific one in the same development. Interesting avenues of future work are indicated.

6 Related Work

Formal modelling of SPLs is not a new area and work has been done to formally specify requirements and reusing these to produce variants of a product line [18]. HATS [19] provides a methodology for applying formal methods at different stages of SPL development cycle. This seems to be a promising work to bring together the domains of formal methods and SPL. All the existing techniques for composing Event-B specifications have been discussed in this paper and we have not seen any work being done for modelling SPLs in Event-B. Lau et al. [20] proposed component-based verification approach which allows the composition of existing verified components and support proof reuse. This is different to our approach because an Event-B component is not a single model but a chain of refinements. We need to compose models at different refinement levels and also preserve the refinement relationship between the abstract and concrete composite models. Some work has been done by Sorge et al. [21] which deals with invariant proof obligations for composing features. This does not support feature refinement and event fusion which is required to complement our feature modelling framework. FEATUREHOUSE [22] is another tool that allows the composition of artefacts and supports various languages with option to include more. It would be very useful to see if Event-B can be included in this framework and whether the composition of Event-B refinement chains can be achieved with proof reuse.

7   Conclusion and Future Work

We have given an overview of the two case-studies that we have modelled to explore existing capability for feature-based development in Event-B. We sought to identify patterns of refinement, generic instantiation, decomposition and composition that could be exploited for reuse. Further, we sought to identify further requirements for tooling, and further research - both experimental and theoretical - to develop a feature-based reuse capability for Event-B/Rodin.

In the component-based PC model we explored SVD. Then considering the option of modelling physical components as features, it appeared that generic elements defining the connection of these features could be instantiated from contextual data about the topology/connectivity of the cell. This idea is close to the shared-event composition of such features and needs further examination.

In the controller-based modelling approach to the PC we found a finer-grained set of generic template models which could be instantiated and composed into physical features, which could then be further composed as above. However, this freer form of composition (which we call feature composition) carries no "correct-by-construction" guarantee, and thus a full reproof burden. It may be that this is an opportunity for fusion composition, which remains to be investigated. Investigation is also needed to find modelling and composition patterns that will give partial PO reuse, thus partial "reproof-for-free". For example, guard-strengthening of events preserves simple refinement, but can introduce deadlock problems.

In the ATM case, we explored one specific pattern of mixed decomposition-recomposition - SVD followed by SED and then SVC. This looks like a promising pattern for composition of abstract features followed by architectural design, subject to structural constraints about shared variables. Future work will reveal exactly what those constraints are, and will explore other such patterns of refinement and (de)composition for feature-based modelling. It would also be interesting to explore how to deal with feature interactions using our case-study work.

References

1. Abrial, J.R.: Modeling in Event-B: System and Software Engineering, 1st edn., Cambridge University Press, Cambridge (2010)
2. Abrial, J.R.: The B-book: assigning programs to meanings. Cambridge University Press, New York (1996)
3. Clements, P., Northrop, L.: Software Product Lines: Practices and Patterns. Addison-Wesley Professional, Reading (2001)
4. Lee, K., Kang, K.C., Lee, J.J.: Concepts and guidelines of feature modeling for product line software engineering. In: Gacek, C. (ed.) ICSR 2002. LNCS, vol. 2319, pp. 62–77. Springer, Heidelberg (2002)
5. Bosch, J.: Design and use of software architectures: adopting and evolving a product-line approach. ACM Press/Addison-Wesley (2000)
6. Snook, C., Poppleton, M., Johnson, I.: Rigorous engineering of product-line requirements: a case study in failure management. IST 50(1-2), 112–129 (2008)
7. Abrial, J.R., Hallerstede, S.: Refinement, Decomposition, and Instantiation of Discrete Models: Application to Event-B. Fundam. Inf. 77(1-2), 1–28 (2007)
8. Butler, M.: Synchronisation-based Decomposition for Event-B. In: RODIN Deliverable D19 Intermediate report on methodology (2006)
9. Hoare, C.A.R.: Communicating sequential processes. Prentice-Hall, Inc., Upper Saddle River (1985)
10. Back, R., von Wright, J.: Trace refinement of action systems. In: Jonsson, B., Parrow, J. (eds.) CONCUR 1994. LNCS, vol. 836, pp. 367–384. Springer, Heidelberg (1994)
11. Silva, R., Pascal, C., Hoang, T.S., Butler, M.: Decomposition tool for event-b. In: Workshop on Tool Building in Formal Methods - ABZ Conference (January 2010)
12. Poppleton, M.R.: The composition of event-B models. In: Börger, E., Butler, M., Bowen, J.P., Boca, P. (eds.) ABZ 2008. LNCS, vol. 5238, pp. 209–222. Springer, Heidelberg (2008)
13. Gondal, A., Poppleton, M., Snook, C.: Feature composition - towards product lines of Event-B models. In: MDPLE 2009 CTIT Workshop Proceedings (June 2009)
14. Gondal, A., Poppleton, M., Butler, M., Snook, C.: Feature-Oriented Modelling Using Event-B. In: SETP-10, Orlando, FL, USA (2010)
15. Czarnecki, K., Helsen, S., Eisenecker, U.: Staged configuration through specialization and multilevel configuration of feature models. Software Process: Improvement and Practice 10(2), 143–169 (2005)
16. Lindner, T.: Task description. In: Lewerentz, C., Lindner, T. (eds.) Formal Development of Reactive Systems. LNCS, vol. 891, Springer, Heidelberg (1995)
17. Butler, M.: Towards a cookbook for modelling and refinement of control problems (2009), http://deploy-eprints.ecs.soton.ac.uk/108/
18. Kishi, T., Noda, N.: Formal verification and software product lines. Commun. ACM 49(0001-0782), 73–77 (2006)
19. Clarke, D., Diakov, N., Hähnle, R., Johnsen, E.B., Puebla, G., Weitzel, B., Wong, P.Y.H.: HATS-a formal software product line engineering methodology. In: Proc. Intl. Workshop on Formal Methods in SPL Engineering, South Corea (2010)
20. Lau, K.K., Wang, Z., Wang, A., Gu, M.: A component-based approach to verified software: What, why, how and what next? In: Chen, X., Liu, Z., Reed, M. (eds.) Proc. 1st Asian Working Conference on Verified Software, pp. 225–229 (2006)
21. Sorge, J., Poppleton, M., Butler, M.: A basis for feature-oriented modelling in event-B. In: Frappier, M., Glässer, U., Khurshid, S., Laleau, R., Reeves, S. (eds.) ABZ 2010. LNCS, vol. 5977, pp. 409–409. Springer, Heidelberg (2010)
22. Apel, S., Kastner, C., Lengauer, C.: FEATUREHOUSE: Language-independent, automated software composition. In: ICSE 2009, USA, pp. 221–231 (2009)

A Formal Approach for Incremental Construction with an Application to Autonomous Robotic Systems

Saddek Bensalem[1], Lavindra de Silva[3], Andreas Griesmayer[1], Felix Ingrand[3], Axel Legay[4], and Rongjie Yan[1,2]

[1] Verimag Laboratory, Université Joseph Fourier, Grenoble, CNRS
[2] State Key Laboratory of Computer Science, Institute of Software, CAS, Beijing
[3] LAAS/CNRS, Université de Toulouse
[4] INRIA/IRISA, Rennes

Abstract. In this paper, we propose a new workflow for the design of composite systems. Contrary to existing approaches, which build on traditional techniques for single-component systems, our methodology is incremental in terms of both the design and the verification process. The approach exploits the hierarchy between components and can detect errors at an early stage of the design. As a second contribution of the paper, we apply our methodology to automatically generate C code to coordinate the various modules of an autonomous robot. To the best of our knowledge, this is the first time that such a coordination code is generated automatically.

1 Introduction

Computers play a central role in modern life and their errors can have dramatic consequences. For example, such mistakes could jeopardize the banking system of a country or, more dramatically, endanger human life through the failure of some safety systems. It is therefore not surprising that proving the correctness of computer systems is a highly relevant problem. Checking correctness is becoming more and more challenging as systems now result from the combination of smaller systems developed by independent teams. A major difficulty is that the designer has to provide systematic rules that coordinate the interactions between the various components to make sure that the system will indeed match its objectives.

Most existing approaches work by first producing code (in programming languages such as C or JAVA) to coordinate the components and then applying a software verification technique to decide whether the resulting system behaves properly. This approach usually requires the designer to manually write the code that will coordinate the components. Moreover, it postpones the verification problem to the end of the design, ignoring that errors should be detected as early as possible. Here, we suggest a different workflow that exploits the initial decomposition of the system into subsystems. More precisely, we will use an adequate component-based design language and a verification methodology that permit reasoning on the behavior of the entire system incrementally starting from the subsystems and assembling them hierarchically. We rely on the *BIP* framework [13], a tool set for component-based design. In the *BIP* language, atomic

S. Apel and E. Jackson (Eds.): SC 2011, LNCS 6708, pp. 116–132, 2011.
© Springer-Verlag Berlin Heidelberg 2011

components are represented by transition systems labeled with C/C++ functions. Bigger components are obtained by combining smaller units through a series of interactions and communication primitives. The BIP tool chain can use those communication mechanisms to automatically synthesize C code that coordinate the components. We furthermore show how to verify the models using *DFinder*, a verification tool of the *BIP* framework that effectively exploits the knowledge about the component structure.

The main contributions of this paper are twofold. First, we summarize and formalize results from previous work to a unified workflow that combines *BIP* and *DFinder*. Second, we apply this workflow to automatically produce the code that will synchronize the $G^{en}{}_oM$ [20] modules of the autonomous rover DALA [9,8]. By joining forces, $G^{en}{}_oM$, *BIP* and *DFinder* provide us with a fully automatic technique to generate correct C code to coordinate the various $G^{en}{}_oM$ components in the functional level of the robot. This use of the workflow is a significant contribution with respect to other methodologies to design autonomous robots. Indeed, most other existing work proposes functional levels that are designed without a workflow providing any formal guarantee of correctness. Further contributions of this paper are the extension of the verified model to comprise all main modules of the rover, and the extension of the type of properties that can be checked by *DFinder* to include a number of safety properties.

Related Work. The work presented here uses the incremental design process that exploits the hierarchy between components induced by the *BIP* language. More precisely, *DFinder* allows to reuse the results obtained for sub-components in order to speed up the verification of the global system. The actual C code for coordinating the participating components can then be automatically synthesized from the model [4]. This is in contrast with existing posteriori approaches [3,12,22] where correctness is checked over the complete design. Our experience shows that for those systems that can be described in BIP, it is generally easier to apply the verification process before generating the code rather than after. There are other approaches that generate code from mathematical specifications (e.g., [2]) but to the best of our knowledge, none of them embed an incremental verification procedure. The modeling and verification tools presented in this paper, *BIP* and *DFinder*, are products of continuous research [4,5,6,7,11] aimed at improving the approaches by, e.g., optimizing the verification process through incremental computation of the invariants. Consequently, while parts of the functional level of the DALA rover have been verified in past work, verification of all modules belonging to laser-based navigation was only possible with the most recent version of the tool [10], which we report on for the first time in this paper.

There are some works that attempt to incorporate formal tools into the development of robot software systems. R^2C [23] is a *state checker* used in the LAAS architecture [19]. R^2C encodes user-supplied constraints for the system and continuously checks and ensures at runtime that incoming requests are consistent with those constraints. The ORCCAD system [18] is a development environment to prove various properties of robotic systems, based on the Esterel [15] language. This approach, however, is limited to the synchronous paradigm. The work presented in [1] makes use of an abstract representation of services and allows for validating the resulting automata via model checking techniques. Likewise, the approach proposed in [30] involves abstracting the system into a state-transition-based language and using a controller to execute

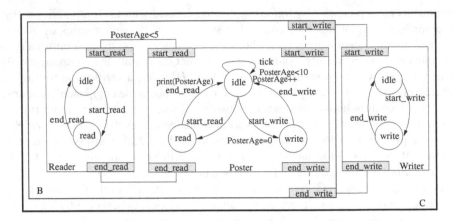

Fig. 1. An example of *BIP* model

the state evolutions while respecting the associated programmer specified invariants. Finally, the CIRCA SSP planner [21] synthesizes off-line controllers from a domain description, and then deduces the corresponding timed automaton for controlling the system at runtime. These automata can be formally validated with model checking techniques. In contrast to the approach that we have applied to the DALA rover, the above works are mostly designed for the decisional level, which plans and executes the task plan, but they cannot address the validation and verification of the underlying functional level, which performs the actual actions. While the R^2C approach aims at enforcing user-supplied safety constraints online, this approach cannot be used to check the functional level for correctness off-line (before execution).

Structure of the paper. In Section 2, we present a language for component-based design. We also survey powerful techniques to verify systems written in this language. Section 3 introduces our workflow based on *BIP* and *DFinder*. Experimental results are presented in Section 4, where we introduce the DALA robot and use our workflow to synthesize code to coordinate its various modules. Section 5 concludes the paper.

2   Background: *BIP* Language and Verification Methodology

In this section, we briefly survey the formal definition of the *BIP* language for component-based design introduced in [4], and give a short introduction to verification of systems described in this language. In Section 3, we will propose a workflow based on this theoretical framework. The basic unit of our language is the atomic component:

Definition 1 (Atomic Component). *An atomic component is a transition system extended with data $B = (L, P, \mathcal{T}, X, \{g_\tau\}_{\tau \in \mathcal{T}}, \{f_\tau\}_{\tau \in \mathcal{T}})$, where:*

- *$(L, P, \mathcal{T})$ is a transition system, where $L = \{l_1, l_2, \ldots, l_k\}$ is a set of control locations, P is a set of ports, and $\mathcal{T} \subseteq L \times P \times L$ is a set of transitions.*
- *$X = \{x_1, \ldots, x_n\}$ is a set of variables and for each $\tau \in \mathcal{T}$ respectively, g_τ is a guard, a predicate on X, and $f_\tau(X, X')$ is an update relation, a predicate on X (current) and X' (next) state variables.*

An atomic component resembles a classical transition system with the addition that one can also attach C/C++ functions and data to the transitions of the component. Each time the transition is taken, the attached code is executed. Coordination between components is described by interactions with strongly synchronized ports, enabling conditions and data exchange between different components.

Definition 2 (Interactions). *Given a set of n components* $B_1, B_2, \ldots, B_n$ *with* $B_i = (L_i, P_i, T_i, X_i, \{g_\tau\}_{\tau \in T_i}, \{f_\tau\}_{\tau \in T_i})$, *an interaction a is a set of ports, i.e., a subset of* $\bigcup_{i=1}^{n} P_i$, *such that* $\forall i \in [1, n]. |a \cap P_i| \leq 1$.

Graphically, interactions will be represented by a line between ports. Parallel composition between components allows to build larger components by combining a series of smaller components. The operation is given by sets of interactions, which are defined by *connector*s. The connection mechanism between the components is also called *glue*. Interactions can be seen as *transitions* of the product of all components and allow enabling conditions and updates in form of C/C++ code.

Example 1. *Figure 1 shows a graphical representation of a BIP model. We use circles to describe locations, arrows between circles for transitions, and squares on components for exported ports (i.e., ports that can synchronize with ports of other components). The example of Figure 1 consists of the atomic components* Poster, Reader *and* Writer. Poster *contains three locations and five transitions, which are labeled by the ports* start_read, end_read, start_write, end_write *and* tick *ports. Note that* tick *is not exported; the associated transition can be executed without synchronization. The component also contains an integer variable PosterAge, which is used by port* start_read. *We use* print *to output the value of PosterAge during the execution of the transition labeled by* end_read. *There are two pairs of interactions. The interaction between two ports* start_read *from* Reader *and* Poster *is only enabled if the guard PosterAge* < 5 *is fulfilled, in which case the two components can synchronously move to their read locations.*

Definition 3 (Parallel Composition). *Given n components* $B_i = (L_i, P_i, T_i, X_i, \{g_\tau\}_{\tau \in T_i}, \{f_\tau\}_{\tau \in T_i})$ *and a set of interactions* γ, *we define* $B = \gamma(B_1, \ldots, B_n)$ *as the component* $(L, \gamma, T, X, \{g_\tau\}_{\tau \in T}, \{f_\tau\}_{\tau \in T})$, *where:*

- (L, γ, T) *is the transition system such that*
  - $L = L_1 \times L_2 \times \ldots \times L_n$ *is the set of control locations,*
  - $T \subseteq L \times \gamma \times L$ *contains transitions* $\tau = ((l_1, \ldots, l_n), a, (l'_1, \ldots, l'_n))$ *obtained by synchronization of sets of transitions* $\{\tau_i = (l_i, p_i, l'_i) \in T_i\}_{i \in I}$ *such that* $I \subseteq \{1, \ldots, n\}, \{p_i\}_{i \in I} = a \in \gamma$ *and* $l'_j = l_j$ *if* $j \notin I$.
- $X = \bigcup_{i=1}^{n} X_i$ *and for a transition* τ *resulting from the synchronization of a set of transitions* $\{\tau_i\}_{i \in I}$, *the associated guard and function are respectively* $g_\tau = \bigwedge_{i \in I} g_{\tau_i}$ *and* $f_\tau = \bigwedge_{i \in I} f_{\tau_i} \wedge \bigwedge_{i \notin I} (X'_i = X_i)$.

Given an interaction a, only those components that are involved in a can make a step. If a component does not participate in the interaction, then it remains in the same state. By adding interactions over different (composite) components incrementally, we obtain a composite component with a layered structure.

2.1 Invariant-Based Verification

In this work, we are mostly interested in checking whether a system is deadlock-free or whether it satisfies some safety requirements. A first solution would be to compute the set of reachable states of the system and then check that any state satisfies the property. Unfortunately, the number of global states is exponential in the number of states of the individual components, which makes the approach intractable.

To avoid this state space explosion problem, we compute an invariant of the system; an over-approximation of the set of reachable states. Let us assume the existence of a predicate that represents all the states that do satisfy the property. If the negation of the predicate is not satisfied by the invariant (i.e., the invariant does not imply the negation), then we can say that the property described by the predicate is correct. Otherwise, we have to compute a stronger invariant with a smaller over-approximation to check the negation of the predicate. Computing invariants for component-based systems is a challenging problem with the major difficulty of optimally exploiting the underlying design to reduce computation time. A compositional verification method based on invariant computation is presented in [6,7]. This method is based on the following rule:

$$\frac{\{B_i < \Phi_i >\}_i, \; \Psi \in II(\|_\gamma \{B_i\}_i, \{\Phi_i\}_i), \; (\bigwedge_i \Phi_i) \wedge \Psi \Rightarrow \Phi}{\|_\gamma \{B_i\}_i < \Phi >}$$

Here, we work with two different kinds of invariants: the *component invariant* Φ for describing restrictions on the state local to the atomic components, and the *interaction invariant* Ψ to cover restrictions imposed by the synchronization of components. In more detail, the rule states that if all components B_i fulfill their respective *component invariants* Φ_i, the composition of all components $II(\|_\gamma \{B_i\}_i, \{\Phi_i\}_i)$ with the interactions γ fulfills an *interaction invariant* Ψ, and if furthermore the conjunction of the invariants $(\bigwedge_i \Phi_i) \wedge \Psi$ implies a predicate on the global system Φ, then also the global system $\|_\gamma \{B_i\}_i$ itself fulfills Φ. This approach was introduced in [7], where we have shown that the invariants can be computed in an efficient manner by using/combining abstraction and fixed-point techniques. This work was further developed and extended in a series of work [5,11] to better exploit the properties of the design, e.g., by using the component structure to compute the invariants incrementally.

The above methodology has been implemented in the *DFinder* tool set [10] which takes as input a program written in the *BIP* language and checks whether it is safe or not. Using the theory introduced in [5], we can in some situations decide if properties remain correct when adding new interactions to the design. This is done by an analysis of the interactions that are added to the system. *DFinder* also allows to directly compute the set of deadlocking states, *DIS*, in a straightforward way by examination of the interactions and its conditions. Building the conjunction of the negation of *DIS* and the computed invariants gives a natural way for verifying the deadlock-freedom of the system. More information on this, and more complex properties are shown in Subsection 4.3.

3 A Workflow for Component-Based Design

The *BIP* framework supports the complete design flow for component-based systems. It provides formal techniques to describe the incremental construction of

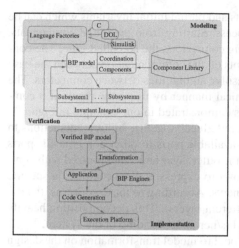

Fig. 2. BIP design flow

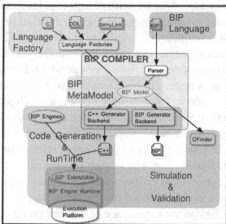

Fig. 3. BIP tool set

component-based systems by adding interactions to the existing set of components and provides methods and tools to analyze, maintain and deploy the models. This section builds on the concepts of the previous sections, introduces the framework in more detail and gives an overview of the tools that support the workflow from the design level to actual C++ code generation for deployment.

3.1 The Design Process

To exploit the *BIP* design methodology in verification, we use an incremental design obtained from identifying and modeling components in a bottom up manner. Certain properties, like causality chains that require some exact order of events $a_1 \rightarrow a_2 \rightarrow a_3 \rightarrow a_4$, can be decomposed into several properties that can be checked on smaller subsystems ($a_1 \rightarrow a_2$, $a_2 \rightarrow a_3$, $a_3 \rightarrow a_4$). If those properties are satisfied on the sub-components (a certain layer in the component hierarchy), the properties are still preserved by adding interactions in a new construction layer. More details on incremental property computations, and the rules to follow for construction and decomposition can be found in [5]. However, since adding constraints (interactions) may introduce deadlocks, the deadlock-freedom cannot be preserved during the construction process and verification is still necessary to obtain a correctness-by-construction system. Over all, the design process can be summarized to the three main steps *Modeling*, *Verification*, and *Code generation* (Figure 2). Each of these steps is assisted by the tool chain (Figure 3):

Modeling. Real world component-based design frameworks usually contain a library for reuse. The starting point for creating a model is therefore to take existing components from a *BIP* component library to build new ones as construction basis. For applications written in supported third party languages like C, G$^{en}_o$M [19] (for the DALA robot) and DOL [28], a series of *Language Factories* help in extracting the control structure and building a component system. The operations and data flow are implemented by C/C++ code embedded in the transitions. Note that this library of *BIP* components may already come with component invariants and partial initial invariants which can be used to speed up the global verification process. Starting from the initial components, the complete *BIP* model is created by adding connectors, the so called *glue*. The connectors implement interactions and constraints on the communication between the base components, and *priorities* can be used to resolve ambiguities between connectors. The components can be connected in a hierarchical manner by using the result of a composition as the new base component. This is demonstrated in our example in Figure 1, where the components *Poster* and *Reader* are "glued" together by two interactions to generate a new component. To provide the available ports to other components, ports *start_write* and *end_write* are exported to the outer layer and synchronized with component *Writer*. The design process also allows to express and concentrate on specific concerns and properties in different components. According to these concerns, the design is decomposed into subsystems (or different layers). This decomposition heavily relies on the experience of the designer and his/her understanding of the system.

The framework also provides tools for model to model transformation on the design level to, e.g., allow architecture optimizations and the automated adaption of the model to distributed settings [16,14]. These transformations are designed to preserve the behavioral properties of the model and therefore do not invalidate verification results that may have been established before.

Verification. *DFinder* works on the *BIP* design and implements the invariant computation techniques summarized in Section 2.1. It directly implements effective deadlock detection, and allows to check for general safety properties by encoding them into a reachability problem. (Section 4 gives more detail on how to encode important properties in the context of the DALA robot.) The invariants of every subsystem (or layer) can be computed and checked locally. Local verification before building the whole system allows to find problems as soon as possible. For example, in the components of Figure 1, we can detect a deadlock in the component composed by *Poster* and *Reader* before we check the deadlock-freedom of the whole system. When we consider this composite component, only ports *start_read* and *end_read* are connected. The deadlock is that both *Poster* and *Reader* stay at *idle* with $PosterAge = 10$. The reason is that port *start_write* is not connected, and the enabling conditions of ports *tick* and *start_read* are not satisfied. Therefore, without checking the whole design, we have already detected a deadlock. To remove the deadlock, we go back to the BIP model and delete the condition either on the interaction between ports *start_write* or on the transition labeled by port *tick*. After computing the invariants and checking the related properties for every subsystem, we compute the invariants of the whole system by reusing the invariants of the subsystems in *DFinder* as shown in Section 2.1. This global invariant is then used to check the deadlock-freedom and the properties not being checked in the subsystems.

Code generation. Verification and modeling steps are iterated until the specification is fulfilled. Having reached a satisfying model, BIP-to-C compilers allow the generation of C++ code for either simulation or deployment on the target platform. Simulation code still contains models that replace the hardware and additionally may provide estimations and monitors to examine nonfunctional properties like power consumption. The simulation code also gives rise to further verification methods like statistical model checking. The deployment code uses low level communication primitives of the destination platform and is compiled to run on the respective hardware. Like for model to model transformation, the different code generation methods preserve the behavioral properties of the model. The preservation of the behavioral properties from design level to executable code is one of the main advantages of the *BIP* tool chain. It enables us to use *DFinder* on the design level to establish important safety properties of the actually implemented application. A rerun of *DFinder* is only required after manual intervention in the models is done to ensure the integrity of the changes. Furthermore, a rerun can make use of previously computed results from other modules.

4 An Application: The Autonomous DALA Robot

Designing and developing software for an autonomous robot is a challenging and complex task. The robotics community has relied on architectures (e.g. CLARATY [26]), and software tools (e.g. OROCOS [17], CARMEN [25], Player Stage [29], Microsoft Robotics Studio [24], and ROS [27]), which provide certain control flow mechanisms to support requests or commands with arguments passed through components, as well as reports sent back to the requesting component. A practical solution is to organize software components into various levels (e.g., decisional level and functional level) that correspond to different temporal requirements or to different abstraction levels. The decisional level of a robot is responsible for producing the task plan and supervising its execution, while being reactive to events from the functional level at the same time. The functional level usually includes all the basic, built-in action and perception capabilities (e.g., image processing, obstacle avoidance, and motion control). It is also necessary to describe constraints between the two levels. For example, the functional level of the robot needs to be safe in the sense that "bad" requests from the decisional level are not executed. Different modeling mechanisms have various ways to implement this feature. Nowadays, one of the most used solutions consists of adding those constraints manually in the form of an extra level between the decisional and the functional level. Unfortunately, there is no way to ensure that those manual constraints are sound, i.e., that those constraints indeed prevent the functional level from acting in an unsafe way. Our objective in this section is to show that this limitation can be overcome by using the *BIP* workflow. In [9], we have already proposed systematic methodologies to synthesize C code to coordinate the functional and the decisional levels of a robot. However, we were unable to complete the verification process as the verification technique we used did not exploit the design of the system. In this paper, we show how *DFinder* can exploit this design to guarantee the correctness of this code. This is also the first time we explain in detail the verification of safety properties by using *DFinder*.

   The next subsection presents our case study in more detail, followed by the encoding of the problem in *BIP* in Section 4.2, which includes a reasoning on the constraints attached to the various modules. Finally, Section 4.3 shows how to use *DFinder* to refine the model and eventually guarantee the correctness of the constraints. After verification with *DFinder*, the *BIP Compiler* generates the C code that coordinates the various modules of the robot. Due to space limitations, we only present a part of the design. The full case study can be downloaded from http://www-verimag.imag.fr/dfinder.

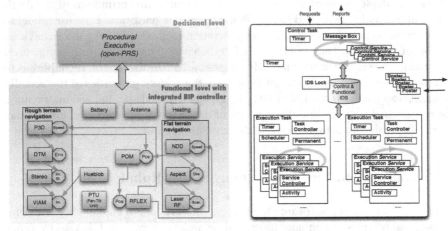

Fig. 4. Two level structure of DALA robot   **Fig. 5.** G^{en}ₒM module internal structure

4.1   The DALA Robot and Its Module Description

The DALA robot is an extraterrestrial rover like autonomous robot that is able to navigate to certain locations to take pictures, while avoiding obstacles. To cope with the various navigation environments, the rover has two *navigation modes*, which are outlined in Figure 4: a laser-based subsystem for flat terrain, and a vision-based subsystem for rough terrain. The boxes are G^{en}ₒM *modules*, which themselves are constructed from a series of *services* to initialize, execute, and stop hardware drivers. The octagons are *Posters*, which store the data produced by modules and used by other modules or the supervisor. In the following we concentrate on the laser-based subsystem, which builds a map (`Aspect`) using laser scans produced by the `LaserRF` module. The `NDD` module navigates by avoiding obstacles in this map and periodically produces a speed reference from the current position (from `POM`). `RFLEX` controls the wheels of the robot using this speed reference and produces the current position of the robot for `POM`. The mode for rough terrain works similarly but uses images from the stereo cameras. Besides the modules involved in the navigation, there are modules for image capture, camera control, orbiter communication, and power and energy management.

The internals of a generic module are shown in Figure 5. Every module provides services to be invoked by requests. The interface is provided by the *Control Task*, and a *Timer* controls and coordinates the communications between the various entities. In addition, there is at least one scheduler with a Timer to control when a service can be executed. An executable service consists of control and execution units. The control unit decides on the execution of a certain code under the supervision of the scheduler and the interface. The execution unit is used to execute pieces of code and to communicate with hardware drivers related to the functionality of the service. Certain constraints may exist between different services (from the same module or from different modules) in order to satisfy specified requirements (see below and next subsection). Posters also own a Timer to track the age of their data and ensure that only fresh data can be read. For functional safety, DALA needs to implement requirements of the following kind:

Causality: A service can be triggered only after certain services have terminated successfully. As an example, a module that needs specific initialization services will not allow any execution service until these services have been completed.

Interrupt activity: Certain services are not allowed to run concurrently. As an example, we require that pictures are not taken with any high resolution camera while the robot is moving, to prevent high resolution pictures from being blurred (this constraint does not apply to low resolution panoramic pictures). If a service is running and a depending one requires to be triggered, either the former is aborted or the latter is rejected.

Data freshness: Data read from posters needs to be fresh, to prevent a service from reading out-of-date data and making wrong actions. We use a variable *PosterAge* in every Poster to record whether the data inside the poster is fresh or not. E.g., an obstacle reference produced by the `Aspect` module is not fresh if it has not been updated for more than five ticks.

In the next subsections, we present a component-based design methodology to build the various modules of the robot in an incremental manner, and show how to add constraints on the interactions that ensure the requirements. Finally, we use *DFinder* to show that those interactions indeed guarantee the correctness of the robot.

4.2   Module Componentization in *BIP*

In recent work [9,8], we developed a systematic incremental approach to build G^{en}_oM modules of the functional level of the DALA robot in *BIP*. More precisely, we have shown that the control and data flow in the robot arise naturally from the *BIP* language and enforce a clear separation between connection and functional elements. Control flow mechanisms provide requests with arguments passed from one component to another, as well as sending back the results to the requester upon completion. Data flow mechanisms offer access to data produced by one component to another component. We sketch how to build the components of the robot in *BIP* and show how to add the constraints to guarantee the requirements outlined in the previous section.

Building components. By inspecting the structure of a G^{en}_oM module, we have identified ten types of atomic components to be described in the *BIP* language. Those atomic components serve as a library of basic units to build composite components according to the hierarchy of a module (Figure 5) and the hierarchy between modules. Each of those atomic components contains both control flow and C code operations. We demonstrate the modeling process on an example of a G^{en}_oM *execution services*; other services can be encoded in a similar manner. A G^{en}_oM execution service is used to execute certain tasks that are specified by a request. It also checks the validity of the request, and controls the execution of the related code. We separate the control flow and the real code execution flow into the *BIP* components *Service Controller* and *Activity* (see Figure 6). The component *Service Controller* checks the validity of the parameters of the request (if any), and decides if a service shall be executed or aborted. The actual execution of these decisions is performed by the component *Activity*, which updates related posters if necessary. A service is initialized by port *start* and executed by *exec*. The locations

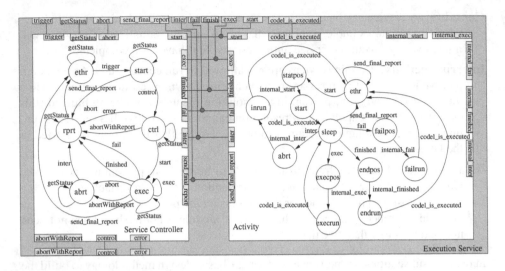

Fig. 6. An Execution Service in DALA

in *Activity* correspond to different execution steps like detection of errors, abort or termination. Interactions or ports are exported to be synchronized with other components according to the requirements.

Adding constraints. Having modeled the components as main building blocks of the system, we use constraints to enforce the requirements presented above. The constraints are implemented using BIP connectors. We illustrate the method using two examples implementing a *causality* and a *data freshness* property. The methods directly extend to the whole group of requirements.

Causality. In module NDD, *SetParams* may only be called when *Init* is successfully finished. This property concerns three components: the internal *Init* and *SetParams* services and the *MessageBox*, which exports the *SetParams* and *rejectSetParams* port to the outside (see also Figure 5). These components communicate through the *Init.getStatus*, *MessageBox.SetParams*, *MessageBox.rejectSetParams* and *SetParams.triggers* ports, which also allow access to the variables in the components. In the following we will sometimes omit the component names for brevity. The simplified definition of the connector is given in Figure 7. Connector *AllowSP* triggers the *SetParams* service ("*do*" clause) only if *getStatus.done* of the *Init* service is true ("*provided*" clause). Otherwise, connector *RejctSP* is enabled and enables *rejectSetParams* in the *Message Box* to reject the request.

Data freshness. When a module tries to read from a poster of certain other modules, the *data freshness* property prevents produced data from being used if the data is not "fresh". E.g., a reference produced by the Aspect module is not "fresh" if it has not been updated for more than five ticks. Variable *PosterAge* keeps track of the time since the last write to the associated Poster. To avoid obstacles, component *Permanent* in the NDD module reads data from component *PolarPoster* in the Aspect module to update the surrounding information. Freshness of the read

connector AllowSP(*getStatus,SetParams, trigger*)
  provided *getStatus.done==true*
  do { *trigger.active=true*}
connector *RejctSP*(*getStatus, rejectSetParams*)
  provided *getStatus.done==false*
  do { *errormsg=INIT-NOT-SET*}

connector *PermSR*(*perm,exec, startread*)
  provided *startread.PosterAge<* 5
  do {}

Fig. 7. Connectors ensuring causality   **Fig. 8.** Connectors ensuring freshness

data is ensured by synchronization of the ports *Scheduler.perm*, *Permanent.exec* and *PolarPoster.startread* as shown in Figure 8.

4.3 Verification

In this section, we report on the validation process conducted with *DFinder*. We focus on the laser-based navigation mode, but similar results can be obtained for the vision-based navigation mode. In Section 4.3.1, we show that the constraints added in the previous section indeed guarantee the requirements introduced in Section 4.1. For doing so, we show how to encode the problem in *DFinder* and then report the results of the tool. In addition to verifying the requirements, we have to make sure that the new constraints did not introduce deadlocks. This problem will be considered in Section 4.3.2. We also show how the design can be refined in the case that *DFinder* finds a violation of the property.

4.3.1 Verification of Safety Properties
To check safety properties, we build the negation of the property and check if there is a state in the invariant computed by *DFinder* which also satisfies this negation. If not, then the property is fulfilled. If there is a state that fulfills the invariant as well as the negation of the property, we have then found a potential violation and need to check if it is reachable.

To illustrate how to check safety properties, we use the causality requirement from the example above. The connectors *AllowSP* and *RejctSP* from Figure 7 involve the two variables *active* and *done* from components *SetParams* and *Init* respectively. We analyze the execution of the components and examine those variables to get a hint of how to write the predicate for this property. We observe the following cases:

1. *Init.done==false* and *SetParams.active==false* when *Init* is not successfully finished.
2. *Init.done==true* and *SetParams.active==false* when *Init* is finished successfully, but there is no request from *SetParams*.
3. *Init.done==true* and *SetParams.active==true* when *Init* is finished successfully, and *Set-Params* is triggered.
4. *Init.done==false* and *SetParams.active==true* when *Init* is re-triggered and aborted while *SetParams* is running.

The last combination is possible because the module allows re-initialization, which could occur during the execution of *SetParams*. During the execution of *Init*, the abort of some services could cause *Init* to be aborted. Then *Init.done* becomes false. This

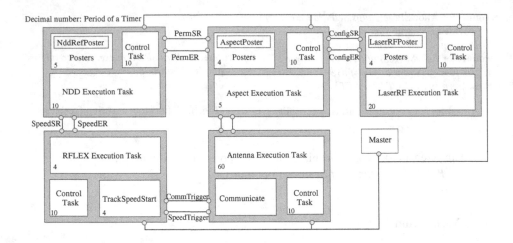

Fig. 9. Interrelation between five modules

behavior prevents us from writing the property purely on the variables, because all the possible combinations are perfectly legal. What we do want to check, however, is that *SetParams* is only *started* in a state where *Init* was executed successfully. To do so, we introduce a new Boolean variable *history* in *SetParams* that is set to true only if *SetParams* was activated when *Init* is done (by adding *trigger.history=true* to the **do** field in *AllowSP* in Fig 7). The property to check is now *active* → *history*, which means that *SetParams* is only active if it was started in a proper state. If the property is false in some state of the system, *SetParams* was started by some connector in an illegal state. *DFinder* took 17 seconds to check that this is not the case and the causality property is satisfied. Observe that when interacting with other modules in the laser-based navigation mode, module NDD will still satisfy the causality requirement. Indeed, using the theory of [5], we observe that adding new constraints between the modules will not falsify the property.

4.3.2   Verification of Deadlock-Freedom
As we have said in Section 4.1, modules LaserRF, Aspect, NDD and RFLEX control the laser-based navigation modes. The relations between the modules are shown in Figure 9. Posters are in charge of data exchange between the modules with the objective of controlling the moves of the robot. More precisely, Aspect reads data from Poster *LaserRFPoster* in LaserRF in order to obtain the surrounding information of the robot to generate a map. Module NDD reads data from Poster *AspectPoster* in module Aspect in order to draw the navigation diagram. Finally, RFLEX obtains the speed reference from Poster *NDDRef* in module NDD to control the wheel. The interactions are in pairs, with a start of reading (similar to the connector in Figure 8) and an end of reading from a poster by some service. In addition to the data shared between different modules, there are also safety requirements between modules RFLEX and Antenna, i.e., the robot can neither move when it is communicating with the orbiter using Antenna, nor communicate with the orbiter when it is moving. In order to take those constraints

into account one has to add two interactions between Execution Service *TrackSpeed-Start* of module RFLEX and Execution Service *Communicate* of module Antenna. The building and verifying process is incremental and local properties are checked as soon as all connectors of the respective layer are added (and exported ports are connected to singleton connectors). Eventually, all five modules of the navigation mode are connected by a global Timer component to control the synchronization of all the Timer components.

As we added extra constraints to guarantee some safety requirements, one also has to check that those constraints do not introduce new deadlocks. Due to the complexity of the interactions between modules, checking for deadlock-freedom is a non trivial process. Since we apply invariants to over-approximate the reachable states, the resulting object may contain false deadlocks that are not reachable. For example, when we update posters in the modules, we will apply a semaphore (*IDS Lock* in Figure 5) to ensure that the operation is *atomic*. The same semaphore is used during the execution of *Execution Services* and *Control Services*. We obtained a deadlock in module Antenna, saying that the semaphore is not occupied when we were updating posters. Therefore, we cannot release it when we try to finish the action. Obviously, the deadlock is not reachable. However, *DFinder* can only remove false deadlocks automatically for finite systems with Boolean variables. The modules in the functional level of DALA robot contain both integer and Boolean variables. We thus have to manually analyze the deadlocks detected by the *DFinder*, and then eventually add invariants that are strong enough to remove those non reachable deadlocks. As it is quite difficult to decide whether a deadlock is false after having composed the five modules, we have first used *DFinder* to remove false deadlocks for each single module. The invariants used in this process have then been used to compute a global interaction invariant for the five modules. As a summary, we conducted the following checks: (1) deadlock-freedom checking on single modules without considering the interrelation between different modules; (2) deadlock-freedom checking between groups of modules by adding interactions between different modules according to data-freshness or interrupt-activity requirements; (3) checking deadlock-freedom of five modules by considering all the constraints over these five modules.

Module NDD contained a deadlock that was caused by the strong synchronization between Timers for *Execution Task*, *Control Task* and *Posters*. It was removed by separating the Timer of *Control Task* from the strong synchronization [8]. We also detected a deadlock between module Aspect and module NDD. This deadlock was caused by thedata-freshness requirement for reading posters. By modifying component *Service Controller* and adding an interaction to deal with the non-fresh data case, we have been able to remove that deadlock. After this correction, we have shown that the flat navigation mode consisting of these five modules is deadlock-free.

Our results are summarized in Table 1 where we show the time consumption in deadlock-freedom checking. *DLcheck new* refers to the latest results. In contrast to previous models (*DLcheck old*), the current version uses a global strategy for the ordering of variables, which helps in finding a good encoding of the model in the underlying data structure of *DFinder*. Moreover, restructuring and improvements in its latest version [10] allow for a better access to the computed invariants to remove false positives

Table 1. Verification times for the DALA robot

module	comps	locs	intrs	vars	states	DLcheck old time	DLcheck new time
RFLEX	56	308	227	35	10^{30}	9:39	3:07
NDD	27	152	117	27	10^{14}	8:16	1:15
LaserRF	43	213	202	29	2.4×10^{21}	1:22	1:04
Aspect	29	160	117	21	1.2×10^{16}	0:39	0:21
Antenna	20	97	73	23	10^{9}	0:14	0:13
Combined	198	926	724	132	2.9×10^{90}	-	5:05

during the incremental computation process, which improves the performance greatly. These optimizations allowed us for the first time to verify all the main modules in parallel. We use *module* for the name of the module; *comps* for the number of components in the module; *locs* for the number of control locations in the module; *intrs* for the number of interactions in the module; *vars* for the number of variables in the modules; *states* for the number of global states in the module; and *time* for the time taken for *DFinder* to return a result.

5 Conclusion

In this paper, we have proposed a new workflow for component-based design of systems. Our approach relies on the powerful language *BIP* that can be used to express the interactions between the various components and define a hierarchy between them. Moreover, BIP can be used to synthesize C/C++ code to coordinate the components by exploiting the interactions. The technique uses *DFinder*, a tool capable of checking the absence of deadlocks by exploiting the hierarchy between the various components. Our methodology has been applied to model, verify and ultimately synthesize the coordination code for an autonomous robot.

There are various directions for future research, such as developing a refinement procedure for false-positive deadlocks in the general setting. Another possibility would be to consider real time in the components. The reader may have observed that although we added constraints to guarantee it (which influence deadlock), we were not able to check the service interruption requirement. Indeed, this would require *DFinder* to reason on executions rather than on states, which the tool cannot currently do.

References

1. Altisen, K., Clodic, A., Maraninchi, F., Rutten, E.: Using controller synthesis to build property-enforcing layers. In: ESOP, pp. 174–188 (April 2003)
2. Amnell, T., Fersman, E., Pettersson, P., Yi, W., Sun, H.: Code synthesis for timed automata. Nordic J. of Computing 9, 269–300 (2002)
3. Ball, T., Cook, B., Levin, V., Rajamani, S.K.: SLAM and static driver verifier: Technology transfer of formal methods inside microsoft. In: Boiten, E.A., Derrick, J., Smith, G.P. (eds.) IFM 2004. LNCS, vol. 2999, pp. 1–20. Springer, Heidelberg (2004)
4. Basu, A., Bozga, M., Sifakis, J.: Modeling heterogeneous real-time components in BIP. In: ICSEFM, pp. 3–12 (2006)

5. Bensalem, S., Bozga, M., Legay, A., Nguyen, T.-H., Sifakis, J., Yan, R.: Incremental component-based construction and verification using invariants. In: FMCAD, pp. 257–265 (2010)

6. Bensalem, S., Bozga, M., Nguyen, T.-H., Sifakis, J.: D-finder: A tool for compositional deadlock detection and verification. In: Bouajjani, A., Maler, O. (eds.) CAV 2009. LNCS, vol. 5643, pp. 614–619. Springer, Heidelberg (2009)

7. Bensalem, S., Bozga, M., Sifakis, J., Nguyen, T.-H.: Compositional verification for component-based systems and application. In: Cha, S(S.), Choi, J.-Y., Kim, M., Lee, I., Viswanathan, M. (eds.) ATVA 2008. LNCS, vol. 5311, pp. 64–79. Springer, Heidelberg (2008)

8. Bensalem, S., de Silva, L., Gallien, M., Ingrand, F., Yan, R.: "Rock solid" software: A verifiable and correct by construction controller for rover and spacecraft functional layers. In: ISAIRAS, pp. 859–866 (2010)

9. Bensalem, S., Gallien, M.: Toward a more dependable software architecture for autonomous robots. Special issue on Software Engineering for Robotics of the IEEE RAM 16(1), 1–11 (2009)

10. Bensalem, S., Griesmayer, A., Legay, A., Nguyen, T.-H., Sifakis, J., Yan, R.: D-Finder 2: Towards Efficient Correctness of Incremental Design. In: Bobaru, M., Havelund, K., Holzmann, G.J., Joshi, R. (eds.) NFM 2011. LNCS, vol. 6617, pp. 453–458. Springer, Heidelberg (2011)

11. Bensalem, S., Legay, A., Nguyen, T.-H., Sifakis, J., Yan, R.: Incremental invariant generation for compositional design. In: TASE, pp. 157–167 (2010)

12. Beyer, D., Henzinger, T.A., Jhala, R., Majumdar, R.: The software model checker BLAST: Applications to software engineering. STTT 9(5-6), 505–525 (2007)

13. BIP Framework,
   http://www-verimag.imag.fr/
   Rigorous-Design-of-Component-Based.html

14. Bonakdarpour, B., Bozga, M., Jaber, M., Quilbeuf, J., Sifakis, J.: From high-level component-based models to distributed implementations. In: EMSOFT, pp. 209–218 (2010)

15. Boussinot, F., de Simone, R.: The ESTEREL Language. Proceeding of the IEEE, 1293–1304 (1991)

16. Bozga, M., Jaber, M., Sifakis, J.: Source-to-source architecture transformation for performance optimization in bip. In: SIES, pp. 152–160 (2009)

17. Bruyninckx, H.: Open robot control software: the orocos project. In: ICRA, Seoul, Korea, pp. 2523–2528 (2001)

18. Espiau, B., Kapellos, K., Jourdan, M.: Formal verification in robotics: Why and how. In: IFRR, editor, The Seventh International Symposium of Robotics Research, Munich, pp. 201–213. Cambridge Press (1995)

19. Fleury, S., Herrb, M., Chatila, R.: $G^{en}{}_{o}M$: A tool for the specification and the implementation of operating modules in a distributed robot architecture. In: IROS, pp. 842–848 (1997)

20. $G^{en}{}_{o}M$, http://www.openrobots.org/wiki/genom

21. Goldman, R.P., Musliner, D.J., Pelican, M.J.: Using model checking to plan hard real-time controllers. In: Proc. of AIPS Workshop on Model-Theoretic Approaches to Planning (2000)

22. Henzinger, T.A., Jhala, R., Majumdar, R., Sutre, G.: Lazy abstraction. In: POPL, pp. 58–70. ACM, New York (2002)

23. Ingrand, F., Lacroix, S., Lemai, S., Py, F.: Decisional autonomy of planetary rovers. Journal of Field Robotics 24(7), 559–580 (2007)

24. Jackson, J.: Microsoft robotics studio: A technical introduction. IEEE RAM 14(4), 82–87 (2007)

25. Montemerlo, M., Roy, N., Thrun, S.: Perspectives on standardization in mobile robot programming: The carnegie mellon navigation (carmen) toolkit. In: Proc. IEEE/RSJ Int. Conf. Intelligent Robots and Systems, Las Vegas, NV, pp. 2436–2441 (2003)
26. Nesnas, I.A., Wright, A., Bajracharya, M., Simmons, R., Estlin, T.: Claraty and challenges of developing interoperable robotic software. In: IROS, Las Vegas, NV (October 2003) invited paper
27. Quigley, M., Gerkey, B., Conley, K., Faust, J., Foote, T., Leibs, J., Berger, E., Wheeler, R., Ng, A.: Ros: an open-source robot operating system. In: International Conference on Robotics and Automation, Kobe, Japan (2009)
28. Thiele, L., Bacivarov, I., Haid, W., Huang, K.: Mapping applications to tiled multiprocessor embedded systems. In: ACSD, pp. 29–40. IEEE, Los Alamitos (2007)
29. Vaughan, R., Gerkey, B.: Reusable robot software and the player/stage project. In: Software Engineering for Experimental Robotics, pp. 267–289 (2007)
30. Williams, B.C., Ingham, M.D., Chung, S., Elliott, P., Hofbaur, M., Sullivan, G.T.: Model-Based Programming of Fault-Aware Systems. In: AI, pp. 61–75 winter (2003)

Towards Incremental Cycle Analysis in ESMoL Distributed Control System Models

Joseph Porter, Daniel Balasubramanian, Graham Hemingway,
and János Sztipanovits

Institute for Software Integrated Systems,
Vanderbilt University,
Nashville TN 37212, USA
jporter@isis.vanderbilt.edu
http://www.isis.vanderbilt.edu

Abstract. We consider the problem of incremental cycle analysis for dataflow models in the Embedded Systems Modeling Language (ESMoL). This is an example of a syntactic property which does not lend itself to compositional analysis. We give a general form of a cycle enumeration algorithm that makes use of graph hierarchy to improve analysis efficiency. Our framework also stores simple connectivity information in the model to accelerate future cycle analyses when additional components are added or modifications are made. An extended version of this work gives a mapping from a term algebraic model of the ESMoL component model and logical dataflow sublanguages to the analysis framework, and an evaluation on a fixed-wing aircraft controller model[7]. Integrated cycle analysis aids well-formedness checking during model construction in the ESMoL tool suite.

Keywords: model-based design, embedded systems, model analysis.

1 Introduction

High confidence embedded control system software designs often require formal analyses to ensure design correctness. Detailed models of system behavior include numerous design concerns such as controller stability, timing requirements, fault tolerance, and deadlock freedom. Models for each of these domains must together provide a consistent and faithful representation of the potential problems an operational system would face. This poses challenges for structural representation of models, as components and design aspects are commonly tightly coupled. The ESMoL embedded software design language is built on a platform which provides inherent correctness properties for well-formed models. We rely on decoupling methods such as passive control design (decoupling controller stability from network effects) and time-triggered models of computation (decoupling timing and fault tolerance from functional requirements) and on compositional and incremental analysis to enable rapid prototyping in our design environment. As design paradigms become more fully decoupled and analysis becomes faster

S. Apel and E. Jackson (Eds.): SC 2011, LNCS 6708, pp. 133–140, 2011.

(and therefore cheaper), we move closer to the goal of "correct by construction" model-based software development.

In compositional analysis for graphical software models, sometimes the nature of the analysis does not easily lead to a clean syntactic decomposition in the models. Examples include end-to-end properties such as latency, and other properties which require the evaluation of particular connections spanning multiple levels of components. One approach for dealing with such properties in hierarchical dataflow designs is the creation of interface data for each component which abstracts properties of that component. Hierarchical schedulability models defined over dataflows are a particular example[9] – each composite task contains a resource interface characterizing the aggregate supply required to schedule the task and all of its children. Extensions to the formalism allow the designer to efficiently and incrementally evaluate whether new tasks can be admitted to the design without recomputing the full analysis[3]. One goal is to see whether this approach can be generalized to other properties that do not easily fit the compositional structure of hierarchical designs.

One particular syntactic analysis problem concerns synchronous execution environments and system assembly. In dataflow models of computation we are often concerned with so-called "algebraic" or delay-free processing loops in a design model. Many synchronous formalisms require the absence of delay-free loops in order to guarantee deadlock freedom [1] or timing determinism [5]. This condition can be encoded structurally into dataflow modeling languages – for example Simulink [11] analyzes models for algebraic loops and attempts to resolve them analytically. In our work we only consider the structural problem of loop detection in model-based distributed embedded system designs.

We propose a simple incremental cycle enumeration technique for ESMoL:

- The algorithm uses Johnson's simple cycle enumeration algorithm as its core engine[4]. Johnson's algorithm is known to be efficient [6]. We use cycle enumeration in order to provide detailed feedback to designers.
- The algorithm exploits the component structure of hierarchical dataflow models to allow the cycle enumeration to scale up to larger models. A small amount of interface data is created and stored for each component as the analysis processes the model hierarchy from the bottom up. The interface data consists of a set of typed graph edges indicating whether dataflow paths exist between each of the component's input/output pairs. Each component is evaluated for cycles using the interface data instead of the detailed dataflow connections of its child components.
- The interface data facilitates incremental analysis, as it also contains a flag to determine whether modifications have been made to the component. We refer to the flag and the connectivity edges as an *incremental interface* for the component. This is consistent with the use of the concept in other model analysis domains, such as compositional scheduling analysis[3]. In order for the incremental method to assist our development processes, the total runtime for all partial assessments of the model should be no greater than the analysis running on the full model. Because the amount of interface data

supporting the incremental analysis is small, the method should scale to large designs without imposing onerous data storage requirements on the model.

– The technique will not produce false positive cycle reports, though it may compress multiple cycles into a single cycle through the interface abstraction. Fortunately, full cycles can be recovered from the abstract cycles through application of the enumeration algorithm on a much smaller graph.

Zhou and Lee presented an algebraic formalism for detecting causality cycles in dataflow graphs, identifying particular ports that participate in a cycle. [14]. Our method traverses the entire model and extracts all elementary cycles, reporting all ports and subsystems involved in each cycle. Our approach is also inspired by work from Tripakis et al, which creates a richer incremental interface for components to capture execution granularity as well as potential deadlock information[13]. Their approach is much more complex in both model space and computation than our approach. Our formalism does not aim to pull semantic information forward into the interface beyond connectivity. In that sense our approach is more general, as it could be applied to multiple model analysis problems in the embedded systems design domain.

2 Background

A number of frameworks and techniques contributed to our solution:

ESMoL Component Model: As the ESMoL language structure is documented elsewhere[8], we only cover details relevant to incremental cycle checking. ES-MoL is a graphical modeling language which allows designers to use Simulink diagrams as synchronous software function specifications (where the execution of each block is equivalent to a single bounded-time blocking C language call). These specifications are used to create blocks representing ESMoL component types. ESMoL components have message structures as interfaces, and the type specification includes a map between Simulink signal ports and the fields of the input and output message structures. The messages represent C structures, and the map graphically captures the marshaling of Simulink data to those structures. ESMoL and its tools provide design concepts and functions for specifying logical architecture and deployment, and performing scheduling analysis.

In ESMoL a designer can include Simulink references from parts of an imported dataflow model, and instantiate them any number of times within the type definitions. ESMoL tasks can distribute functions over a time-triggered network for performance, or replicate similar functions for fault mitigation. This level of flexibility requires automatic type-checking to ensure compatibility for chosen configurations. Beyond interface type-checking, structural well-formedness problems arise during assembly such as zero-delay cycles.

Cycle Enumeration: To implement cycle enumeration we use the algorithm Johnson proposed as an extension of Tiernan's algorithm [12] for enumerating elementary cycles in a directed graph[4]. Both approaches rely on depth-first search with backtracking, but Johnson's method marks vertices on elementary paths already considered to eliminate fruitless searching, unmarking them when a cycle is found. Johnson's algorithm is polynomial ($O((n+e)c)$, where n, e, and c are the sizes of the vertex, edge, and cycle set, respectively), and is considered the best available general cycle enumeration method[6]. We implemented Johnson's algorithm in C++ using the Boost Graph library [10].

Hierarchical Graphs: As a notation for describing our incremental approach we use the algebra of hierarchical graphs introduced by Bruni et al[2]. We will only give a summary of some of the notation here for brevity. The interested reader can refer to [7] (and [2]) for a more detailed account.

$$\mathbb{D} ::= L_{\bar{x}}[\mathbb{G}] \tag{1}$$
$$\mathbb{G} ::= \mathbf{0} \mid x \mid l < \bar{x} > \mid \mathbb{G} \parallel \mathbb{G} \mid (\nu\bar{x})\mathbb{G} \mid \mathbb{D} < \bar{x} >$$

Intuitively, Equation 1 is a grammar defining a simple textual notation for describing typed hierarchical graphs. Within the formalism we can compare equivalence between algebraic descriptions of two hierarchical graphs using reduction rules and a normal form (as in Bruni[2]), though equivalence is beyond the scope of this publication. The algebraic properties are for future use. The other main attraction of this particular formalism is that the notation allows the definition of interface symbols which correspond easily to port objects in a dataflow language, and the hiding of those interfaces as we specialize types. The notation is a compact shorthand for much larger diagrams or mathematical descriptions. The rule $\mathbb{D}$ corresponds to composite types in our dataflow language (which may have other composites as children). The specification for a composite element is $L_{\bar{x}}[\mathbb{G}]$, which means that an element of $\mathbb{D}$ has type L and interface vertices in the list $\bar{x}$ and a corresponding internal graph $\mathbb{G}$ defining the details of the component. The internal graph may also include subcomponents. Gluing of subgraphs only occurs at common vertices. When a composite element from $\mathbb{D}$ of a particular type is used as a child element to form a larger (parent) graph, vertices from the child are possibly renamed in the parent, hence the notation $\mathbb{D} < \bar{x} >$. In a parallel composition, vertices with the same name x are glued together. Finally $[\![\mathbb{G}]\!]$ indicates the graph corresponding to the expression $\mathbb{G}$.

3   Incremental Cycle Analysis

Our intention is to support a design and analysis work flow that includes incremental analysis steps. For example, a designer may analyze part of the design before integrating it into a larger part of the system. In our work flow, we envision storing the results of that first analysis along with some interface data to reduce the cost of the second analysis. The same should hold true for the system design. We should be able to analyze the system design efficiently, calculating incremental analysis interfaces. When the system models are revised, whether by adding, removing, or modifying components we can isolate the effects of the change on the cost of the analysis.

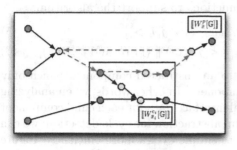 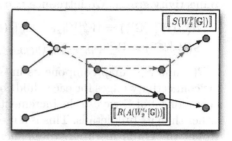

(a) Generic hierarchical graph   (b) Abstract graph

Fig. 1. Simple graph example

Let $\mathbb{G}$ be a well-formed hierarchical graph (as in Bruni [2]). To get more comfortable with the notation, first note that graph $\mathbb{G}$ itself (without hierarchical structure) can be described by the expression:

$$\mathbb{G} = (\| \ x) \ \| \ (\|_{(u,v)\in\mathcal{E}} \ l < u, v >) \tag{2}$$

which is the parallel composition of the graphs induced by individual edges of $\mathbb{G}$, merged at their common vertices.

Let $C(\mathbb{G})$ be the set of elementary cycles in $\mathbb{G}$, and let $P(\mathbb{G}, u, v)$ be the subgraph of $\mathbb{G}$ containing all of the paths from vertex u to vertex v.

Consider a set of components of type W. Let $W_{\bar{x}}^p[G]$ represent a component object in a graph hierarchy with interface vertices $\bar{x}$, and let $W_{\bar{x}_i}^{c_i}[G]$ be the children of W^p ($[\![W^{c_i}]\!] \subset [\![W^p]\!]$) with their respective interface vertices $(\bar{x}_i)$. Then neglecting vertex hiding and renaming to simplify the illustration, we have the following:

$$W_{\bar{x}}^p[\mathbb{G}] = W_{\bar{x}}^p[(\|_h \ x_h) \ \| \ (\|_{(j,k)} \ l < j, k >) \ \| \ (\|_i \ W_{\bar{x}_i}^{c_i}[\mathbb{G}])] \tag{3}$$

Eq. 3 describes the component W^p in terms of its component children W^{c_i}, internal vertices x_h, and edges $l < j, k >$. Fig. 1a gives a simple example of a hierarchical graph with one child component and one cycle which includes vertices and edges within the child component (dashed links).

We introduce a new type of edge l_c into the model, which is used to connect vertices at the boundaries of a component, abstracting the interface connectivity of the component. Introduce a new mapping $A : \mathcal{D} \to \mathcal{D}'$ from the components of $\mathbb{G}$ to components in a new graph $\mathbb{G}'$. $\mathbb{G}'$ is identical to $\mathbb{G}$, but adds the new edge label. This is the interface that we will use for incremental cycle analysis.

$$A(W_{\bar{x}_i}^{c_i}[\mathbb{G}]) = W_{\bar{x}_i}^{c_i}[(\|_h \ x_h) \ \| \ (\|_{(j,k)\in\lfloor\bar{x}_i\rfloor\wedge P(\mathbb{G},j,k)\neq\emptyset} \ l_c < j, k >) \tag{4}$$
$$\| \ (\|_{(j,k)} \ l < j, k >) \ \| \ (\|_m \ W_{\bar{x}_m}^{c_m}[\mathbb{G}])])]$$

In this abstraction function the child components are replaced by a much simpler connectivity graph. We introduce two functions to support the algorithm:

$$R(A(W_{\bar{x}}^{c_i}[\mathbb{G}])) = W_{\bar{x}_i}^{c_i}[(\|_{x \in \bar{x}_i} x) \| (\|_{(j,k) \in l_c} l_c < j, k >)] \tag{5}$$

$$S(W_{\bar{x}}^{p}[\mathbb{G}]) = W_{\bar{x}}^{p}[(\|_h x_h) \| (\|_{(j,k) \in \lfloor \bar{x} \rfloor} l < j, k >) \| (\|_i R(A(W_{\bar{x}_i}^{c_i}[\mathbb{G}])))] \tag{6}$$

$R(\cdot)$ and $S(\cdot)$ map components in $\mathbb{G}$ to an abstracted component which only has connectivity edges for each child component. In other words, when analyzing a component of $\mathbb{G}$ we use the incremental interface data for each child component rather than its full details. This is a useful abstraction for cycle detection: we can exploit the graph hierarchy to enumerate simple cycles more efficiently. Figure 1b gives an example of the transformation defined by $A(\cdot)$, $R(\cdot)$, and $S(\cdot)$. The child graph is replaced by its abstracted correspondent, which only preserves connectivity between interface vertices in the child component.

Assume we have a function FINDALLCYCLES : $\mathbb{G} \to 2^{\mathbb{G}}$ which enumerates all elementary cycles in a graph $\mathbb{G}$, returning sets of subgraphs. Then Algorithm 1. adapts the general algorithm FINDALLCYCLES to the hierarchical graph structure described above. We assume that $\mathbb{G}$ has a unique root component, and that we have a function $modified : \mathbb{D} \to boolean$ which indicates whether a particular hierarchical component has been modified since the last run. New components in the model are considered modified by default.

The runtime for the extended algorithm should be slightly worse than Johnson's algorithm in the worst case, as it must also compute the interface graphs. In the average case the cycle checking proceeds on graphs much smaller than the global graph, offsetting the cost of finding paths in each subgraph. Further, if the incremental interface edges are stored in the model following the analysis, then scalability is enhanced when incrementally adding functions to a design. Cycle analysis is then restricted to the size of the new components together with the stored interfaces.

Algorithm 1. Hierarchical cycle detection

1: $cycles \leftarrow []$
2: $ifaces \leftarrow \{\}$
3: **function** FINDHCYCLES($[\![W_{\bar{x}}^{p}[\mathbb{G}]]\!]$)
4:    **for all** $W_{\bar{x}_i}^{c_i}[\mathbb{G}] \in W_{\bar{x}}^{p}[\mathbb{G}]$ **do**
5:       FINDHCYCLES($[\![W_{\bar{x}_i}^{c_i}[\mathbb{G}]]\!]$)
6:    **end for**
7:    $modified(W_{\bar{x}}^{p}[\mathbb{G}]) \leftarrow (modified(W_{\bar{x}}^{p}[\mathbb{G}]) \vee (\vee_{c_i} modified(W_{\bar{x}_i}^{c_i}[\mathbb{G}]))$
8:    **if** $modified(W_{\bar{x}}^{p}[\mathbb{G}])$ **then**
9:       $T \leftarrow [\![S(W_{\bar{x}}^{p}[\mathbb{G}])]\!]$
10:      $cycles \leftarrow [cycles; \text{FINDALLCYCLES}(T)]$
11:      $ifaces[p] \leftarrow A(T)$
12:   **end if**
13: **end function**
14: FINDHCYCLES($\mathbb{G}$)

- (Lines 1-2) Initialize a list to hold the resulting cycles, and an associative list to contain the component interface data.
- (Lines 3-6) Perform a depth-first search on the hierarchical graph, recursively visiting all of the child components ($W_{\bar{x}_i}^{c_i}[\mathbb{G}]$) for the current (parent) component ($W_{\bar{x}}^p[\mathbb{G}]$).
- (Line 7) The modification status is propagated up the hierarchy as the algorithm progresses. Each component which has a modified child will also be marked as modified.
- (Lines 8-12) If the current component has been modified, we use the previously computed incremental connectivity interface for each subcomponent to check for cycles in the current component – the connectivity graph interface is substituted for each subcomponent. The cycles are accumulated as the algorithm ascends to the top of the model, and a connectivity interface is created for the current component before returning.

4   ESMoL Language Mapping

To find delay-free loops for a given ESMoL model, we must first map a well-formed ESMoL model to the generic hierarchical graph model (as in [7]), remove all delay elements from the model, and then invoke the algorithm. For any cycle found in a component we can construct a more detailed cycle by substituting paths using the connectivity edges with their more detailed equivalents in the descendants of the component (recursively descending downwards until we run out of cycle elements). Call this subgraph the *expanded cycle*. Repeating the cycle enumeration algorithm on these structures yields the full set of elementary cycles, and should still retain considerable efficiency as we are only analyzing cycles with possible subcycles, which can be a relatively small slice of the design graph. [7] includes an example.

5   Conclusion

One interesting observation is the generality of the approach. Algorithm 1. very nearly captures a generic procedure for bottom-up incremental syntactic analysis of hierarchical graphical models. Note that two small contributions may emerge from this observation 1) we have a structure to which we can adapt some other model analysis techniques for incremental operation, if an appropriate component interface can be found for the particular analysis in question, and 2) this approach could lead to a tool for efficiently specifying such analyses, from which we could generate software code to implement the analysis.

Acknowledgements

This work is sponsored in part by the National Science Foundation (grant NSF-CCF-0820088) and by the Air Force Office of Scientific Research, USAF (grant/contract number FA9550-06-0312).

References

1. Benveniste, A., Caspi, P., di Natale, M., Pinello, C., Sangiovanni-Vincentelli, A., Tripakis, S.: Loosely time-triggered architectures based on communication-by-sampling. In: EMSOFT 2007: Proc. of the 7th ACM & IEEE Intl. Conf. on Embedded Software, pp. 231–239. ACM, New York (2007)
2. Bruni, R., Gadducci, F., Lafuente, A.L.: An Algebra of Hierarchical Graphs and Its Application to Structural Encoding. Scientific Annals of Computer Science 20, 53–96 (2010)
3. Easwaran, A.: Advances in hierarchical real-time systems: Incrementality, optimality, and multiprocessor clustering. Ph.D. thesis, Univ. of Pennsylvania (2008)
4. Johnson, D.B.: Finding all the elementary circuits of a directed graph. SIAM J. Comput. 4(1), 77–84 (1975)
5. Lee, E.A., Messerschmitt, D.G.: Synchronous data flow. Proc. of the IEEE 75(9), 1235–1245 (1987)
6. Mateti, P., Deo, N.: On algorithms for enumerating all circuits of a graph. SIAM J. Comput. 5(1), 90–99 (1976)
7. Porter, J., Balasubramanian, D., Hemingway, G., Sztipanovits, J.: Towards Incremental Cycle Analysis in ESMoL Distributed Control System Models (Extended Version) (April 2011), http://www.isis.vanderbilt.edu/sites/default/files/incr_cycle_analysis.pdf
8. Porter, J., Hemingway, G., Nine, H., vanBuskirk, C., Kottenstette, N., Karsai, G., Sztipanovits, J.: The ESMoL Language and Tools for High-Confidence Distributed Control Systems Design. Part 1: Language, Framework, and Analysis (September 2010), http://www.isis.vanderbilt.edu/sites/default/files/ESMoL_TR.pdf
9. Shin, I.: Compositional Framework for Real-Time Embedded Systems. Ph.D. thesis, Univ. of Pennsylvania, Philadelphia (2006)
10. Siek, J.G., Lee, L.Q., Lumsdaine, A.: The Boost Graph Library: User Guide and Reference Manual. Addison-Wesley Professional, Reading (2001)
11. The MathWorks, Inc.: Simulink/Stateflow Tools, http://www.mathworks.com
12. Tiernan, J.C.: An efficient search algorithm to find the elementary circuits of a graph. Commun. ACM 13, 722–726 (1970), http://doi.acm.org/10.1145/362814.362819
13. Tripakis, S., Bui, D., Geilen, M., Rodiers, B., Lee, E.A.: Compositionality in Synchronous Data Flow: Modular Code Generation from Hierarchical SDF Graphs. Tech. Rep. UCB/EECS-2010-52, Univ. of California, Berkeley (2010)
14. Zhou, Y., Lee, E.: Causality interfaces for actor networks. ACM Trans. on Emb. Computing Systems 7(3) (April 2008)

Assuring Architectural Properties during Compositional Architecture Design

Constanze Deiters and Andreas Rausch

Department of Informatics – Software Systems Engineering
Clausthal University of Technology
Julius-Albert-Str. 4, 38678 Clausthal-Zellerfeld, Germany
{constanze.deiters,andreas.rausch}@tu-clausthal.de
http://sse.in.tu-clausthal.de

Abstract. Nowadays, software architectures are built by reusing proven architectural building blocks. The several building blocks are composed together to form the desired software architecture. Each block has its specific architectural properties which were maybe also responsible for its choice. But these properties could be violated during composition with impact on the architecture's quality. Therefore, this paper proposes an approach to assure architectural properties of architectural building blocks during the compositional design of software architectures. This approach describes properties of architectural building blocks as assurances. Assurances as well as the descriptions of architectural building blocks themselves are formalised in the same way. Furthermore, the assurances of the chosen architectural building blocks are examined in composed architectures.

Keywords: Software Architecture, Architecture Composition, Architectural Building Block.

1 Introduction

A software architecture defines the basic organization of a system by structuring the different software elements and the relationships between them [1]. With increasing dimension of a software system also its architecture's dimension and complexity increase. To handle this complexity software architectures are composed of **architectural building blocks** (ABBs), which summarize joint architectural elements and their relationships under abstract entities [2]. Such ABBs are approved templates like architectural patterns, architectural principles and reference architectures:

- *Architectural pattern.* The solution part of a pattern defines roles for architectural elements and dependencies between them. Examples of architectural patterns are the Layers pattern or the Pipes and Filter pattern [3].
- *Architectural principle.* Architectural principles are architectural rules which are applied cross-cutting to the decomposition structure. They can be applied

S. Apel and E. Jackson (Eds.): SC 2011, LNCS 6708, pp. 141–148, 2011.

globally to the whole architecture as well as only on single components. An example of an architectural principle is the separation of business and technical concerns [4].

- *Reference architecture.* Reference architectures describe a mapping of divided functionality onto the parts of a system [1]. An example is the 3-Layer Architecture [5] with the separation of data, application and presentation functionality and the mapping to the corresponding layers.

In its capacity as framework for further design and implementation a software architecture has an high impact on the quality of the software system [6]. Accordingly, ABBs forming an intended architecture has also to be chosen depending on how well their properties meet desired quality requirements. For this purpose, Herold et al. [7] proposed to choose the different building blocks based on GOAL models. Required properties are derived from high-level requirements. ABBs with suited properties are chosen from a repository and are composed to architecture alternatives. Similar, but on the level of design patterns, Gross and Yu [8] and Araujo and Weiss [9] use the non-functional requirements (NFR) framework to build a force hierarchy for each design pattern and map properties of these patterns to functional and non-functional aspects of the system.

These approaches are suited to choose appropriate ABBs. But composing selected ABBs could lead to conflicts in the resulting architecture because these ABBs maybe have contradictory properties. Hence, the aim of this work is to provide a seamless approach for composing software architectures out of ABBs which avoid defective composition results by checking them against ABBs and their properties. As a result, this approach can support software architects during architectural design to compose ABBs.

The remaining paper is structured as following: Section 2 describes the fundamental problem of composing architectural building blocks. Basic notions and first ideas are represented in Section 3. This problem and its solution are touching different fields of related work over which Section 4 gives an overview. Section 5 concludes this paper and gives an outlook on further work.

2   Problem Statement

ABBs - architectural patterns, architectural principles or reference architectures - by themselves are not software architectures. As aforementioned, they rather serve as proven solution templates to recurring problems of architecture design. To create a software architecture a software architect chooses ABBs according to the system's needs and composes them.

The structure of the ABB *Layers Pattern* is shown in Figure 1. Both layers, *lowerLayer* and *upperLayer*, are arranged hierarchically, whereby the dependency between them is directed from *upperLayer* to *lowerLayer*. This unidirectional dependency from the upper to the lower layer is one essential property of this pattern and drives to some advantages. For example, exchanging the implementation of a layer does not affect layers above. Additionally, correct usage of the ABB *Layers Pattern* shall avoid cyclic dependencies between layers.

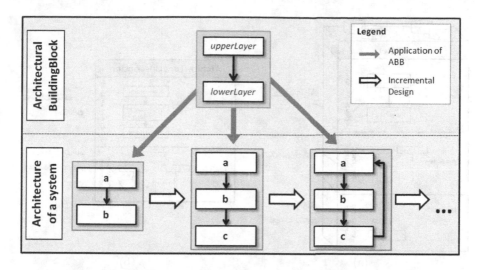

Fig. 1. Multiple application of ABB *Layers Pattern* during incremental design

Assuming, this ABB is applied stepwise and repeatedly to create a software architecture with the three layers *a*, *b* and *c* and the resulting dependencies as depicted in the lower part of Figure 1. Then, the last application of this ABB creates a dependency from layer *c* to layer *a* and leads to a cyclic dependency in this example architecture. Hence, the essential property of the ABB *Layer Pattern* - noncyclic dependencies - is not valid and the advantages of the ABB can no more be warranted.

This simple example illustrates the fundamental problem, we are faced to in this work: architects choose ABBs based on their architectural properties which the ABBs assure when considered in isolation. Out of selected ABBs the architect composes a software architecture. During ABB composing especially the properties which guide the ABB choice could be violated. Therefore, the proposed approach in this paper aims at how ABB can be composed with guaranteeing at the same time that their properties also hold in the composed architecture.

3   Overview of the Approach

In this approach an ABB is represented by a formalised ***structure description*** as well as a formalised ***behaviour description***. To describe structure and behaviour of an ABB, ***ABB roles*** and ***ABB relationships*** are introduced, for example, the two layers named *upperLayer* and *lowerLayer* and the use relationship from *upperLayer* to *lowerLayer*, respectively (see Figure 2a). As explained in Section 2, it is important to preserve the architectural properties of the single ABBs during the compositional design of software architectures. These properties are therefore described as ***ABB assurances*** within an additional ***assurance description***. For example, such an assurance is the absence of cycles between layers of the *Layers Pattern*.

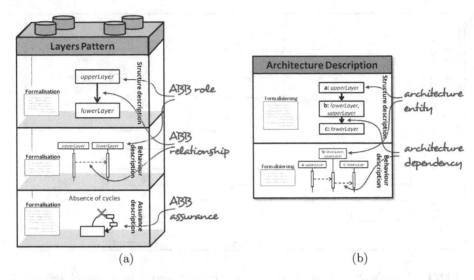

(a)   (b)

Fig. 2. Concept of an architectural building block (ABB) with description separation into structure, behaviour and assurance (a); concept of an architecture description with separation into structure and behaviour (b)

A concrete architecture is also represented by a formalised **structure description** as well as a formalised **behaviour description**. Similar to an ABB description an **architecture description** consists of different notational elements: **architecture entities**, for example, the layers a, b and c, and **architecture dependencies**, for example, between the layers a and b or b and c (see Figure 2b).

Software architectures are now created stepwise by applying ABB by ABB. ABB roles and relationships are taken on by architecture entities and dependencies, respectively (ABB instantiation). Instantiating ABB roles and relationships implies ABB structure and behaviour to the corresponding architecture elements.

Thereby, an architecture entity can at the same time assume roles of several (different or equal) ABBs. As a result the corresponding ABBs are not only instantiated but also composed. Such a composition result is depicted in Figure 2b: ABB *Layers Pattern* from Figure 2a was two times applied in such a way that the architecture entity b is an instance of the ABB roles *lowerLayer* as well as *upperLayer*. In our approach we call this combination of composition and instantiation **instance composition**.

ABBs can also be used to describe architectures at different levels of detail by applying **hierarchical composition**. This means, that an instance of one ABB or an instance composition of several ABBs specifies the interior of an already existing architecture entity.

According to our proposed approach, a software architecture is created stepwise with examining after every step the assurance of architectural properties owned by applied ABBs (see Figure 3): an architect chooses ABB by ABB from an ABB repository and assembles the selected by instance or hierarchical

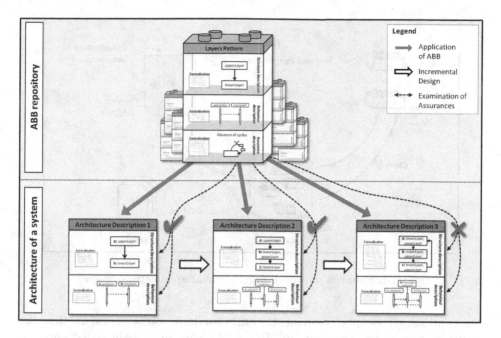

Fig. 3. Instance composition of ABBs and examination of assurances

composition. After each composition the architectural assurances of all applied
ABBs are examined once again. Thereby, this procedure exploits the formalised
descriptions of ABBs, their instantiations and assurances which are related by
preceding compositions. Violations of assurances can be discovered in this way
and presented to the architect. The architect is now able to decide whether this
violation is acceptable or not. In the later case he has to change the architecture
so that no violations are left behind.

This presented approach is embedded into a seamless process (see Figure 4)
for architectural design. ABBs and their assurances are formalised and stored
within a repository. According to the needs of the intended system architecture
suitable ABBs are chosen and composed by instance or hierarchical composition.
These compositions can result in a complete architecture or even an incomplete
architecture which needs to be composed with further ABBs to get finished.
However, results of this approach can be stored as new ABBs into the repository
and can be reused within another architecture design.

4   Related Work

Elaborating an approach for the problem illustrated in Section 2 covers a lot of
different areas of research within the software architecture community. An architecture is characterised by its structural elements and also by the behaviour
of its parts. Therefore, an adequate description language needs to handle both.
Common architecture description languages (ADLs) usually define at least the

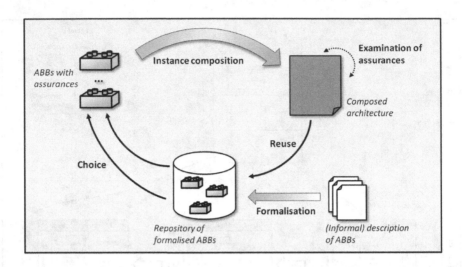

Fig. 4. Seamless process of compositional architecture design

three primary concepts component, connector and configuration to describe structure as well as behaviour [10]. But ADLs vary in their intended purpose, for example, focusing on distinct system categories or following certain programming languages and their paradigms [11,10,12].

Important for the approach proposed in this paper is the ability to describe an ABB as a kind of template which combines different components, connectors and so on. Furthermore, to build software architectures these templates need to instantiate and to compose. Most ADLs do not explicit support template mechanism or even support only distinct architectural patterns [13,14]. Only a few ADLs, like WRIGHT [15] or Alloy [16], offer an explicit template mechanisms but with the limitation that an architecture can base on just one template.

The ability to implement only one ABB at the same time requires combining ABBs first on an abstract level with, for example, defining new merged ABB elements. Even then the new ABBs can be instantiated. This procedure is also followed by [17]. Other approaches treat applied instantiated ABBs as separate parts of an architecture which are coupled by connectors [18,19,17]. Only considering this kind of composition does not allow overlapping ABB elements, like an architecture entity assumes roles from different ABBs. But this does not represent reality in software architectures. Similar to the aforementioned strategy another strategy composing architectures from ABBs is to handle instantiated ABBs as own subsystems which are linked by connectors [18,19]. But, this also does not allow overlapping ABBs as in the case before. Additionally, the architectural elements which are bind to ABB elements are settled on a lower decomposition level. Description approaches which consider ABB elements as role [20,21] prevent the mentioned shortcomings. They allow that architectural entities belong to instances of different ABBs by assuming multiple roles and that instantiated ABBs can be intertwined.

Furthermore, ABBs also specify assurances which constrain their usage. An appropriate formalism has to include structure and behaviour elements and has to have sufficient expressive power. Constraints can be expressed in a lot of ADLs but with varying expressive power. Furthermore, these constraints are usually limited by focusing on behavioural aspects like a kind of communication protocol [10,14]. Other approaches use constraints to limit the kind of entities that are bound to a role [17].

5 Conclusion and Further Work

In this paper, we proposed an approach to assure architectural properties of ABBs during compositional architecture design and pointed out how this approach can be embedded into an architecture design process. We presented in which description parts we intent to divide ABBs and architectures and we analysed which basic architectural elements are used to describe ABBs and architectures. Furthermore, we introduced two kinds of composition: instance composition and hierarchical composition. Architectural properties, like absence of cycles, are expressed as constraints over the elements of ABBs and are checked for compliance during the architecture design process.

As described in Section 4 some ADLs support the definition of ABBs but allow the use of only one ABB per architecture description. In contrast, our approach is intended to explicitly support multiple ABBs per architecture description without creating new ABBs first. Furthermore, our approach does not consider instantiated ABBs as separate blocks which are linked by connectors. The ability that architectural elements can assume roles from different ABBs allows various integrations and combinations of ABBs.

We illustrated the proposed approach using only one specific ABB, namely the Layers pattern. It is undenied that there are more ABBs that must be considered to prove the practicability of this approach. They need to be summarised, analysed for their elements and properties and formalised. Then, it is possible to build and study larger examples of composed ABBs.

A next step planned is to define a first metamodel for the description of ABBs. Furthermore, to formalise ABBs and software architectures an adequate description language has to be chosen or adapted.

References

1. Bass, L., Clements, P., Kazman, R.: Software Architecture in Practice, 2nd edn. Addison-Wesley, Reading (2003)
2. The Open Group, (ed.): The Open Group Architecture Framework (TOGAF). 8 edn. Van Haren Publishing (August 2007)
3. Buschmann, F., Meunier, R., Rohnert, H., Sommerlad, P., Stal, M.: Pattern-Oriented Software Architecture: A System of Patterns, 1st edn. Software Design Patterns, vol. 1. Wiley & Sons, Chichester (1996)

4. Bergner, K., Rausch, A., Sihling, M., Vilbig, A.: Putting the Parts Together - Concepts, Description Techniques, and Development Process for Componentware. In: Proceedings of the 33rd Hawaii International Conference on System Sciences, HICSS 2000, vol. 8. IEEE Computer Society Press, Washington, DC, USA (2000)
5. Fowler, M.: Patterns of Enterprise Application Architecture. Addison-Wesley Professional, Reading (2002)
6. Garlan, D., Shaw, M.: An Introduction to Software Architecture. In: Ambriola, V., Tortora, G. (eds.) Advances in Software Engineering and Knowledge Engineering, pp. 1–39. World Scientific Publishing Company, Singapore (1993)
7. Herold, S., Metzger, A., Rausch, A., Stallbaum, H.: Towards Bridging the Gap between Goal-Oriented Requirements Engineering and Compositional Architecture Development. In: Proceedings of the Second SHARK-ADI Workshop at ICSE. IEEE Computer Society, Washington, DC, USA (2007)
8. Gross, D., Yu, E.: From Non-Functional Requirements to Design through Patterns. Requirements Engineering 6(1), 18–36 (2001)
9. Araujo, I., Weiss, M.: Linking Patterns and Non-Functional Requirements. In: Proceedings of the 9th Conference on (PLoP 2002), Monticello Illinois (USA) (2002)
10. Medvidovic, N., Taylor, R.N.: A Classification and Comparison Framework for Software Architecture Description Languages. IEEE Trans. Softw. Eng. 26(1), 70–93 (2000)
11. Kamal, A.W., Avgeriou, P.: An Evaluation of ADLs on Modeling Patterns for Software Architecture. In: Proceedings of the 4th International Workshop on Rapid Integration of Software Engineering techniques (RISE). LNCS. Springer, Heidelberg (2007)
12. Vestal, S.: A Cursory Overview and Comparison of Four Architecture Description Languages. Technical report, Honeywell Technology Center (1993)
13. Clements, P.C.: A Survey of Architecture Description Languages. In: Proceedings of the 8th IWSSD. IEEE Computer Society, Los Alamitos (1996)
14. Nitto, E.D., Rosenblum, D.: Exploiting ADLs to Specify Architectural Styles Induced by Middleware Infrastructures. In: Proceedings of the 21st ICSE, pp. 13–22. ACM, Los Angeles (1999)
15. Allen, R.J.: A Formal Approach to Software Architecture. Ph.D. Thesis, Carnegie Mellon University (May 1997)
16. Kim, J.S., Garlan, D.: Analyzing Architectural Styles. Journal of Systems and Software 83, 1216–1235 (2010)
17. Hammouda, I., Koskimies, K.: An Approach for Structural Pattern Composition. In: Lumpe, M., Vanderperren, W. (eds.) SC 2007. LNCS, vol. 4829, pp. 252–265. Springer, Heidelberg (2007)
18. Abd-Allah, A.A.: Composing Heterogeneous Software Architectures. Ph.D. thesis, University of Southern California (1996)
19. Gacek, C.: Detecting Architectural Mismatches During Systems Composition. Ph.D. thesis, University of Southern California (1998)
20. Riehle, D.: Describing and Composing Patterns Using Role Diagrams. In: Proceedings of the 1996 Ubilab Conference, Universitätsverlag Konstanz, pp. 137–152 (1996)
21. Zdun, U., Avgeriou, P.: Modeling Architectural Patterns Using Architectural Primitives. In: Proceedings of the 20th OOPSLA, vol. 40, pp. 133–146. ACM, New York (2005)

Coherence and Performance for Interactive Scientific Visualization Applications

Sébastien Limet, Sophie Robert, and Ahmed Turki

Laboratoire d'Informatique Fondamentale d'Orléans, Université d'Orléans, France*

Abstract. This paper addresses the use of component-based development to build interactive scientific visualization applications. Our overall approach is to make this programming technique more accessible to non-computer-scientists. Therefore, we present a method to, out of constraints given by the user, automatically build and coordinate the dataflow of a real-time interactive scientific visualization application. This type of applications must run as fast as possible while preserving the accuracy of their results. These two aspects are often conflicting, for example when it comes to allowing message dropping or not. Our approach aims at automatically finding the best balance between these two requirements when building the application. An overview of a prototype implementation based on the FlowVR middleware is also given.

Keywords: Composition, Coherence, Coordination, Synchronization.

1 Introduction

The interactive visualization of simulations helps scientists better understand the phenomena they study. In [5] for example, biochemists describe how it can unveil some interactions between complex molecular assemblies. The observer can then become an actor by applying forces to the atoms. The intended interactivity in these applications is not limited to a passive manipulation of the graphical output. It is rather active and its effects are propagated throughout the whole running application. As an example, one can think of pushing and pulling atoms during a molecular simulation.

The development of interactive scientific visualizations is however hampered by the complexity of the software developments it needs. Scientific simulation specialists are seldom experts in 2D/3D visualization or in control device programming. Component-based development promotes collaborative work in this area since it allows each specialist to independently develop the parts he is skilled in. The component approach has been widely studied for scientific computing. These approaches generally follow a workflow model. A variety of Scientific Workflow Management Systems (SWMSs) [17] are proposed to design, generate, deploy and execute scientific applications which consists in carrying out an overall process over a dataset through a sequence of finite steps [4,7,8].

---

* This work is supported by the french ANR project FvNano.

S. Apel and E. Jackson (Eds.): SC 2011, LNCS 6708, pp. 149–164, 2011.

Some of them are extended to provide control constructs that allow branching, looping and parallelism. These control constructs are based on control nodes in [15], on control links in [11], on directors in [12] or on adaptation connectors in [6]. But, in all cases, the user has the task of manually specifying the control behaviour of the components and of the overall application by instanciating these control constructs. Moreover, the lack of explicit support of data streams in SWMSs hampered application development in some scientific domains. Now, initiatives are being taken, either by extending a current workflow paradigm [2,3,9] or by defining a whole new model [16]. While these developments were mostly motivated by the need to integrate continuous sensor feeds as inputs to workflows, we claim that some iterative scientific simulators like Gromacs [10] need a similar attention in order to be integrated into a scientific workflow. We also argue that a dataflow model of iterative components suits better the performance requirements of interactive visualization. In addition, the components may run at different rates. Simulations often run slowly while components handling control devices run very fast. The composition work consists then in focusing on inter-component communication and synchronization. It must guarantee that the whole constructed application remains fast enough to process interactions in a reasonable time so that the user can observe their effects on the simulation. Finally, the scientific nature of the applications requires a specific attention to the data carrying. While some of the data can be dropped to speed the application up -e.g. the positions of the atoms in a molecular simulation has not necessarily to be frame-accurate at display-, the wholeness of other data may be essential to the coherence of the application. In [14], the authors stress the importance of well formalized coordination mechanisms in the coherence of simulations.

So the construction of a component-based real-time interactive application must deal with heterogeneous components and data and try to reach the best compromise between speed and coherence. The accessibility of the composition task must also remain a prerogative.

In this paper, we present a framework to specify dataflow component-based interactive scientific visualization applications. It consists in

- a component specification taking into account its iterative process,
- a composition model focused on data communication and synchronization constraints,
- an automatic method to deduce inter-component communications and synchronizations that fit the user's requirements at best and allow the components to run as fast as possible.

This paper is organized as follows: Section 2 introduces our component model and specifically its set of connectors. Section 3 explains the specific coordination challenges of real-time interactive scientific visualization and Section 4 our methodology to address them. Section 5 presents the results of our approach applied to a real world application. In Section 6, we evaluate our method and give the axes of our future work.

2   Component Model

We define a composition model to automatically build high-performance interactive applications. Its objectives are to

- formalize a component definition from an iterative process and heterogeneous code,
- formalize an application construction based on additional elements to express inter component connections able to ensure coherence and performance,
- propose a composition model to automatically construct the intented applications.

2.1   Components

Unlike scientific computing pipelines, data-driven interactive visualization applications are meant to run continuously along with the simulation or interaction components at the heart of them. Looping is thus inherent to all of the components and can directly be encoded inside them just like the *Push* behaviour described in [13]. A *component* encapsulates a specific task in the data processing pipeline. Formally, it is a quintuplet $A = (n, I, O, C, f)$ where n is the name of the component and I and O two sets of user defined input and output ports. I and O respectively include s (for *start*) and e (for *end*), two default triggering input and output ports. e, at the end of an iteration, emits a signal that can be used to trigger another object. s is the port that receives such signals. C contains the coherence constraints of A. It is a set of disjoint subsets of $I - \{s\}$. Finally, f is a boolean to indicate that the component must run *freely*. We indeed distinguish special components called *interactive components* that capture user interaction. Typically, they can manage control devices. Specifying that a component is interactive (setting f to true) means that its iteration rate must only depend on its processing rate. This ensures that the component will not miss any interaction event. For a component A, $name(A)$ denotes its name, $I(A)$ and $O(A)$ its set of input and output ports respectively, $cstr(A)$ its set of coherence constraints, and $f(A)$ its type.

Components work iteratively. The *behavior* of the component A consists in: (1) waiting until all of its connected input ports are supplied with data and that s, if connected, receives a new signal (2) performing its computation task which can be a parallel task and (3) producing new data on all of its output ports and a signal on e. This process is called an *iteration* of A. Each component numbers its iterations. $i(A)$ is the *iteration rate* of the component. $i(A)$ depends, of course, on the time the component needs to perform its task but it could also depend on the time data takes to arrive to the input ports since A must wait until all of its connected input ports are fed. *input* and *output ports* are identified by a *name*. Data circulating between ports are called *messages*. For a message m, $it(m)$ is the iteration number of the component that produced m. The components of our model can also handle empty messages, i.e. containing no data. This allows a component to go out of the waiting state as soon as all of its input ports are fed, even if not all with fresh data.

2.2   Application Construction

Constructing an application consists in defining the components and the connectivity between their ports. To express this connectivity we define *Connectors* and *Links* in order to describe exactly how data is transmitted from an emitter component to a receiver component.

Connectors. Our component model adopts a set of *exogeneous connectors* [6] designed to support iterative components of different rates anywhere in the application graph. For example, with respect to recent approaches [6,13,16], it adds the ability to choose between blocking and non-blocking connections in order to let the end-user decide which processes should constantly be kept alive and which ones do not need to reprocess already processed data. Similarly, we introduce filtering connections comparable to the filtering nodes in [9] because they appear to be an essential alternative, for the sake of performance, to the systematic buffering of all the messages in use in [16]. On the other hand, we chose not to include explicit time parameters for activity triggering to keep our model the most generic possible. Connectors must be set between two components to determine the communication policy between them, i.e. the type of synchronization and the possibility to loose messages or not. A connector c is a quadruple $c = (n, \{s, i\}, o, t)$ where t is its type (see Figure 1) and i is an input port and o an output port. n and s are similar to their homonyms in the component. We use the same notations $name(c)$, $I(c)$, $O(c)$ and $type(c)$ as for components. c can contain several messages. When the sender writes a message on an output port, it simply adds this message to the connector and when the receiver reads its input port, the connector delivers one of its messages.

Because the components might run at different rates, the connectors need to avoid the overflow of messages when the receiver is slower than the sender. On the other hand, the sender might also slow the receiver down if its iteration rate is lower. To tackle these problems, we propose five connection patterns. *sFIFO*, *bBuffer* and *bGreedy* are similar to patterns described in [13].

- In a plain FIFO connection, the sender dispatches messages at its own rate without considering the receiver. To prevent overflows, this pattern adds a new condition to leave the waiting state. In addition to new input data, the sender must wait for a triggering signal usually sent by the receiver. This connector is called **sFIFO**, *s* standing for *synchronized*. However, as observed in [13], it can make slow components block their predecessors and, recursively, the entire application. This is particularly annoying in visualization applications where display components, that can be slow, are always at the end of the pipeline.
- Buffered FIFO connections can be useful to absorb overflows when one of the two components has an irregular iteration rate. When ready, the receiver triggers the sending of the oldest message in the buffer. We define the **bBuffer**, where *b* stands for *blocking*, because, in the lack of new incoming messages, it will block the receiver. The **nbBuffer**, with *nb* standing for *non-blocking*, can, in contrast, dispatch empty messages when it is empty.

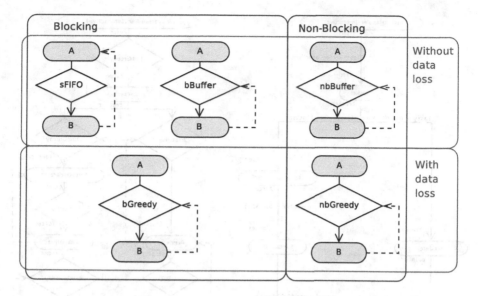

Fig. 1. The five connectors of our framework.

- A Greedy connector keeps only the last message provided by the sender and sends it upon the receiver's request. It is usually used to avoid overflows when it is not required that all messages are processed. The **bGreedy** and the **nbGreedy** are, respectively, the blocking and the non-blocking variants of this pattern.

Links. Links connect components or connectors together through their ports. They are denoted by (x^p, y^q) with x, y components or connectors, $p \in O(x)$ and $q \in I(y)$. There are two types of links:

- **A data link** transmits data messages. For a data link (x^p, y^q), we impose that $p \neq e$, $q \neq s$ and at least x or y is a connector. Indeed, as a connector is always required to define a communication policy, a data link cannot be directly set between two components.
- **A triggering link** transmits *triggering signals*. For such a link (x^p, y^q), we impose that x is a component, $p = e$ and $q = s$. The triggering links are illustrated by dashed lines in Figure 1. Please note that, to avoid deadlocks, neither components nor connectors wait for a triggering signal before their very first iteration.

2.3 Application Graph

With these elements, the application construction can be represented by a graph called the *application graph*. The vertices of this graph are the components and the connectors. The edges represent the links.

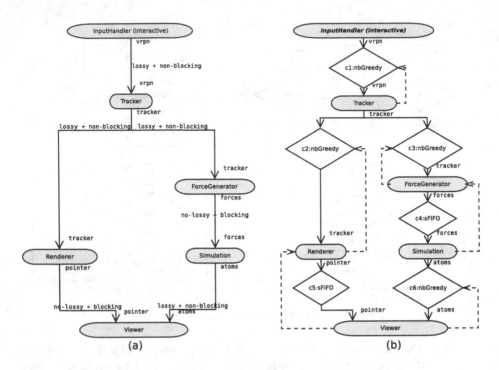

Fig. 2. (a) A specification graph (b) A corresponding application graph

Definition 1. *Let Cp be a set of components, Cn a set of connectors, Dl a set of data links and Tl a set of triggering links. The graph* $App = (Cp \bigcup Cn, Dl \bigcup Tl)$ *defines an* application graph. *In the remainder of this article, we call a* data path *of App an acyclic path in the graph* $(Cp \bigcup Cn, Dl)$.

Figure 2(b) illustrates the application graph of an interactive molecular dynamics application. An *InputHandler* communicates with a hardware controller like an Omni®Phantom. It transforms interaction events into streams that are filtered by the *Tracker* component to forward only the position of the pointer. This position is then used to compute, in real-time, the forces injected into the simulation in order to be applied to the molecule. It is also passed to a *Renderer* that computes the graphical representation of the pointer. We use an *nbGreedy* after the *InputHandler* because it iterates brokenly and with high frequency. Then, while *ForceGenerator* and *Simulation* are synchronized thanks to blocking patterns, the *Viewer* is separated from them by an *nbGreedy* to obtain the smoothest display possible. Building a whole application by putting together components, connectors and links is not easy for beginners, especially considering the specific requirements detailed in Section 3. In Section 4, we present a method to automate this construction.

3   Introducing Coherence

When building his application, the user makes local decisions by choosing the connectors to set between pairs of components. Controlling the coordination of the whole graph this way remains a difficult task that can become unsolvable as the number of graph edges increases. Of course, one can set non-blocking connections everywhere to avoid slow downs. Nevertheless, this would lead to a rash global coordination which is contradictory with the precision expected from scientific applications. Alternatively, one can tie everything up with blocking and non-lossy patterns to ensure coherence but this would result in a general performance drop to the frequency of the slowest component. Our goal is to propose a composition model able to construct, from a user specification, an application ensuring performance and result reliability. To introduce our concepts, we first need a few preliminary definitions.

Definition 2. *Let App be an application graph. We call* segment *a data path in App. The start vertex is called the* source, *denoted $src(s)$, and the end vertex is called the* destination, *denoted $dest(s)$. A message arriving at $dest(s)$ is called a* result *of s. The message from the source that originates this result is denoted by $ori_s(r)$. A segment whose source and destination are both components is called a* pipeline.

Definition 3. *Two pipelines p_1 and p_2 are* parallel *if and only if $src(p_1) = src(p_2)$ and $dest(p_1) = dest(p_2)$ and they do not share any other component.*

In interactive scientific visualization, result reliability can be achieved, from a coordination point of view and apart from data type matters, by enforcing coherence constraints on the data streams coming to a component from different input ports. In the application of Figure 2(b), the user might want the data issued by *Renderer* and *Simulation* to be synchronized at display, i.e. to come from the same iteration of the *Tracker*. More generally, the coherence between two input ports i_1 and i_2 means that if the two messages arriving at the same time at i_1 and i_2 are the results of two parallel pipelines starting at a single component A, then they are the "products" of the same iteration of A.

Definition 4. *Let A be a component and i_1, $i_2 \in I(A)$. i_1 and i_2 are said* coherent *if, for all pairs of parallel pipelines (p_1, p_2) such that the last edge of p_1 connects to i_1 and the last edge of p_2 connects to i_2, we can ensure that $it(ori_{p_1}(r_1)) = it(ori_{p_2}(r_2))$ where r_1 and r_2 are two results of p_1 and p_2 read at the same iteration by A.*

In Figure 2(b), the coherence between the input ports *pointer* and *atoms* of the *Viewer* is not achieved. Indeed, as the *nbGreedy* connectors c2, c3 and c6 deliver only the last stored message and as the modules of the two pipelines run at different rates, *Viewer* can receive two messages that are not initiated by the same iteration of *Tracker*.

4   Automatic Composition

This section describes how the user specifies constraints on his application and the way is automatically built an application graph that ensures input port coherence while trying to preserve performance.

4.1   Application Specification

The application specification helps the user focus on the expected properties of the communications in the application, avoiding technicalities. It is done by a directed graph called the *specification graph*. Its vertices are the components of the application. Its edges, directed from the sender to the receiver, are labelled with the names of the output and input ports and the constraints on the communications. These constraints are of two types: (1) the *message policy*, i.e. can this communication drop messages or not, and (2) the *synchronization policy*, i.e. should the receiver of the message be blocked when no new messages are available. Our aim is to compute an application graph that implements the specifications given by the user. The first step of the process consists in computing a preliminary application graph by replacing each edge of the specification graph with a connector following the rules of Table 1. As in many cases, several connectors fit the same combination, this table itself was created following the overall rule: *The generated application has to be, first of all, as safe as possible and then, as fast as possible.*

The application graph of Figure 2(b) is obtained from the specification graph of Figure 2(a).

Table 1. The choice of communication patterns

	Blocking policy		Non-blocking or Interactive receiver
Msg loss	bGreedy		nbGreedy
	Sender is interactive	Sender not interactive	
No msg loss	bBuffer	sFIFO	nbBuffer

Next, the preliminary graph is transformed to implement first the coherence constraints and then to optimize the running time of the application. We first present how coherence can be implemented in an application graph then we explain the different steps of the process.

4.2   Input Port Coherence

The coherence of two or more input ports of a component depends on the coherence of pairs of parallel pipelines that end at these input ports. The latter relies on a few basic concepts illustrated in Figure 3.

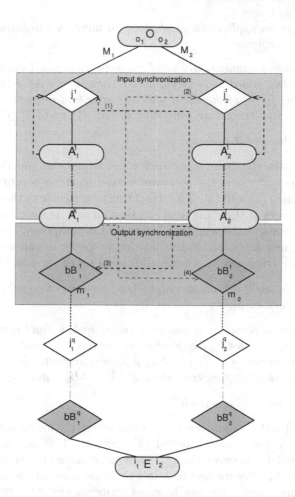

Fig. 3. Ensuring Coherence

Definition 5. *A segment* $(A_1, c_1, \ldots, A_{n-1}, c_{n-1}, A_n)$ *where* A_i $(1 \leq i \leq n)$ *is a component and* c_i $(1 \leq i \leq n-1)$ *is either a sFIFO or a bBuffer connector is called a* synchronous segment.

Property 1. Let $s = (A_1, c_1, \ldots, A_{n-1}, c_{n-1}, A_n)$ be a synchronous segment and m_n a message produced by A_n, $it(m_n) = it(ori_s(m_n))$.

The property is obvious since no message is lost inside a synchronous segment. Indeed A_n generates as many messages as A_1.

Definition 6. *A junction is a bGreedy, an nbGreedy or an nbBuffer connector between two consecutive synchronous segments making them* independent.

The more synchronous segments an application has, the faster it can run. However, the junctions between the segments of a pipeline are also the points where coherence can be lost.

Definition 7. *In an application graph App, an* input synchronization *is a composition pattern involving*

- *two synchronous segments s_1, s_2 of respectively k and l components which are distinct and ended respectively by the components A_1^k and A_2^l,*
- *two junctions j_1, j_2 of the same type and preceding respectively s_1 and s_2,*
- *a* backward cross-triggering *consisting of (A_1^e, j_2^s) and (A_2^e, j_1^s).*

This pattern is denoted $J * (s_1, s_2)$.

Figure 3 illustrates the *input synchronization* where the junctions j_1^1 and j_2^1 are of same type and where the *backward cross-triggering* is represented by the two arrows labelled (1) and (2). This synchronization ensures that the junctions select their messages at the same time and that no new messages are accepted by the first components of the segments before all the components of the segments are ready for a new iteration. Note that this property is maintained when the two junctions are triggered by a same additional set of signals.

Definition 8. *In an application graph App, an* output synchronization *is a composition pattern involving*

- *two synchronous segments s_1 and s_2 of respectively k and l components which are distinct and ended by components respectively A_1^k and A_2^l,*
- *two bBuffer connectors bB_1 and bB_2 following respectively s_1 and s_2,*
- *a* forward cross-triggering *consisting of $(A^k{}_1{}^e, bB_2^s)$ and $(A_2{}^{l^e}, bB_1^s)$.*

This pattern is denoted $(s_1, s_2) * bB$.

Figure 3 illustrates the *output synchronization* where the forward cross-triggering is represented by the arrows labelled (3) and (4). This composition pattern ensures that the delay between the synchronous segments to produce messages is absorbed. As the bBuffer connectors select their messages at the same time when all the last components of the synchronous segments are done, the messages are also delivered at the same time. Note that this property is maintained when the two bBuffer connectors are triggered by a same additional set of signals.

Definition 9. *In an application graph App, the composition $J * (s_1, s_2) * bB$ where s_1 and s_2 are two synchronous segments with no common components, is called a pair of* coherent *segments. $[J * (s_1, s_2) * bB]^q$ denotes the composition of q coherent segments $J^1 * (s_1^1, s_2^1) * bB^1 * \cdots * J^q * (s_1^q, s_2^q) * bB^q$.*

We denote by M a series of messages, $|M|$ is the length of this series, and M^i denotes its ith message. A set of series of messages $\{M_1, \ldots, M_n\}$ are said coherent if $|M_1| = \cdots = |M_n|$ and $\forall j \in [1, |M_1|]$, $it(M_1^j) = \cdots = it(M_n^j)$.

Theorem 1. *Let App be an application graph and $(S_1, S_2) = J * (s_1, s_2) * bB$ a pair of coherent segments of App. If the series of messages M_1 and M_2 stored in the junctions j_1 and j_2 are coherent, then the set of messages m_1 and m_2 stored respectively in the bBuffer connectors bB_1 and bB_2 are such that $it(m_1) = it(m_2)$ and $it(ori_{S_1}(m_1)) = it(ori_{S_2}(m_2))$ when the bBuffers are triggered.*

Proof. Since the series of messages stored in j_1 and j_2 are coherent and that they are triggered at the same time, the messages M_1^i and M_2^i that they deliver respectively have the same iteration number k_1. After this operation, the new series of messages stored in j_1, j_2 are still coherent. By construction, the first components of the two segments begin a new iteration at the same time. So, their iteration numbers are always equal and denoted k_2. From Property 1, we know that the iteration number of each message delivered at the end of both segments, is equal to the iteration number of the message produced by the first components of the segments, i.e. k_2. Since the message m_1 stored in bB_1 and m_2 stored in bB_2 are made available only when both the last components of s_1 and s_2 finish their iterations, we do have that $it(m_1) = it(m_2) = k_2$ at this moment and $it(ori_{s_1}(m_1)) = it(ori_{s_2}(m_2))$.

Theorem 2. *Let App be an application graph and $(S_1, S_2) = [J * (s_1, s_2) * bB]^q$ two segments in App. If the series of messages M_1 and M_2 stored in the junctions j_1^1 and j_2^1 of the first coherent segments are coherent then the set of messages m_1 and m_2 stored respectively in the bBuffer connectors bB_1^q and bB_2^q of the last coherent segments are such that $it(m_1) = it(m_2)$ and $it(ori_{S_1}(m_1)) = it(ori_{S_2}(m_2))$ when the bBuffers are triggered.*

Proof. According to Theorem 1, if the series of messages stored in the junctions are coherent then the messages delivered by the bBuffer connectors have the same iteration number. Therefore, the series of messages stored in the next junctions are coherent. An easy induction on q proves the theorem.

Figure 3 gives an example of two parallel pipelines p_1 and p_2 that ensure the coherence of two ports. This application graph is composed of an initial component O (for origin), of a composition pattern $[J*(s_1, s_2)*bB]^q$ such that $(O^{o_1}, j_1^{1^i})$ and $(O^{o_2}, j_2^{1^i})$ and of a final component E such that $(Bb_1^{q^o}, E^{i_1})$ and $(Bb_2^{q^o}, E^{i_2})$. The junctions are such that j_2^l and j_1^l $1 \le l \le q$ are of the same type. If M_1 and M_2 denote the series of messages coming from the output ports of the component O, M_1 and M_2 are coherent. So the messages stored in the first junctions j_1^1 and j_1^2 are coherent. According to Theorem 2, for the messages delivered by the bBuffers bB_1^q and Bb_2^q, $it(m_1) = it(m_2)$. Moreover if S_1 denotes the data path from j_1^1 to bB_1^q and S_2 the one from j_2^1 to bB_2^q then $it(ori_{S_1}(m_1)) = it(ori_{S_2}(m_2))$. This means that $ori_{S_1}(m_1)$ and $ori_{S_2}(m_2)$ come from the same iteration of O and, hence, that $it(ori_{p_1}(r_1)) = it(ori_{p_2}(r_2))$ which corresponds to the definition of the coherence.

To build an application graph under coherence contraints, we propose to transform the preliminary application graph into a new one such that the data paths involved in a coherence constraint are composed of coherent segments.

4.3 Transformations for Coherence Construction

The different steps of our construction are illustrated by the specification graph of Figure 2(a) where the user wants coherence between ports *pointer* and *atoms* of component *Viewer*. Figure 2(b) gives the preliminary application graph of this application.

Coherence graphs. The first step of the transformation consists in looking for parallel pipelines that must be coherent. They are collected in coherence graphs.

Definition 10. *Given an application graph G and a coherence constraint C of the component A in G, the* coherence graph *of C in G is the subgraph of G that contains all the parallel pipelines of G with the members of C as destinations.*

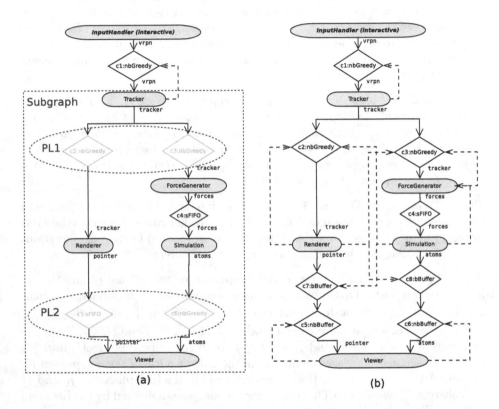

Fig. 4. Application graph before (a) and after (b) equalization and synchronization

Our example application has one coherence constraint {*pointer, atoms*}. Its coherence graph is inside the frame in Figure 4(a).

Path segmentation. As seen in Section 4.2, our construction is based on parallel pipelines which have the same number of independent segments. So, the purpose of this step is to create, if necessary, new segments, i.e. switch some connectors from {sFIFO or bBuffer} to nbBuffer, or from {bGreedy or nbGreedy} to {sFIFO, bBuffer or nbBuffer}. This is possible because we allow the system to relax blocking, non-blocking or lossy constraints of the specification graph. In contrast, no-lossy constraints are never relaxed.

Instead of making coherent each pair of parallel pipelines, the process is done on the whole application at the same time. This allow it to take into account all the constraints and avoid backtrackings in the process. For that, we use a linear system where each variable is associated to a connector. The domain of the variables is $\{0, 1\}$. 0 means that the connector is either a sFIFO or a bBuffer, and 1 any of the three other patterns. Since these other patterns define junctions, it is sufficient to impose that the sums of the variables of the parallel pipelines are equal to ensure that they have the same number of segments.

Formally, let App be an application graph and $C_1, \ldots, C_n$ the set of coherence constraints of the modules in App. We denote by $G|_{C_i}$ the coherence graph of C_i in App. For each component A of App, we denote by $PP_A(App|_{C_i})$ the set of parallel pipelines coming from A and leading to C_i. To each connector c of App, we associate the variable v_c of domain $\{0, 1\}$. For each path p in App that contains the sequence of connectors $c_1, \ldots, c_k$, we define $Sum(p) = v_{c_1} + \cdots + v_{c_k}$. For each component A and each of its constraints C, we define the set of equations $Eq(PP_A(App|_c)) = \{Sum(p_1) = \cdots = Sum(p_l)|\, p_j \in PP_A(App|c), 1 \leq j \leq l\}$. The set of equations corresponding to the problem is then $Eq_{App} = \bigcup\{Eq(PP_A(C)|A \in App, C \in cstr(A)\}$.

Additional constraints are also added to the problem to avoid misleading solutions. For each connector c of App, according to the properties of the corresponding connection in the specification graph and those of the sender and the receiver, we determine the set of compatible patterns. If this set contains only elements of $\{$nbBuffer, bGreedy, nbGreedy$\}$, we add $v_c = 1$ to the linear system. The set of these additional equations is denoted by Fix_{App}. Most of the time, the system has many solutions that are not equivalent from a performance point of view. We give then priority to those that maximize the application's performance, i.e. that preserve at best the initial junctions. This is expressed by the following objective function $Maximize(Sum(J_{App}))$ where J_{App} is the set of junctions initially set in App and $Sum(J_{App}) = \Sigma_{c \in J_{App}}(v_c)$. So the linear problem we want to solve is $Eq_{App} \bigcup Fix_{App} \bigcup Maximize(Sum(J_{App}))$.

For the application of Figure 4(a), this process produces the following problem $\{c_2 + c_5 = c_3 + c_4 + c_6\} \bigcup \{\emptyset\} \bigcup Maximize(c_2 + c_3 + c_6)$ and its solution is $\{c_2 = 1, c_3 = 1, c_4 = 0, c_5 = 1, c_6 = 1\}$.

Plateau equalization. It remains now to definitively set the pattern of each junction. For that, we define the notion of *plateau*.

Definition 11. *Let App be an application graph, $O * [J * (s_1, s_2) * bB]^q * E$ two parallel pipelines whose last edges connect to two ports of the same coherence constraint of E. We say that the junctions j_1^i and j_2^i ($i \in [1, q]$) are of the same level, which is denoted by $j_1^i \leftrightarrow j_2^i$. The reflexive-transitive closure of $\leftrightarrow$ is denoted by $\leftrightarrow^*$. A plateau is the set of the junctions of the same equivalence class of $\leftrightarrow^*$.*

It can be proved that two different junctions j_l^i and j_l^k that belong to the same pipeline involved in at least one coherence constraint cannot be in the same plateau. This avoids interblocking input-output synchronizations.

The connectors of a given plateau must be of the same type to ensure a coherence constraint. This is the object of the next step. To solve the problem on the whole graph, we group all the plateaus that have connectors in common into a single subset of connectors. When a subset contains connectors of different types, we either set all the connectors of the subset to nbBuffer if this subset contains at least a nbBuffer or we set a nbGreedy otherwise. Figure 4(a) shows that our example application has two plateaus *PL1* and *PL2*. *PL1* will be kept as it is because the connectors are already of the same type. In *PL2* however, the non-lossy constraint on c5 enforces *nbBuffer* as the only possible option.

At the end of this step, we first add the backward cross-triggerings to the junctions. Since a plateau may involve more than two segments, our construction generalizes Definition 7. For a plateau $j_1, \ldots, j_n$ and the segments $s_1, \ldots, s_n$ ending with components $A_1, \ldots, A_n$ we add the set of edges $\{(A_i^e, J_j^s) | i \neq j\}$. Moreover to implement the output synchronization, we add one bBuffer connector just after each A_i ($i \in [1, n]$) and add the edges for the forward cross-triggerings. This ensures the required coherences.

Finalization and optimization. To finalize the application graph, our system adds all the missing trigger links, factorizing those that can be. For example, in the application graph in Figure 4(b), *Simulation* triggers *ForceGenerator* which triggers c3. This boils down to *Simulation* triggering c3. Finally, the system outputs an XML file that can be used to generate the concrete application.

5   Experimental Results

To validate our component-based model, we use FlowVR [1], a middleware to develop and run high-performance interactive applications. It is based on a component called *module* which consists in an iterative process with input and output ports and can model our component. It also offers an assembly model expressed as a communication network of connection elements covering standard communication or synchronization patterns. For specific needs, it is also possible to develop ad hoc connection elements and, in particular, our connector elements have been developed and integrated into FlowVR.

Concerning our automatic application construction, we implemented a software prototype that parses a user specification XML file and generates the adequate application graph according to the given information and constraints. This application graph is then transformed into a FlowVR assembly model which can be processed by FlowVR to execute the application on a cluster architecture.

We have been testing our software prototype on the example application used throughout this paper. This application is representative as it contains connections with different arities and a coherence constraint between the input ports *pointer* and *atoms* of the display component. The simulation component in the implementation is run by Gromacs, a very popular molecular dynamics engine and the other components have been specifically implemented. The tests were run with a 3000 atom molecule on a 2x2.5Ghz CPU.

We tested several versions of the graph, including one with only bBuffers and sFIFOs as we suppose it would be set by hand by someone unfamiliar with the connection patterns and unsure of the impact of message dropping on the coherence. As this graph has only one-segment pipelines, it doesn't need any specific coherence processing. However, the overall performance drops to the iteration rate of the slowest component, i.e. the *Viewer* in this case, so around 14.8 it/sec. In contrast, the implementation of the automatically generated application graph of Figure 4(b) keeps the display component loosely connected to the rest and the simulation can run at up to 154.2 it/sec. The coherence between the input ports *atoms* and *pointer* is also maintained.

6 Discussion and Future Work

Coherence - along with performance and simplicity - is a major criteria for scientists when building their own software. To our knowledge, coherence as we mean it in this paper and its automatic fulfillment by graph modification has not been explored yet. We proved that a complex application can be automatically constructed from a user specification expressed in terms of communication and coherence constraints. Not only do the generated applications ensure the coherence of data input wherever it is requested but they also guarantee the safest -in terms of overflows or unwanted output overwriting- and the fastest execution possible. A software prototype used on a real world scientific application validates our approach.

The focus of our future research will be to enrich our model with component hierarchy and define a coherence that supports not only regular message streaming but also event-based message emission. Moreover we plan to enrich the coherence model. For example, the user might need other coherence constraints such as allowing a gap of up to n iterations between two components or coherence with respect to messages produced by two different components. We also plan to implement a composition UI and deal with data type compatibility and adaptation still in the perspective of simplifying the assembly of heterogeneous software components.

References

1. Allard, J., Gouranton, V., Lecointre, L., Limet, S., Melin, E., Raffin, B., Robert, S.: FlowVR: a middleware for large scale virtual reality applications. LNCS, pp. 497–505 (2004)
2. Barseghian, D., Altintas, I., Jones, M.-B., Crawl, D., Potter, N., Gallagher, J., Cornillon, P., Schildhauer, M., Borer, E.-T., Seabloom, E.-W.: Workflows and extensions to the Kepler scientific workflow system to support environmental sensor data access and analysis. Ecological Informatics 5(1), 42–50 (2010)
3. Bkörnstad, B.J.: A Workflow Approach to Stream Processing. PhD thesis, Zürich (2007)
4. Callahan, S.P., Freire, J., Santos, E., Scheidegger, C.E., Silva, C.T., Vo, H.T.: VisTrails: visualization meets data management. In: Proceedings of the 2006 ACM SIGMOD international conference on Management of data, p. 747. ACM, New York (2006)

5. Delalande, O., Férey, N., Grasseau, G., Baaden, M.: Complex molecular assemblies at hand via interactive simulations. Journal of Computational Chemistry 30(15) (2009)
6. Velasco Elizondo, P., Lau, K.-K.: A catalogue of component connectors to support development with reuse. Journal of Systems and Software 83(7), 1165–1178 (2010)
7. Gil, Y., Ratnakar, V., Kim, J., Gonzalez-Calero, P., Groth, P., Moody, J., Deelman, E.: Wings: Intelligent workflow-based design of computational experiments. IEEE Intelligent Systems 99 (2010)
8. Goodale, T., Allen, G., Lanfermann, G., Masso, J., Radke, T., Seidel, E., Shalf, J.: The cactus framework and toolkit: Design and applications. In: Vector and Parallel Processing, pp. 1–31 (2002)
9. Herath, C., Plale, B.: Streamflow Programming Model for Data Streaming in Scientific Workflows. In: 2010 10th IEEE/ACM International Conference on Cluster, Cloud and Grid Computing, pp. 302–311 (May 2010)
10. Hess, B., Kutzner, C., van der Spoel, D., Lindahl, E.: GROMACS 4: Algorithms for Highly Efficient, Load-Balanced, and Scalable Molecular Simulation. Journal of Chemical Theory and Computation 4(3), 435–447 (2008)
11. Hull, D., Wolstencroft, K., Stevens, R., Goble, C., Pocock, M.R., Li, P., Oinn, T.: Taverna: a tool for building and running workflows of services.. Nucleic acids research 34(Web Server issue), W729–W732 (2006)
12. Ludascher, B., Altintas, I., Berkley, C., Higgins, D., Jaeger, E., Jones, M., Lee, E.A., Tao, J., Zhao, Y.: Scientific workflow management and the Kepler system. Concurrency and Computation: Practice and Experience 18(10), 1039–1065 (2006)
13. Pautasso, C., Alonso, G.: Parallel computing patterns for grid workflows. In: Proceedings of the Workshop on Workflows in Support of Large-Scale Science, pp. 19–23 (2006)
14. Siebert, J., Ciarletta, L., Chevrier, V.: Agents & artefacts for multiple models coordination. In: Proceedings of the 2010 ACM Symposium on Applied Computing, pp. 20–24 (2010)
15. Taylor, I., Shields, M., Wang, I., Harrison, A.: Visual Grid Workflow in Triana. Journal of Grid Computing 3(3-4), 153–169 (2006)
16. Wombacher, A.: Data Workflow-A Workflow Model for Continuous Data Processing. Data Processing (2010)
17. Zhao, Z., Belloum, A., Wibisono, A., Terpstra, F., de Boer, P.T., Sloot, P., Hertzberger, B.: Scientific workflow management: between generality and applicability. In: Quality Software (QSIC 2005), pp. 357–364. IEEE, Los Alamitos (2006)

Toward Validated Composition in Component-Based Adaptive Middleware

Annie Ressouche[1], Jean-Yves Tigli[2], and Oscar Carrillo[1]

[1] INRIA Sophia Antipolis
2004, route des Lucioles, BP 93
06902 Sophia Antipolis, Cedex France
annie.ressouche@inria.fr, ocrozo@gmail.com
[2] I3S Laboratory, Nice Sophia University
CNRS, Polytech'Sophia SI 930 route des Colles, BP 145
06903 Sophia Antipolis, Cedex, France
tigli@polytech.unice.fr

Abstract. Nowadays, adaptive middleware plays an important role in the design of applications in ubiquitous and ambient computing. Currently most of these systems manage the adaptation at the middleware intermediary layer. Dynamic adaptive middleware are then decomposed into two levels : a first one to simplify the development of distributed systems using devices, a second one to perform dynamic adaptations within the first level. In this paper we consider component-based middleware and a corresponding compositional adaptation. Indeed, the composition often involves conflicts between concurrent adaptations. Thus we study how to maintain consistency of the application in spite of changes of critical components and conflicts that may appear when we compose some component assemblies. Relying on formal methods, we provide a well defined representation of component behaviors. In such a setting, model checking techniques are applied to ensure that concurrent access does not violate expected and acceptable behaviors of critical components.

Keywords: component-based middleware, adaptive middleware, validation, formal methods, synchronous modelling.

1 Introduction

1.1 Component-Based Adaptive and Reactive Middleware

Ubiquitous computing follows an evolution of computer science introduced by Weiser [21] two decades ago. A major consequence is the arrival of applications more and more opened on every day environment relying on objects supposedly communicating and intelligent. Devices managed in ubiquitous computing are nowadays *heterogeneous*, *variable*, and *interacting with a physical environment*. Moreover, applications in this domain must often face some *variability* during execution time. Moving with a mobile user, such applications have not always

S. Apel and E. Jackson (Eds.): SC 2011, LNCS 6708, pp. 165–180, 2011.

access to the same devices. Thus, it turns out that the appearance and disappearance of these latter need a dynamic evolution of the application. Hence, evolving in a real environment, ubiquitous applications must be able to react to changes in the surrounding *physical environment*.

Then, it is a real challenge to address these constraints for middleware. Indeed, now they must support a stable applicative model in spite of a heterogeneous and variable software infrastructure. Actually, middleware must be *reactive* (they must react to context change) and *adaptive* (they must adapt themselves continuously to context changes).

Historically, [18] defines two extremes in the range of strategies for adaptation. At one extreme, adaptation is entirely the responsibility of individual applications. The other extreme of application-transparent adaptation places entire responsibility for adaptation on the system. Currently most of the work converge to manage the adaptation at the middleware intermediary layer [1]. In this last case dynamic adaptive middleware are then decomposed into two levels [7]. The primary level of middleware is to simplify the development of distributed systems [10]. The second level performs dynamic adaptations within middleware.

Because ubiquitous computing is based on preexisting devices, middleware must manage legacy of black-box of software pieces. Three kinds of approaches are well suited to manage such constraints : component oriented middleware, service oriented middleware and more recently new popular approaches using components assembly to compose preexisting services like, SCA or SLCA ([19]).

The second level of adaptive middleware manages dynamic modifications of the first one to perform adaptation. According to [14] we can distinguish two main approaches to implement software adaptation. The first one is *parameter adaptation*. For component based middleware this approach consists in modifying components variables that determine their behavior. The second one is *compositional adaptation*. This approach allows component-based middleware to change dynamically components with others in response to changes in its execution environment. In this paper we study how to maintain consistency of the application in spite of critical components changes and conflicts that may appear when we superpose component assemblies in mechanisms for compositional adaptation. Indeed in such cases, we need to use verification techniques to check safety and various other correctness properties of the evolving application.

1.2   Need for Validation

Then, the main motivation appears when we introduce new requirements for ubiquitous applications such as *safety*. Indeed, few research works in ubiquitous computing address some partly critical applications. For example, many ubiquitous applications address health care domain without validating some critical functionalities. Anyway, *safety* is an important concern in adaptive middleware. Applications may intervene in critical systems (i.e. system whose failure or malfunction may result in death or serious injury to people, or loss or severe damage to equipment or environmental harm). Components may have to satisfy stringent constraints related to security and should be submitted to formal verification and validation. Moreover, context change adaptation should preserve safety rules. Then key problems are :(1) how to specify and validate the behavior of one assembly connected to a critical component (Cf. section 3), (2) in case of multiple assemblies sharing a critical component (see the end of section 1.1), how to compose them and validate properties of the overall application (Cf. section 4).

1.3 Our Proposal

To address these problems, we introduce a means to describe critical component behaviors as synchronous monitors for which formal methods and model checking techniques apply. Nevertheless, our major contribution is the definition of a sound composition operation also lying on formal methods and useful to perform context adaptation. We prove safety property preservation through this operation, hence we offer the ability to perform verification over assembly composition. Thus we extend our component-based adaptive middleware with specific tools to allow validation of local composition on critical devices and services, using model checking techniques.

The paper is organized as follows: next section (2) briefly describes the component-based middleware use we consider and introduces the example we rely on all along the paper to illustrate our approach. It is extracted from a use case in the domain of health care for elderly. Then section 3 presents our solution which introduces synchronous monitors to model critical devices expected behaviors. They support formal validation. In section 4 we introduce a composition operation between synchronous monitors preserving validated properties. Such an approach allows us to offer a deterministic solution to multiple access to critical devices. We discuss the practical issues of our work in section 5. We introduce our reactive adaptive middleware for ubiquitous computing, named WComp and also its extension with verification facilities. Then we describe the implementation of the example in our middleware. In section 6 we compare our approach with different works which address the problem of reliability of middleware for ubiquitous computing. Finally, section 7 concludes and opens the way for future works.

2 Component-Based Middleware Use

In this work, we consider middleware where communication means are event-based. Of course event-driven systems are not suitable for very complex design, but adequate for reactivity, dynamicity and high adaptability. In our approach such components are often proxies for services for device and then must reflect the device behavior. Some of them are critical and we want to validate their usage within some middleware assemblies.

We illustrate our approach with the design of (a small part of) an application in the domain of health care for elderly. The purpose is to monitor old adult in an instrumented home, using sensing technology. There are different kinds of sensors in the environment: video cameras, contact sensors to indicate closed or opened status of equipment, wearable sensors, etc. In this framework, we are deep in the domain where reactive and adaptive middleware solutions apply, since some sensors can appear and disappear (particularly wearable ones). In this example, we show the design of a small part of a project dedicated to observe activities of daily living (ADLs) in an equipped home [1]. We consider the recognition of activities related to kitchen usage. The goal is to send several kinds of alarms depending on sensor observation results. Component proxies are associated to four sensors: a contact sensor on the fridge which indicates the state of the door (opened or closed); a timer which sends a minute information; a camera which locates a person; a posture sensor which tells if the person is standing, sitting or lying. This latter is a wearable device composed by accelerometers.

In this application, an *Alarm* component proxy receives three kinds of alarms: *warning*, *weak_alarm* and *strong_alarm*. It is linked with assemblies of components for fridge and timer sensors, camera sensor and posture sensor. This *Alarm* component is critical and we will ensure that it raises the appropriate alarm in the designed application. To this aim, we offer a mean to ensure that each output event coming from one of the designed assemblies for sensors is correctly sent. Indeed, we supply a new component reflecting the behaviors of (assemblies of) components and we check that these latter are used out of harm's way (see section 3.2). Moreover, it is not sufficient to individually prove that each new component outputs are not misused. We also must ensure that the combination of two output events coming from two different assemblies and linked with the same input event of *Alarm* component works correctly. Thus we introduce a safe composition between components (see section 4.2).

3   Components with Validated Behaviors

To validation purpose, we introduce models to describe the behavior of application components. Finite automata are well adapted to the representation of device behaviors and moreover provide a lot of verification tools based on efficient model-checking techniques to verify properties.

3.1   Component Behavior as Synchronous Models

The goal is to define means to represent component behavior. These components listen to events coming from other components or from an input environment and will provide output events in reaction. They have to satisfy stringent constraints (correctness, response time) and they should be submitted to formal verification and validation as they may intervene in a critical decision. Thus determinism would be an important advantage. A way of reducing the complexity of behavior description is to consider them evolve through successive phases. During one phase, only the external events which were present at the beginning of the phase

---

[1] http://gerhome.cstb.fr/

and the internal events that occurred as a consequence of the first ones are considered. The phase ends when some stability has been achieved (or when an external clock decides that it is over). We call such a phase an instant. Such an instant-based representation will be called a *synchronous* model. In such models, a reaction has *no duration* because its real duration is delayed to the next clock cycle or next instant of the system. This issue characterizes the *synchronous hypothesis* on which all synchronous models rely. A significant way well suited to validation is to express these models as Mealy machines [15]. Mealy machines are both finite automata and synchronous models. Indeed a transition in Mealy machines corresponds to a reaction or an instant of the system.

The Mealy machines we consider are 5-uple of the shape:

$< Q, q^{init}, I, O, \mathcal{T}, \lambda >$, where Q is a finite set of states; $q^{init} \in Q$ is the initial state. I (resp. O) is a finite set of input (resp. output) events; $\mathcal{T} \subseteq Q \times Q$ is the transition relation. λ is a labeling function: $\lambda : \mathcal{T} \times I^B \mapsto 2^O_\epsilon$ [2] where I^B is the set of Boolean expressions over I [3]. It is a Boolean algebra with standard interpretation for $true, false, \cdot, +$ and $\neg$ [4]. In short, $q \xrightarrow{i/o} q'$ will denote a transition with the agreement: $(q, q') \in \mathcal{T}$ and $\lambda((q, q'), i) = o$. Furthermore, according to the synchronous hypothesis, we want our model deterministic and reactive:

1. $q \xrightarrow{i/o_1} q_1$ and $q \xrightarrow{i/o_2} q_2 \in \mathcal{T} \Rightarrow q_1 = q_2$ and $o_1 = o_2$ (determinism)

2. $\forall i \in I^B, \forall q \in Q, \exists q \xrightarrow{i/o} q' \in \mathcal{T}$ (reactivity)

Critical components will provide a synchronous model of their behavior and some additional properties (constraints) checked when component is used. This model is designed as a Mealy machine where each output is connected with an input event of the critical component. Indeed, let us consider a synchronous monitor specified as the Mealy machine $M =< Q, q^{init}, I, O, \mathcal{T}, \lambda >$ and connected to a critical component with I_C as input event set. There must exist an injective mapping : $in : O \mapsto I_C$.

3.2 Use Case Synchronous Monitor Definition

In the application introduced in section 2, there is an assembly related to the *posture* sensor and connected to the *Alarm* component. According to section 3.1, we will define a synchronous monitor to describe the behavior of the assembly. This *posture* monitor listens to $I_3 = \{sitting, standing, lying\}$ input event set. Its output event set is $O_3 = \{warning3, weak\_alarm3\}$. It emits a $warning_3$ event when the person is sitting or standing and a $weak\_alarm_3$ event when

---

[2] $2^O_\epsilon = 2^O \cup \{\epsilon\}$ and ϵ represents an undefined event.

[3] Its elements are built according to the following grammar: $e := true \mid false \mid I \mid e \cdot e \mid e + e \mid \neg e$.

[4] We will consider usual Boolean algebra rules to infer equality between two elements of I^B.

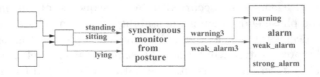

Fig. 1. A synchronous monitor to manage the access to the critical alarm proxy component from the posture sensor assembly

he(she) is lying [5] . This monitor is the Mealy machine $< Q_3, q_3^{init}, I_3, O_3, \mathcal{T}_3, \lambda_3 >$ with an only state and two transitions:

$$q_3^{init} \xrightarrow{(standing\ or\ sitting)\ and\ not\ lying/warning_3} q_3^{init}$$

$$q_3^{init} \xrightarrow{(not\ standing\ and\ notsitting)\ and\ lying/weak\_alarm_3} q_3^{init}$$

Finally, the critical *Alarm* proxy component has
$I_A = \{warning, weak\_alarm, strong\_alarm\}$ as input event set and there is an

injection $in_3 : O_3 \mapsto I_A$: $\begin{cases} in_3(warning_3) = warning \\ in_3(weak\_alarm_3) = weak\_alarm \end{cases}$

Figure 1 shows the assembly we get in the application for this *posture* synchronous monitor. Then, safety and liveness properties concerning critical component usage can be verified using model-checking tools ([3] among a lot of them).

3.3   Component Behavior Validation

Among others validation techniques, the *model-checking* approach [13] requires a model of systems against which formulas are checked for satisfaction. The model must express all the possible behaviors of the system, the formulas depict required properties of such behaviors. Synchronous Mealy machines are well suited to express these behaviors and they are relevant models to apply model checking techniques. The properties may be formalized as formulas of a formal logic interpreted over automata. In order to benefit from well-known results about the preservation of properties through composition, we will consider the $\forall CTL^*$ logic [13]. It is a formal language where assertions related to behavior are easily expressed. It is based on first-order logic and offers temporal operators that make it possible to express properties holding for states and paths. Nowadays, almost all model checking tools check $\forall CTL^*$ properties against automata models.

The logic is interpreted over *Kripke structures* [6] in order to express model checking algorithms and satisfaction of a state formula is defined in a natural inductive way (see [13] for complete definitions). A Mealy machine M can be

---

[5] It is a weak alarm since lying posture is not dangerous in all contexts.

[6] A   *Kripke structure K* is a tuple: $K =< Q, Q_0, A, R, L >$ where: (1) Q is a finite set of states; (2) $Q_0 \subseteq Q$ is the set of initial states; (3) A is a finite set of atomic propositions; (4) $R \subseteq Q \times Q$ is a transition relation that must be total: for every state $q \in Q$, there is a state q' such that $R(q, q')$; (5) $L : S \mapsto 2^A$ is a labeling function that labels each state by the set of atomic propositions true in that state.

mapped to a Kripke structure $\mathcal{K}(M)$, which is also a state machine. We don't detail this adaptation, it is fully described in [17].

Definition 1. *We say that a Kripke structure K satisfies a state formula ψ ($K \models \psi$) if property ψ is true for the initial states of K. This definition is extended to Mealy machines: $M \models \psi$ iff $\mathcal{K}(M) \models \psi$;*

In our approach, several synchronous monitors can drive the same proxy component corresponding to several sub-assemblies respectively managing different concerns. Indeed, there is no communication between these monitors and their output event sets are disjoint. But we need to compose them and specify a composition mechanism.

4   Synchronous Model Composition

When a critical component has multiple synchronous monitors corresponding to several concern managements in the application, we want to build an only synchronous model component which agrees with all these primitive synchronous monitors and whose output event set is related to the input event set of the critical component by an injection. We continue to rely on our use case (see section 2) to illustrate such a situation.

4.1   Use Case Multiple Access

In our use case, there are three sub-assemblies linked to the critical *Alarm* component. Thus, we introduce three synchronous monitors in this assembly.

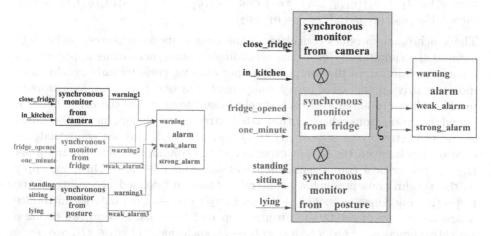

Fig. 2. Multiple access to alarm proxy component

Fig. 3. Composition of multiple access to connect the alarm proxy component

The first synchronous monitor describes the behavior of *Alarm* component with respect to the sub assembly managing the *camera* device; the second is defined with respect to the sub assembly related to the *door fridge* and *timer* sensors; and the third tells the behavior of *Alarm* when it is related to a sub assembly managing a *posture detection* sensor. The *camera* monitor is a Mealy machine with $\{in\_kitchen, close\_fridge\}$ as input set, $\{warning_1\}$ as output set. When both of its inputs are present, $warning1$ is emitted. The *fridge* monitor reacts to $\{fridge\_opened, one\_minute\}$ input events and sends a $warning_2$ event when the fridge door is opened and a $weak\_alarm_2$ event when it is opened for more than one minute. The *posture* monitor has been described in section 3.2. Thus, we get the assembly described in figure 2. We can see that *warning* and *weak_alarm* entries have multiple access. Our method will replace these three components by a single component : $camera \otimes fridge \otimes posture \mid_\varsigma$ (see figure 3).

4.2   Multiple Access to Components

To specify how output events sent by different synchronous monitors and connected to a critical component, we introduce an operation of *composition under constraints* of synchronous models. We achieve this composition operation relying on the well-defined synchronous product ($\otimes$) of synchronous models and we replace the outputs of this latter with respect to a set of constraints (ς).

Definition 2. *The synchronous product of two Mealy machines ($M_1 \otimes M_2$) is defined as follows: assume that*

$M_1 = \langle Q_1, q_1^{init}, I_1, O_1, T_1, \lambda_1 \rangle$ and $M_2 = \langle Q_2, q_2^{init}, I_2, O_2, T_2, \lambda_2 \rangle$,
then $M_1 \otimes M_2 = \langle Q_1 \times Q_2, (q_1^{init}, q_2^{init}), I_1 \cup I_2, O_1 \cup O_2, T, \lambda \rangle$
where $T = \{((q_1, q_2), (q_1', q_2')) \mid (q_1, q_1') \in T_1, (q_2, q_2') \in T_2\}$ *and*
$\forall (q_1, q_1') \in T_1 \mid \lambda_1((q_1, q_1'), i_1) = o_1)$ *and* $\forall (q_2, q_2') \in T_2 \mid \lambda_2((q_2, q_2'), i_2) = o_2)$
then $\lambda(((q_1, q_2), (q_1', q_2')), i_1 \cdot i_2) = o_1 \cup o_2)$.

The synchronous product considers all the combinations of states, taking into account the simultaneity of events according to our synchronous approach. As already mentioned, in the composition operation we consider only synchronous monitors driving the same proxy component. On one hand, the synchronous product allows to agree with each synchronous monitor. On the other hand, it introduces transitions whose output label carry events belonging to the union of the respective event sets of M_1 (O_1) and M_2 (O_2). But we want that the relationship between the output event set of the composition and the input set (I_C) of the critical component will be at least an injection. Thus, we apply to the synchronous product a "constraint function" defined according to the respective injections $in_1 : O_1 \mapsto I_C$ and $in_2 : O_2 \mapsto I_C$. First, we introduce a new output event set O and an injection $in : O \mapsto I_C$. Second, we define a surjective function $\gamma : O_1 \cup O_2 \cup O_1 \times O_2 \mapsto O_\epsilon$ such that: (1) $\forall o_1 \in O_1, \gamma(o_1) = o$ and $in(o) = in_1(o_1)$; (2) $\forall o_2 \in O_2, \gamma(o_2) = o$ and $in(o) = in_2(o_2)$.

From these definitions, a "constraint" function $\varsigma : 2^{O_1 \cup O_2} \mapsto 2^O$ is deduced: $\forall o \in 2^{O_1 \cup O_2}$, if $\exists o_1, o_2 \in o$ such that $\gamma(o_1, o_2) \neq \epsilon$ then $\gamma(o_1, o_2) \in \varsigma(o)$; else $\gamma(o_1) \in \varsigma(o)$ and $\gamma(o_2) \in \varsigma(o)$.

This constraint function is applied to the output label sets of of the synchronous product:

Definition 3. *Assume that* $M_1 \otimes M_2 = < Q_1 \times Q_2, (q_1^{init}, q_2^{init}), I_1 \cup I_2, O_1 \cup O_2, \mathcal{T}, \lambda >$, *then* $M_1 \otimes |_\varsigma M_2 = < Q_1 \times Q_2, (q_1^{init}, q_2^{init}), I_1 \cup I_2, O, \mathcal{T}_\varsigma, \lambda_\varsigma >$ *where* $\mathcal{T}_\varsigma = \mathcal{T}$ *and* λ_ς *is defined as follows:*
$\lambda_\varsigma(((q_1, q_2), (q_1', q_2')), i) = o$ *iff* $\lambda(((q_1, q_2), (q_1', q_2')), i) = o_1 \cup o_2$ *and* $\varsigma(o_1 \cup o_2) = o$
(assuming that λ *is the labeling function of* $M_1 \otimes M_2$ *).*

The synchronous product of two Mealy machines yields a Mealy machine. It is a well-known result of the synchronous framework. Constraint function application modifies only output event sets of labels and thus our composition operation constructs a Mealy machine.

4.3   Composition and Validation

Our composition operation allows to solve the multiple access to a given proxy component problem. The result of this operation is a Mealy machine against which model-checking techniques apply as for any synchronous monitor (see 3.3). Moreover, we also want the preservation of properties under composition: if M_1 verifies a $\forall CTL^*$ formula Φ ($M_1 \models \Phi$) then this latter also holds for a composition where M_1 is part of ($M_1 \otimes |_\varsigma M_2 \models \Phi$). To prove such a feature, we show that $\mathcal{K}(M_1)$ can be viewed as an "approximation" of $\mathcal{K}(M_1 \otimes |_\varsigma M_2)$.

Definition 4. *Let* $K_1 = < Q_1, Q_1^0, A_1, R_1, L_1 >$ *and* $K_2 = < Q_2, Q_2^0, A_2, R_2, L_2 >$ *be two kripke structures and* h_a *a surjection from* A_1 *to* A_2. *We say that* K_2 *approximates* K_1 *(denoted* $K_1 \sqsubseteq_h K_2$*) when*

1. *It exists a surjection* $h : Q_1 \mapsto Q_2$ *such that:* $h(q_1) = q_2 \Rightarrow \forall a_2 \in L_2(q_2), \exists a_1 \in L_1(q_1)$ *and* $h_a(a_1) = a_2$.
2. $\forall q_2 \in Q_2^0, \exists q_1 \in Q_1^0$ *and* $h(q_1) = q_2$; *and*
3. $\exists q_1, q_1'(h(q_1) = q_2, h(q_1') = q_2'$ *and* $R_1(q_1, q_1') \Rightarrow R_2(q_2, q_2'))$.

Now we make more precise what does mean $\forall CTL*$ properties are preserved through our composition operation. In [12], Clarke and all show that $\forall CTL*$ formulas are preserved for transition system approximations. We use the same method to prove that $\forall CTL*$ formulas are preserved through Kripke structure approximations. Let K_1 and K_2 be two Kripke structures and $h_a : A_1 \mapsto A_2$ a surjective mapping such that there is a surjection h from Q_1 to Q_2 and $K_1 \sqsubseteq_h K_2$. The method consists in (1) define a translation (τ) from formulas expressing properties in K_2 and formulas expressing properties in K_1 and to prove that if a property ϕ holds for K_2, $\tau(\phi)$ holds for K_1. For lack of space, we do not detail the proof but it is an induction on the structure of formulas and it is told in detail in [17]. We apply these results to synchronous monitors.

For short, we will denote $M_1 \otimes |_\varsigma M_2$ as M_ς. $\mathcal{K}(M_1) = < \mathcal{K}Q_1, Q_1^0, A_1, L_1, R_1 >$ and $\mathcal{K}(M_\varsigma) = < \mathcal{K}Q_\varsigma, Q_\varsigma^0, A_\varsigma, L_\varsigma, R_\varsigma >$ are built according to the translation operation (fully described in [17]). Then we define (1) a surjective $\hat{h}_a$ from A_ς

to A_1 and a surjective mapping: $\hat{h} : \mathcal{K}Q_\zeta \mapsto \mathcal{K}Q_1$ and we prove that $\mathcal{K}(M_\zeta) \sqsubseteq_{\hat{h}}$ $\mathcal{K}(M_1)$ (see [17]). By construction A_ζ is composed of elements of the form $i_1.i_2$ (i_1 belongs to I_1 the input event set of M_1 and i_2 to I_2) and of elements belonging to O. Indeed, $\hat{h}_a$ is defined as follows: $\hat{h}_a(i_1.i_2) = i_1$ and $\hat{h}_a(o) = o_1$ if $\gamma(o_1) = o$. Now, we define a translation mapping τ_ζ between formulas related to $\mathcal{K}(M_\zeta)$ and those related to $\mathcal{K}(M_1)$. This mapping is first defined on atomic formulas :

$$\tau_\zeta(true) = true; \; \tau_\zeta(false) = false; \; \forall a_1 \in A_1, \tau_\zeta(a_1) = \bigvee_{a_\zeta \in A_\zeta} a_\zeta \mid \hat{h}_a(a_1) = a_\zeta.$$

Then it is structurally extended to all formulas according to the syntax of the logic.

Now, we get the main preservation theorem:

Theorem 1. *Let M_1 and M_2 be two Mealy machines and ϕ a $\forall CTL*$ formula related to M_1, then $M_1 \models \phi \Rightarrow M_1 \otimes \mid_\zeta M_2 \models \tau_\zeta(\phi)$*

The proof of this theorem is also detailed in [17]. It is a corollary of the general result about the preservation of $\forall CTL*$ formulas through Kripke structure approximations touched on just before.

4.4 Adaptivity

Supporting both adaptation and safe composition lays down that synchronous monitors and constraint functions are available at runtime. The drawback of this approach is the exponential number of constraint functions due to the different combination of synchronous monitor composition. Constraint functions describe how the different outputs of synchronous monitors linked with the same input of a critical component are reconciled. As monitor output events are disjoint, it is easy to define default combination rules for outputs in order to reduce the number of constraint functions. Moreover, we can compose monitors in an incremental way, hence runtime adaptation is made more efficient. Then, the preservation theorem ensures us that properties holding locally are still valid after an incremental composition process.

5 Practical Issues

5.1 Our WComp Middleware

Relying on this theoretical approach, we improve our *WComp*([19]) middleware to support synchronous component design and validation of behaviors for critical components. WComp is a reactive and adaptive middleware approach which takes into account the principles for ubiquitous computing described in section 1.1. The first level of WComp corresponds to a component-based middleware to compose services for device. The composition is then implemented as a lightweight component assembly. Components interact through events and some of them are connected to services for devices. The second level of WComp use an adaptation paradigm with the original concept named Aspect of Assembly.

Because such a mechanism produces sub-assemblies of components to be superimposed (weaved in our case) to produce the appropriate application, we leverage the work presented in this paper to preserve the safety of the evolving application.

5.2   WComp Critical Component Specification

In section 3, we have shown that the introduction of specific synchronous components is an answer to address the multiple access to critical component problem. Nevertheless, these synchronous components represent the behaviors of critical components as Mealy machines. These latter are models very well suited to formally prove the soundness of our approach, but they are not convenient to deal with. Thus we rely on the Lustre [16] *synchronous languages*. It respects the *synchrony* hypothesis which divides time into discrete instants. It is a data flow language offering two main advantages: (1) It is a *functional* language with no complex side effects. This makes it well adapted to formal verification and safe program transformation. Also, reuse is made easier, which is an interesting feature for reliable programming concerns; (2) it is a *parallel* model, where any sequencing and synchronization depends on data dependencies. We choose this language because, first, Mealy machines are models for it and its compilation provides an implicit representation of them. Second, the synchronous product we rely on to perform the composition of synchronous monitors is expressed naturally in the language. Third, constraint functions can be expressed as equations, thanks to the equational nature of the language.

To perform safety properties validation we rely on the model-checking tool Lesar [9], a symbolic, BDD-based model-checker for Lustre. It is based on the use of *synchronous observers* [8], to describe both the properties to be checked and the assumptions on the program environment under which these properties are intended to hold. An observer of a safety property is a program, taking as inputs the inputs/outputs of the program under verification, and deciding (e.g., by emitting an alarm signal) at each instant whether the property is violated. Running in parallel with the program, an observer of the desired property, and an observer of the assumption made about the environment one has just to check that either the alarm signal is never emitted (property satisfied) or the alarm signal is emitted (assumption violated), which can be done by a simple traversal of the reachable states of the compound program. Hence, using observer technique allows to express the property in the same language used to design our synchronous components and avoid to express $\forall CTL*$ formulas. Verification with Lesar is performed on an abstract (finite) model of the program. Concretely, for purely logical monitors the proof is complete, whereas in general (in particular when numerical values are involved) the proof can be only partial. In our approach, component events are associated with two Lustre variables, a Boolean variable is related to the presence of the event, the other carries it's value. Thus, properties related to presence or absence of events can be proved, but properties related to values depend on the abstraction performed by the tool.

5.3 Use Case Implementation

Now we sketch how we implement the use case in WComp. First, we describe the three synchronous monitors as Lustre programs (called *camera*, *fridge* and *posture*). Figure 4 illustrates this implementation. As described in section 4.2, the composition under constraints of *camera*, *fridge* and *posture* components is a Mealy machine, which has for input event set the union of their respective input event sets components. The output set of the composite component we built is {*warning*, *weak_alarm*, *strong_alarm*} [7] (we will call it *O*). We provide a constraint function to specify how these multiple access are managed and we use it to build the composite component *camera* ⊗ *fridge* ⊗ *posture* $|_\varsigma$. Informally, it maps all combinations of *warning*1, $warning_2$ and $warning_3$ to *warning* event. As soon as either $weak\_alarm_2$ or $weak\_alarm_3$ are emitted, ς maps the output set to *weak_alarm* and if both of them belong to an output set, then a *strong_alarm* is sent since that means that the door of the fridge is opened for more than one minute and the person kept under watch is lying. Of course, different constraints could be defined. For instance, instead of considering that a $warning_i$ is sufficient to launch a warning, we could consider that the *camera* and *fridge* components must agree and emit respectively *warning*1 and $warning_2$. This would yield another composition result.

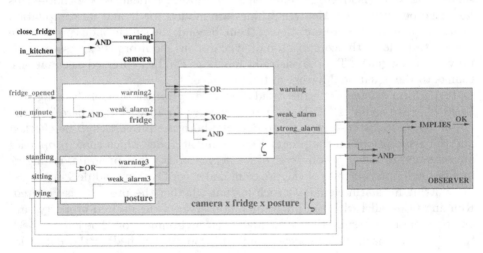

Fig. 4. The implementation in Lustre of the use case. The overall implementation (the composed synchronous monitor + the observer) feeds the Lesar model-checker. The composed synchronous monitor is plugged in the application.

Now, we verify the *camera* ⊗ *fridge* ⊗ *posture* $|_\varsigma$ component before introducing it in the assembly. Thus, we use the observer technique previously described to prove that if the fridge is opened for more than one minute and the person is lying, then a strong alarm is sent. We define an observer which listen

---

[7] As it is in bijection with the input set of *Alarm* component, we keep the same name to an easier identification of connections.

fridge_open, *one_minute*, *lying* and *strong_alarm* events and which computes a Boolean variable *ok* and we prove with Lesar that *ok* is always true, assuming that *lying*, *standing* and *sitting* are exclusive.

On another hand, we just want to touch on the application of theorem 1. Assume that with Lesar, we prove that for *fridge* component, the property: *fridge_opened* $\Rightarrow$ *warning*$_2$ holds. Clearly, from the definition of constraints in *alarm_comp*, we have $\tau_\zeta(warning_2) = warning$.

Thus, we can deduce that *fridge_opened* $\Rightarrow$ *warning* also holds in *alarm_comp*.

After this verification, we automatically generated WComp input code for node *alarm_comp*. Indeed a new component has been automatically weaved in the assembly designing the application in WComp.

6 Related Works

In this work, we rely on a synchronous modelling to verify the functional correctness under concurrency of component behavior and component assemblies in a reactive and adaptive middleware. Other works address the reliability of middleware. For instance, in [20], the authors propose the TLAM (two-level actor model) approach for specifying and reasoning about components of open distributed systems. They show, using the QoS broker MM architecture, how the TLAM framework can be used to specify and reason about distributed middleware services and their composition. They have also shown how specifications in the TLAM framework can lead to implementations. They proved that the implemented middleware correctly works (provided that middleware services respect a set of constraints) and they planned to rely on a theorem prover to achieve these proofs and automate their method.

In the same vein as our approach, some works rely on model-checking techniques to ensure the reliability of middleware solutions. For instance, *PolyORB* is a schizophrenic ("strongly generic") middleware offering several core functions and a Broker design pattern to coordinate them. In [11], Hugues and al, generate Petri nets to model the Broker design pattern of *PolyORB* and use model checking techniques relying on Petri nets models to verify qualitative properties (deadlock, bounds of buffers, appropriate use of critical section,...). We don't use such a modelling because (1) we want to rely on a user-friendly method to describe critical unknown component behaviors; (2) properties we consider don't require Petri nets modelling to be checked. Thus, we prefer to rely on a language allowing to express both component behavior and properties to be verified.

Some other approaches like product line engineering, consider that systems are developed in families and differences between family members are expressed explicitly in terms of features. From this hypothesis, lots of works propose formal modelling and model-checking techniques to describe and verify the combined behavior of a whole system family (for example [4] and [6]). In our approach we do not yet consider dependencies between different configurations of the application, like software product line families. In the same way, in [2] the authors present a compositional reasoning to verify middleware-based Software Architecture.

They take advantage of the particular structure of applications due to their middleware-based approach to prove a global property by decomposition into local properties verified at sub component level. In our approach, we don't yet have such decomposition algorithms to split a global property. By the time, we have a bottom-up reasoning and our preservation theorem is sufficient.

In [5], Delaval and all also use a synchronous data flow language complemented with a mechanism to depict component contrats (BZR) to extend a high level component-based model (Fractal) in order to enforce safety properties concerning component interactions during dynamic reconfiguration. Indeed from Fractal specification it is possible to extract a BZR program made of the automata representation of the component behavior and the component contract. Then, using an ad-hoc discrete controller synthesis tool, they generate in a target executive middleware of Fractal an additional validated controller. But, common component-based middleware as WComp do not supply enough information to deduce component behaviors and contracts. Then, we solve the problem of safe reconfiguration in relying on sound composition of user-defined synchronous monitors, which preserves component properties already proved.

7   Conclusion and Future Works

The work described in this paper is derived from our experience in providing support for correct assembly of components in an event-based reactive and adaptive middleware. In this latter, we solved the adaptation paradigm using the Aspect of Assembly concept. When using our middleware, a developer benefits from a composition mechanism between different component assemblies to adapt his application to context change. While defining this composition mechanism, we realized the need to formalize and verify the multiple access to a critical component (i.e related to a critical device). The corresponding formalism, the topic of this paper, relies on formal methods. Our approach introduces in a main assembly, a synchronous component for each sub assembly connected with a critical component. This additional component implements a behavioral model of the critical component and model checking techniques apply to verify safety properties about it. Thus, we consider that the critical component is validated. Then we proposed a sound (with respect to our mathematical formalism) composition operation between synchronous components. We proved that this operation preserves already separately verified properties of synchronous components. This operation is an answer to the multiple access to critical components. Our aim is to improve our middleware WComp with a dedicated tool. Currently, we supply a graphical interface to design both critical component behaviors and properties as observers in the synchronous language Lustre (see section 5). Then the validation of properties and the creation of the validated synchronous component is automatic. But, designing with Lustre language is not obvious for any expert user and Lesar model-checker does not allow to verify properties related to events carrying data of complex type. Thus, in the future we aimed at providing a user-friendly interface to express critical component behaviors and properties.

This interface will report about violation of properties relying on powerful model checker as *NuSMV* [3] and straightly (without using the Lustre compiler) generate internal code to implement synchronous monitors. Moreover, to validate properties dealing with data, we must study how abstraction techniques apply in our approach or how we can adapt them.

References

1. In: ARM 2010: Proceedings of the 9th International Workshop on Adaptive and Reflective Middleware. ACM, New York (2010)
2. Caporuscio, M., Inverardi, P., Pelliccione, P.: Compositional verification of middleware-based software architecture descriptions. In: ICSE 2004: Proceedings of the 26th International Conference on Software Engineering, pp. 221–230. IEEE, Washington, DC, USA (2004)
3. Cimatti, A., Clarke, E., Giunchiglia, E., Giunchiglia, F., Pistore, M., Roveri, M., Sebastiani, R., Tacchella, A.: NuSMV 2: An OpenSource Tool for Symbolic Model Checking. In: Brinksma, E., Larsen, K.G. (eds.) CAV 2002. LNCS, vol. 2404, pp. 359–364. Springer, Heidelberg (2002), http://nusmv.irst.itc.it
4. Classen, A., Heymans, P., Schobbens, P.-Y., Legay, A., Raskin, J.-F.: Model checking lots of systems: efficient verification of temporal properties in software product lines. In: Proceedings of the 32nd ACM/IEEE International Conference on Software Engineering, ICSE 2010, vol. 1, pp. 335–344. ACM, New York (2010), http://doi.acm.org/10.1145/1806799.1806850 http://doi.acm.org/10.1145/1806799.1806850
5. Delaval, G., Rutten, É.: Reactive model-based control of reconfiguration in the fractal component-based model. In: 13th International Symposium on Component Based Software Engineering (CBSE 2010), Prague, Czech Republic (June 2010), http://pop-art.inrialpes.fr/people/delaval/pub/delaval-cbse10.pdf
6. Fisler, K., Krishnamurthi, S.: Modular verification of collaboration-based software designs. In: Proceedings of the 8th European Software Engineering Conference held Jointly with 9th ACM SIGSOFT International Symposium on Foundations of Software Engineering, Vienna, Austria. ESEC/FSE-9, pp. 152–163. ACM, New York (2001), http://doi.acm.org/10.1145/503209.503231, doi:10.1145/503209.503231
7. Grace, P.: Dynamic adaptation. In: Miranda, H., Garbinato, B., Rodrigues, L. (eds.) Middleware for Network Eccentric and Mobile Applications, pp. 285–304. Springer, Heidelberg (2009)
8. Halbwachs, N., Lagnier, F., Raymond, P.: Synchronous observers and the verification of reactive systems. In: Nivat, M., Rattray, C., Rus, T., Scollo, G. (eds.) Third Int. Conf. on Algebraic Methodology and Software Technology, AMAST 1993. Springer, Heidelberg (1993)
9. Halbwachs, N., Raymond, P.: Validation of synchronous reactive systems: From formal verification to automatic testing. In: Thiagarajan, P.S., Yap, R.H.C. (eds.) ASIAN 1999. LNCS, vol. 1742, p. 1. Springer, Heidelberg (1999)
10. Issarny, V., Caporuscio, M., Georgantas, N.: A perspective on the future of middleware-based software engineering. In: 2007 Future of Software Engineering, pp. 244–258. IEEE Computer Society Press, Los Alamitos (2007), http://dx.doi.org/10.1109/FOSE.2007.2 http://dx.doi.org/10.1109/FOSE.2007.2

11. Hugues, J., Pautet, L., Kordon, F.: Refining middleware functions for verification purpose. In: Proceedings of the Monterey Workshop 2003 (MONTEREY 2003), Chicago, IL, USA, pp. 79–87 (September 2003)
12. Clarke Jr., E.M., Grumberg, O., Long, D.E.: Model checking and abstraction. ACM Transactions om Programming Languages and Systems 16(5), 1512–1542 (1994)
13. Clarke Jr., E.M., Grumberg, O., Peled, D.: Model Checking. MIT Press, Cambridge (2000)
14. McKinley, P.K., Sadjadi, S.M., Kasten, E.P., Cheng, B.H.C.: Composing adaptive software. IEEE Computer 37(7), 56–64 (2004), http://portal.acm.org/citation.cfm?id=1008751.1008762, doi:10.1109/MC.2004.48
15. Mealy, G.: A method to synthesizing sequential circuits. Bell Systems Technical Journal, 1045–1079 (1955)
16. Lagnier, F., Halbwachs, C.R.N.: Programming and verifying critical systems by means of the synchronous data-flow programming language lustre. IEEE Transactions on Software Engineering (1992); Special Issue on the Specification and Analysis of Real-Time Systems
17. Ressouche, A., Tigli, J.-Y., Oscar, C.: Composition and Formal Validation in Reactive Adaptive Middleware. Research report, PULSAR - INRIA Sophia Antipolis - INRIA - Laboratoire d'Informatique, Signaux, et Systèmes de Sophia-Antipolis (I3S) / Equipe RAINBOW - Université de Nice Sophia-Antipolis - CNRS: UMR6070, 02 (2011), Available from: http://hal.inria.fr/inria-00565860/en/
18. Satyanarayanan, M.: Fundamental challenges in mobile computing. In: Proceedings of the Fifteenth Annual ACM Symposium on Principles of Distributed Computing, PODC 1996, pp. 1–7. ACM, New York (1996), http://doi.acm.org/10.1145/248052.248053 http://doi.acm.org/10.1145/248052.248053
19. Tigli, J.-Y., Lavirotte, S., Rey, G., Hourdin, V., Cheung, D., Callegari, E., Riveill, M.: Wcomp middleware for ubiquitous computing: Aspects and composite event-based web services. In: Annals of Telecommunication, vol. 6, Springer, Paris (2009) ; ISSN 0003-4347 (Print) 1958-9395 (Online)
20. Venkatasubramanian, N., Talcott, C., Agha, G.A.: A formal model for reasoning about adaptive qos-enabled middleware. ACM Trans. Softw. Eng. Methodol. 13(1), 86–147 (2004), http://doi.acm.org/10.1145/1005561.1005564http://dx.doi.org/http://doi.acm.org/10.1145/1005561.1005564
21. Weiser, M.: The computer for the twenty-first century. Scientific American Ubicomp Paper 265, 94–104 (1991)

Author Index

Balasubramanian, Daniel   133
Bensalem, Saddek   116
Bliudze, Simon   51
Butler, Michael   100
Bynens, Maarten   68

Carrillo, Oscar   165

Danylenko, Antonina   18
Deiters, Constanze   141
de Silva, Lavindra   116
Du Bois, André Rauber   34

Gondal, Ali   100
Griesmayer, Andreas   116

Hemingway, Graham   133

Ingrand, Felix   116

Joosen, Wouter   68

Kessler, Christoph   18

Legay, Axel   116
Limet, Sébastien   149
Lorenz, David H.   84
Löwe, Welf   18

Ndjatchi, Mbe Koua Christophe   1

Poppleton, Michael   100
Porter, Joseph   133

Rausch, Andreas   141
Ressouche, Annie   165
Robert, Sophie   149

Sifakis, Joseph   51
Sztipanovits, János   133

Tigli, Jean-Yves   165
Trakhtenberg, Victor   84
Truyen, Eddy   68
Turki, Ahmed   149

Velasco Elizondo, Perla   1

Yan, Rongjie   116